The Poetic Memoirs
of
Lady Daibu

The Poetic Memoirs of Lady Daibu

TRANSLATED,

WITH AN INTRODUCTION,

BY

Phillip Tudor Harries

STANFORD UNIVERSITY PRESS

STANFORD, CALIFORNIA

1980

Stanford University Press
Stanford, California

© 1980 by the Board of Trustees of the
Leland Stanford Junior University

Printed in the United States of America
ISBN 0-8047-1077-5
LC 79-65519

To my parents

Acknowledgments

In preparing this book I have benefited not only from the work of Japanese scholars whose commentaries and articles I have consulted, but also from the personal guidance of many people, both in Japan and in the West. I particularly wish to thank Professor Earl Miner of Princeton University for his constant advice and encouragement, Professor Karen Brazell of Cornell University for reading the manuscript and suggesting useful improvements, Professor Ikari Masashi of Nihon University for making time to see me and answer questions at an early stage in my work, and especially Professor Kubota Jun of Tokyo University for giving very generously of his time, energy, and encyclopedic knowledge in helping me with difficult problems of interpretation. I would also like to record my gratitude to Dr. D. E. Mills of Cambridge University and Drs. B. W. F. Powell and I. J. McMullen of Oxford University for their kindness and guidance over a period of many years. Special thanks are due to my wife, Anne, for advice and support at all stages of the work and for her invaluable help in preparing the final manuscript. I have benefited much from the editorial advice of Barbara Mnookin of Stanford University Press. I am also indebted to the Center for East Asian Studies, Stanford University, for a grant towards the cost of typing the manuscript.

P. T. H.

Contents

Translator's Note

A steady interest in the *Poetic Memoirs of Lady Daibu* has led to the production of a moderately large number of texts and a variety of modern editions of the work. For my translation, I have used the text in Hisamatsu et al., eds., *Heian Kamakura shikashū* (Iwanami Shoten, 1964, *Nihon koten bungaku taikei*, vol. 80), based on the Kyushū Daigaku Text, which is considered the most authoritative manuscript. I have also benefited greatly from a number of other annotated editions and commentaries, and I here gratefully acknowledge my indebtedness to the many Japanese scholars without whose works my task would have been considerably more difficult. I have felt free to choose textual variants not in my base text but favored by some Japanese scholars, and wherever I have departed in this way from the base text, I have made it clear in a note. I have also noted the existence of variants that lead to different interpretations, but I have not noted minor variations that do not affect the essential meaning.

The text abounds in official titles and names of government posts. These, particularly the military titles, often sound awkward or inappropriate in English, so I have omitted them and used simply the names of persons involved, except where the sense requires the translation of a title. Wherever a title has been omitted in the translation, I have provided the original form in the notes.

For the convenience of readers using the Index, dates have been given for persons on their first appearance in the Introduction or notes. I have relied on standard Japanese reference works for these dates, and there may sometimes be a discrepancy of one year, owing to the overlapping of years in the Japanese and Western systems. For dates that I consider important I have supplied the exact equivalent in the Western calendar. Ages, where given, are in Western count, not Japanese count, which usually runs one in advance of the Western age-counting system. Where an author and his work are both cited, I have given only the author's dates unless the exact date of the work is significant or the author's dates are unknown.

I have used the Hepburn system of romanization in transcribing names and quotations in Japanese, with the following modifications: *n* rather than *m* is used before *p*, *b*, or *m*; and a hyphen rather than an apostrophe is used where one syllable of a word ends in *n* and the following syllable begins with a vowel.

I have used the following abbreviations in the notes. Publication data on these works and others cited in short form will be found in the Bibliography, pp. 305–11.

GSRJ	*Shinkō gunsho ruijū*
Hyōkai	Murai Jun, *Kenreimon-in Ukyō no Daibu shū hyōkai*
"Hyōshaku"	Kubota Jun, "Kenreimon-in Ukyō no Daibu shū hyōshaku"
Zenshaku	Hon-iden Shigeyoshi, *Hyōchū Kenreimon-in Ukyō no Daibu shū zenshaku*

Introduction

INTRODUCTION

Lady Daibu: Her Life and Times

The Poetic Memoirs of Lady Daibu cover a period of about fifty years at the end of the twelfth century and the beginning of the thirteenth. Lady Daibu lived through one of the most momentous periods of change in Japanese history, but of the historical events of the time she makes only the briefest mention here and there. Her main theme is her own personal life and her emotions, her love affairs, and her sufferings. As a court lady writing in the tradition of court literature, she was concerned not at all with politics or history, but only with a lyrical portrayal of life at court, her brief happiness, the bitter-sweet sadness of her love affair, and finally her despair when it ended with her lover's death in battle. This element of war begins to move her work away from the gentle world of the court and towards the rougher world of a new age.

A new and different literary mode from that of the court ladies has given us spirited military tales from this new period. Thanks to the epic story *The Tale of the Heike* (c. 1222), which recounts in the most beautiful and moving language the courageous deeds, the glory, the pathos, and the tragedy of those troubled times, the late twelfth century has come to seem a period of incomparable romance. Whatever sober historians may tell us of the historical facts, in the popular consciousness at least it is a time when dashing, courtly knights rode out to battle with fierce, barbarian warriors from the eastlands and were swept to destruction, victims of their own sensitivity and cultivation, as well as of their overweening pride.

It is against such a background that *The Poetic Memoirs of Lady Daibu* have enjoyed a quiet popularity for over seven centuries. Lady Daibu shares in the romance of the period. But not for her are the tales of glorious deeds. She tells of the other side of war: the loss of a way of life that seemed good and beautiful; the patient waiting of a woman left behind; and the grief that is the true product of war. For this reason, her work has always attracted readers in times of upheaval, not least during the 1940's, when many people in Japan found themselves suffering through the same horrors as Lady Daibu had experienced many centuries before.

This view from behind the scenes, this domestic picture of the times, gives to her work a special interest, for there we see portrayed famous persons who are known mostly through the military tales or historical records. In her work we often see a completely different side of the great figures of the age: a monster of destructiveness, Taira no Shigehira (1157–85), whose forces laid waste the Tōdaiji Temple in Nara, is seen as a cheerful and charming friend, a man of culture, sensitivity, and thoughtfulness; and many of the persons who are well known from *The Tale of the Heike* are seen in a more human light, emerging as more complete and attractive men and women.

The *Memoirs*, then, are intimately connected with the background of the times, as any autobiography must be. Though Lady Daibu does not write much about specific events, she does mention them, and she writes with a consciousness, however vague, of what was happening beyond the fringes of her own relatively sheltered world. The work will inevitably be read against this background, and any reader who wishes to understand the *Memoirs* must know something of the history of the times and of the course of Lady Daibu's life.

At the end of the twelfth century, Japan was swept violently out of the age of aristocratic, courtly government and into the age of feudal, military rule. The process of change had been gradual; the violent upheaval was merely the final stage, the final struggle for supremacy between two rival military families that had already established their power.

The era thus brought to an end was known as the Heian period, from the name of the country's capital city and cultural center, Heian-kyō the City of Peace and Tranquility. From the beginning of the period, 794, until well into the eleventh century, the name had been apt enough. The hallmark of Heian culture was a pacific, aristocratic aestheticism, courtly almost beyond belief, in which value was determined by birth, rank, and good taste, and in which success, both in society and in one's career, depended on the ability to dress well, comport oneself correctly, compose poetry, write in a good hand, perform music, and display sensitivity to the beauty and sadness of nature in its changing seasons and to the feelings of one's fellow aristocrats. Wit, decorum, good taste, and gentleness were valued. Rude violence was abhorred. Officers of the guards coveted the high social standing that went with their military titles, but they would have been shocked at the idea of having to fight.[1]

This very pacifism and dislike of violence were responsible in part for the decline of Heian culture, though the major cause was economic and demographic. The history of the Heian period can be viewed as a gradual removal of land from

1. For descriptions of Heian society, see "The Rule of Taste," chap. 11 of Sansom, *History of Japan*, vol. 1; and Morris, *World of the Shining Prince*.

the public, tax-producing domain and the expansion of large, tax-exempt, effectively private estates, with a consequent impoverishment of the public exchequer. The process began early in the period and continued at an increasing pace, despite hastily issued government decrees aimed at ending it. Not only was the central government deprived of income, but effective control of land and its revenues—and hence real power—tended to move from the court towards the provinces where the estates were situated; and it was there, in response to a need for self-protection, that the military families gathered strength.

Two clans came in time to dominate the military class: the Minamoto, also known as the Genji, and the Taira, also known as the Heike. These two clans in their various branches spread rapidly, taking other military families and small landowners under their aegis and creating for themselves great power and wealth. They were as much aristocrats as provincials, for they were descended from the imperial family; and in addition to having close ties with the provinces at a local level, they held government positions, notably in the provincial bureaucracy. But they were unable to rise to the highest positions at court because of their provincial ties. The true courtiers looked with disdain on all things provincial: to be outside the capital was to be cut off from all civilization and culture, and a short journey of only a few miles was for them an arduous trip into the wilds. Even provincial governors, though they were members of the central bureaucracy, never rose above middling rank in the all-important court ranking system that governed status, and they were viewed by the other courtiers as an inferior class.[2]

2. The status of courtiers was governed by a system of eight numbered ranks and one preliminary rank, each of which was further subdivided into two grades for ranks one to three and four grades for all ranks below. Ranks one to three constituted the upper class, ranks four and five the middle class, and ranks six and below the lowest class. Most provincial gover-

It was to this class of provincial governors that the leaders of the Minamoto and Taira families belonged. By the early twelfth century they had secured enormous wealth and power in the provinces. With impressive military forces at their command, they had also made themselves indispensable to the government, quelling insurrections in the provinces and policing a capital increasingly threatened by a lawlessness and violence that the peaceloving courtiers were powerless to resist. But they remained in inferior positions, using their power on behalf of the court or ruling factions at court.

By the middle of the twelfth century, however, the Taira had not only made themselves an essential part of the government machinery; they had also begun to ingratiate themselves with the court, cultivate courtly manners and learning, and break through the barrier of being provincial. This was due in large measure to Taira no Tadamori (1096–1153), who rose to be Minister of Justice and put himself on terms of easy intimacy with many courtiers and—most important to success—with court ladies.

For most of the Heian period, the government was effectively in the hands of one family, the Fujiwara, who by a system of marriage politics controlled the Emperor and acted as Regents and Chancellors, with a virtual monopoly of the highest government posts. Within the family itself there were rival factions, and by their own policy of making Emperors abdicate young, the Fujiwara had helped to create a system in which abdicated Emperors tried to rule from retirement. The second half of the twelfth century was dominated by one such figure, Goshirakawa (1127–92), who reigned only three years, from

---

nors belonged to the sixth rank, although those of very large or important provinces could rise to the lower grades of the fifth rank. Lesser provincial officials, of course, belonged to even lower ranks. It was rare, therefore, for a provincial officer to enter even the middle range of the aristocracy.

1155 to 1158, but was a master of intrigue and exercised considerable power from the time of his abdication until his death. It was by supporting him in his various intrigues that the Taira rose to extremely high positions (and arguably, it was by alienating him that they speeded their subsequent downfall). Tadamori's son Kiyomori (1118–81), by making use of the rivalries in the court and by ingratiating himself and his family still further with powerful aristocrats, was able to bring the Taira to supreme power, and eventually he and other members of his family held posts that had once been almost exclusively the right of the Fujiwara.

The peaceful life of the Heian court had not been greatly disturbed by the violence in the provinces or the occasional lawlessness and armed incursions in the streets of the capital. But in 1156, with the Hōgen Insurrection, came the first unmistakable sign of a change in the times. For the first time in over three hundred years a succession dispute was settled by armed conflict, open violence, and bloodshed. The punishment of the insurgents was brutal and bloody; large numbers were executed in a revival of capital punishment that, for courtiers at least, had been in abeyance for the whole of the Heian period. The Taira emerged in a much stronger position. Kiyomori, who was on very close terms with the leaders of the winning faction, was raised in rank, and his family gained entry into high court circles. The Minamoto were weakened, for many of their leaders had chosen to support the insurgents.

Only three and a half years later, in January 1160, another power struggle, the Heiji Insurrection, left Kiyomori in a supreme position. He rose rapidly in rank and became Prime Minister in 1166, though he resigned the position shortly afterwards, once it had served to demonstrate his power. He consolidated his position by marrying his sons and daughters into influential court families and eventually into the imperial family: in 1172 his daughter Tokuko (1157–1213) became consort to Emperor Takakura (1161–81), whose mother was Kiyomori's sister-in-law. In 1178 a son, Antoku (d. 1185), was born to Tokuko and was immediately named Crown Prince. As grandfather of the prospective Emperor, Kiyomori had raised himself to the powerful position once held by Fujiwara leaders.

In the exercise and enjoyment of the power that was now theirs, the Taira were essentially Heian courtiers, even if some of the more conservative aristocrats continued to look on them as provincial upstarts. They had merely taken over positions that had for a long time been the prerogative of the Fujiwara, but they did not change the government except in so far as they had a secure hold on the provincial source of their wealth and were not averse to the use of force in achieving their ends. The life of the court went on as before, with the Taira, as close relatives of the reigning Empress, filling many high positions with no less refinement and elegance than their predecessors.

However, there was much resentment against the Taira, who did not help matters by their often arrogant and overbearing behavior. Following the Shishigatani Affair, a plot that was easily crushed in 1177, the Taira emerged with even greater strength, but also with more enemies, including, most notably, their former ally Goshirakawa. A disagreement with him in 1179 gave Kiyomori an excuse for a minor coup d'état in which he dismissed many officials and promoted members of his family to the vacant posts. Feeling against the Taira grew still more intense.

In 1180 a serious insurrection broke out supported by Minamoto no Yorimasa (1104–80), an important Minamoto leader who had remained neutral in the Heiji Insurrection, but who now called on all Minamoto to unite against the Taira. Though he was defeated, in the autumn of the same year, Minamoto no Yoritomo (1147–99), whose father had been executed after the Heiji Insurrection, raised troops and began a long campaign against the Taira, the Genpei War of 1180–85.

In those five years of intermittent warfare a few events stand out. In 1181 Kiyomori died and was succeeded by his son, Munemori (1147–85), who was quite unequal to the task he faced. In 1183, following a series of Taira defeats, the capital itself was threatened by Minamoto forces, and in the seventh month of that year the whole Taira clan fled the city, seeking the safety of their estates in the west. In the spring of the next year they suffered a major defeat at the battle of Ichinotani, in which many of their leaders were killed. Others were brought back as prisoners to the capital, to be paraded through the streets along with the heads of the slain. Then, in the third month of 1185, the Taira armies were finally destroyed at the battle of Dannoura.

The Taira had exercised their power in and through the court. They had become part of the old order rather than instituting a new one, and some historians believe their very adoption of courtly ways caused them to lose their military prowess and aided in their downfall. But with their destruction the change of government from civil and courtly to feudal and military was completed. Yoritomo set up his own government at Kamakura, some 300 miles to the east of the capital, and though he was nominally a servant of the Emperor, and the court retained the apparatus of government it had always had, power was firmly in the hands of the Minamoto leader. The life of the court continued: it retained its social and cultural prestige, the ceremonies went on, the artistic pursuits were the same, and courtiers intrigued for office as always—but with a consciousness now of the watchful eye of the military government in Kamakura and in a very different atmosphere from before.[3]

3. This account of the complex events and processes of the late Heian period is very brief and ignores many important aspects. For a fuller treatment of this period, the reader may profitably consult such general histories as Sansom, *History of Japan*, vol. 1, and Hall, *Japan from Prehistory*

It was in the midst of these events that Lady Daibu spent the first half of her life. She grew up as the Taira were rising to power at court, and she was herself in service at court during their heyday. Since she had never known a court without the Taira, for her they were a central and normal part of the aristocracy, in fact, the epitome of courtliness and elegance. Their destruction must have seemed to her truly the end of an age.

As with so many women writers of the Heian court, Lady Daibu herself is something of a mystery. We do not know exactly when she was born or when she died, or even what her personal name was. And what little is known of her life must be gleaned from scanty references to her or to her family in various documents and by conjecture from her *Memoirs*—a dangerous procedure, for it is impossible to tell how much her work has been fictionalized and how distorted the facts may be, whether for the sake of art or because of hazy memories.

Both her parents belonged to families with long artistic traditions. Her father was Fujiwara no Koreyuki (1123?–75),[4] a descendant of Fujiwara no Yukinari (972–1027), founder of the renowned Sesonji school of calligraphy. Koreyuki himself was a skilled calligrapher and received many honors from the court. He was also a talented musician, wrote a treatise on music (probably as an instruction manual for his children), and is noted in one document as the music teacher of Lady Daibu.[5] He was, in addition, a literary scholar of repute, the author of the *Genji monogatari shaku*, the first commentary on *The Tale of Genji*, and compiler of a collated edition of *The Tales of Ise*, a tenth-century collection of poem-tales. His eldest son,

to Modern Times; and such specialized studies as Hall and Mass, *Medieval Japan*, and Mass, *Warrior Government*.

4. See Kusakabe, pp. 37–38, for a discussion of his date of birth.

5. *Shinsōsōshōkechimyaku* in GSRJ, 15: 477. His musical treatise is called the *Yakakuteikinshō*.

Koretsune (d. 1227), is particularly mentioned as a poet in the family genealogy.

On her mother's side, Lady Daibu came from a renowned family of court musicians, the Ōmiwa, who had for many generations served in the Bureau of Music, the Gagakuryō. Her grandfather, Ōmiwa no Motomasa (1079–1138), was a flautist of high repute, and Lady Daibu's mother, Yūgiri (d. 1180?),[6] appears to have studied under him, as well as under other teachers. Yūgiri herself was a highly renowned player of the thirteen-stringed zither and had numerous important pupils, including, according to one source, her husband, Koreyuki.[7] It is inconceivable that she did not pass on her skills to her daughter.

With such a background, we would find it strange indeed if Lady Daibu had not shown some artistic inclinations, especially in that age, when families felt a jealous pride in the artistic traditions of their house and passed on skills from one generation to the next. There are signs enough in her *Memoirs* that Lady Daibu enjoyed a considerable reputation for both her calligraphy and her zither-playing, and it is possible that these talents helped her to secure a position as a lady-in-waiting; they certainly must have stood her in good stead while she was at court. It is likely also that her interest in literature was fostered by the activities of her father and brother. In any event, her writing shows by its allusions and its style a very thorough grounding in the classics of Japanese literature, though such knowledge would be normal for any well-educated lady of the time.

6. There was obviously a very close relationship between mother and daughter, since Lady Daibu mentions Yūgiri's death more than once. Honiden suggests 1124–79 as Yūgiri's dates, whereas Kusakabe makes a persuasive case for 1116 as her date of birth. *Zenshaku*, pp. 16–19; Kusakabe, pp. 38–41.

7. GSRJ, 15: 477.

In a society that emphasized artistic pursuits, Lady Daibu came of a family that was more artistic than most, but in general her background and education must have been those of a typical lady of the middle aristocracy. Her father's family, a minor branch of the powerful Fujiwara clan, had for some generations held the fourth or fifth rank. They were thus securely in the middle class at court, though, for the most part, they held no distinguished positions.[8] Lady Daibu would have assumed the same status on entering court, relatively obscure but comfortable. Her life before entering court would probably have equipped her well for the life she would lead there, for her parents' household must have been quite busy, with many a distinguished visitor coming to enjoy the skills of her parents or to learn from them.

Unfortunately, nothing of her early life can be discovered. Much effort and many pages of scholarly discussion have been expended on fixing her date of birth, but no year has been identified with certainty. All suggestions are based on conjecture and circumstantial evidence, and the only thing that can be said with confidence is that she was born between 1150 and 1160. Many scholars favor the year 1157, though there is good reason to put the date as early as 1151.[9] She was, at all events, born close to the time of the Hōgen Insurrection, which marked the emergence of the warrior classes into positions of real power in the aristocracy.

That she entered court service as a lady-in-waiting to Kiyomori's daughter, Empress Tokuko, is certain, but when and under what circumstances is far from clear. It cannot have been

8. *Sonpibunmyaku* in Kuroita, 58: 383–85.

9. I shall not repeat here the complicated circumstantial evidence adduced by Hon-iden for 1157 or by Kusakabe for 1151: neither can make the case conclusively. *Zenshaku*, pp. 15–21; Kusakabe, pp. 46–66. Hisamatsu and Kubota favor the early 1150's, which is as precise as it is wise to be (p. 199).

later than the autumn of 1173, for she herself mentions New Year's Day, 1174, as the probable date of Poem 2 of her *Memoirs*. From the position of this poem at the beginning of her work and the feelings of wonder and joy it expresses, most commentators feel it was written soon after Lady Daibu's entry into court. That, however, is no more than conjecture, and she may well have entered court earlier. It is even possible—though we have no evidence for this, only conjecture—that she was first in service in the household of the Regent Fujiwara no Motozane (1143–66) in the early or middle 1160's, then entered court as early as 1166, following the death of Motozane.[10] There is an intriguing reference to a "Lady Daibu, lady-in-waiting," in the records of a poetry contest held in 1166 at the home of the well-known poet Fujiwara no Shigeie (1128–80.)[11] Despite certain similarities between the third poem of this Lady Daibu and Poem 49 in the *Memoirs*, many commentators refuse to believe that the two poets are one and the same, mostly on grounds of age. But if we put Lady Daibu's date of birth as early as 1151, she could certainly have participated in the poetry contest,[12] though this could have been either before or after she entered court. The interesting possibility raised here is that she may have begun to participate in literary activities at an early age and before entering court service. But all that can be said is that she entered court no later than autumn 1173 (autumn was a common time for beginning service) and probably no earlier than 1166, and she may already have been in service in a private household before this time.

10. Kusakabe, pp. 54–56.

11. *Chūgū no suke Shigeie no Ason no ie no utaawase*, GSRJ, 8: 590–606, where one of the participants is listed as Ukyō no Daibu Denka Nyōbō. The term *denka nyōbō* means a lady-in-waiting either to a member of the imperial family other than the Emperor or at the mansion of a Regent or Chancellor.

12. Kusakabe, p. 50. Kubota also considers it highly probable. Hisamatsu and Kubota, p. 199.

It was from her days at court that she gained the name by which she is now known to the world, the unwieldy title of Kenreimon-in Ukyō no Daibu. The first element, Kenreimon-in, is the name Empress Tokuko received on becoming a Retired Empress, and it serves to define Lady Daibu as one who was in service with Tokuko, rather than some other Lady Daibu in service to another Empress. The second half of the name, Ukyō no Daibu, is a source of trouble. Normally, when a woman entered court, she was sponsored by some influential male relative—often adoptive—and was known by the title or position of her sponsor, not by her own personal name. *Ukyō no daibu* means Superintendent of the Right-hand Half of the Capital, and it is reasonable to assume that Lady Daibu's sponsor held this title. However, only two close relatives of hers are shown in any document to have held the title, and neither of them could have been her sponsor. Her great-grandfather Sadasane retired from public life and took the tonsure in 1119, and though his dates are uncertain, he was probably dead by the time Lady Daibu went into service; her nephew Yukiyoshi (b. 1179) was not promoted to that position until 1235. Who then was her sponsor? Some scholars have taken an easy way out and suggested that her father held the title even though there is no record of his having done so.[13] This is highly unlikely. If Koreyuki had held the post of *ukyō no daibu*, we would expect to find at least one reference to it in some record. Moreover, his rank would have been higher, for the post seems invariably to have been given to men of considerably higher rank than it strictly demanded.

Two men served as *ukyō no daibu* during the period when Lady Daibu is thought to have gone into court service. Fujiwara no Kunitsuna (1122–81) held the post from 1161 to 1168, then Fujiwara no Toshinari (1114–1204) from 1168 to 1175;

13. E.g. Tomikura 1942, p. 8.

either might have been her sponsor, depending on the exact date of her entry into court service. Elaborate arguments have been put forward on behalf of both men.[14] However, the evidence is highly circumstantial and the theories full of conjecture, so that they must remain only attractive possibilities. There are certainly entries in the *Memoirs* suggesting that Lady Daibu was on friendly terms with members of Toshinari's family, in particular her exchange of poems with Toshinari on his ninetieth birthday (Poems 355–56) and with his son, Sadaie (1162–1241), when she was asked for poems for an imperial anthology that Sadaie was compiling (Poems 358–59).

This request for contributions to Sadaie's volume was what ensured that she would be known to posterity by the name Kenreimon-in Ukyō no Daibu. She was probably known at various times in her life by her personal name and perhaps by some other title that she received when she reentered court service late in life. In 1232 Sadaie began collecting poems for the ninth imperial anthology, the *Shinchokusenshū*, which was completed in 1235. He hoped to include some of Lady Daibu's poems, and when he asked her for some, he also inquired under what name she would like to be known. Her answer was, "Just as I was known in those days." There can be no doubt that her time in service with Tokuko is what is meant by "those days." Thus it is that two of her poems appear in the *Shinchokusenshū* under the name of Kenreimon-in Ukyō no Daibu, the earliest known use of the name.[15]

Some scholars have been worried by the fact that Empress Tokuko did not receive the name Kenreimon-in until 1181, by

14. *Zenshaku*, pp. 22–33; Kusakabe, pp. 54–57. Kusakabe demonstrates that Kunitsuna and Toshinari were closely connected, so that the circumstantial evidence for Lady Daibu's close connection with Toshinari's family would support his theory. Hon-iden's theory has doubtful points, and Kusakabe's makes some rather large assumptions for which there is no real evidence.

15. *Shinchokusenshū* 844 and 1100.

which time Lady Daibu had left her service; Lady Daibu would think of herself as being associated with the name Tokuko rather than with Kenreimon-in, they argue.[16] But it was normal to call people by their most recent title, and it is most unlikely that in 1232, when this exchange occurred, anyone—even Lady Daibu—referred to the former Empress as anything other than Kenreimon-in. Sadaie himself probably added the first element in the name for the sake of clarity.

Thus it is that Lady Daibu's name was fixed for posterity. The colophon to the text of her *Memoirs* specifically calls it "The Collection [*shū*] of Kenreimon-in Ukyō no Daibu." This colophon, however, is dated 1260, and we cannot know how much earlier the work was known by that name. As for Lady Daibu's other names, they are likely to remain a mystery.[17]

In the first half of her *Memoirs*, Lady Daibu presents a vivid picture of her life at court: parties with music and poetry, casual musical and literary gatherings, visiting noblemen, gossip with her friends, exchanges of gifts and elegant messages, outings for flower viewing, sitting up all night to see the moon, visits of the Emperor and other illustrious personages to the Empress's apartments, and, of course, love affairs.

Many of the important personages and attractive young noblemen she mentions are members of the Taira family, and her descriptions certainly reinforce the commonly accepted view that the formerly warlike Taira lapsed into luxurious and over-refined ways during their brief spell as the central figures of the Heian court. This familiarity with the Taira family, which she inevitably gained from being a member of Empress Tokuko's entourage, was an integral part of her experience at

16. E.g. Kusakabe, pp. 12–13.

17. Kusakabe identifies Lady Daibu with a lady-in-waiting called Fujiwara no Yoshiko, and Murai Jun suggests that during her time at the court of Retired Emperor Gotoba she was known as Ichi no In no Ukyō no Daibu. Kusakabe, pp. 53–55; "Hyōkai," p. 215; Murai 1963, pp. 233–35.

court and adds greatly to the interest of her work, for many of her descriptions of well-known Taira figures add a new dimension to the descriptions found in other sources.

Lady Daibu cannot have been long at court before she was involved in flirtation. Many of her early entries give a delightful picture of the gallantry and coquetry that was such a common diversion of Heian courtly society. She claims (foreword to Poem 61) that though she was amused by seeing it all, she was determined not to become involved in such affairs herself. But one affair she did have, and it seems to have been the great passion of her life. She does not mention her lover by name, but there is no doubt that he was Taira no Sukemori (1161?–85), a grandson of Kiyomori.[18] It is this love affair that forms the central theme of the *Memoirs*.

For a long time, Lady Daibu was thought to have had only the one affair with Sukemori. But in 1934 the exciting discovery was made that some of her poems were to be found in the collection of Fujiwara no Takanobu (1142–1205), a distinguished literary figure and renowned portrait painter.[19] It is clear that the two had some kind of liaison, but how serious the affair was no one can really say. It may have been a mere flirtation, no more than a conventional exchange of amorous poems between two people who were more friends than lovers. There are several such exchanges with other men (e.g. Poems 59–60). However, Lady Daibu usually names such correspondents, whereas she nowhere mentions Takanobu, and the only other man to receive such anonymity was Sukemori.

If, as seems probable, she did have a real affair with Takanobu, it would have been of a different quality from her affair with Sukemori. Takanobu was considerably older than she was,

18. See *Zenshaku*, pp. 39–40, for an examination of the evidence for this.
19. Shimada, 1934, pp. 36–39. See GSRJ, 12: 56–57, for the poems in Takanobu's collection.

a man of the world and a well-known womanizer, and if we accept the hypothesis of her close connection with the family of Fujiwara no Toshinari, a family friend, since he was Toshinari's stepson.[20] The poems exchanged with Takanobu are wittier, more rhetorically complex, and more conventional, in essence more artificial, than those about or exchanged with Sukemori; but this distinction may be due to the process of selection for her *Memoirs*, and does not necessarily indicate what the real relationships were like. In any case, it is impossible to know how accurately the *Memoirs* reflect the realities of Lady Daibu's love affairs.

The difficulties are compounded because only a few poems are clearly identifiable as coming from or being sent to Takanobu, and there are others that could apply to either man. There are also discrepancies between the forewords to the poems in the *Memoirs* and the forewords to the same poems in the collection of Takanobu, which raises the unanswerable question of whether Lady Daibu purposely altered events or was merely recalling them from a different perspective. Conscious and unconscious artistry in autobiography are often difficult to distinguish.

What seems most likely from the text is that Lady Daibu was merely amusing herself in dalliance with Takanobu, and was not carrying on a real love affair with him when she fell in love with Sukemori. It is Sukemori whom she introduces first (Poem 61), but later she goes on to tell of the affair with Takanobu, saying "sometime prior to that I had been approached by a man" (Poem 135). It seems clear, therefore, that her flirtation with Takanobu came first. She embarked on the affair with Sukemori much against her own judgment but was powerless to resist. She often talks of the affair as being unexpected or an unwelcome but inevitable destiny. To judge from

20. Tomikura 1942, p. 31; Kusakabe, pp. 84–92.

her own words, the course of the affair was far from smooth. She obviously suffered the long periods of neglect that seem to have been the lot of many Heian mistresses. Whether she exaggerates her sufferings, it is impossible to say, but in view of their difference in status and the calls on his time that Sukemori must have had, she probably had to go for longish periods without seeing him. If her affair with Takanobu did become serious, it was doubtless during one such period of neglect, when she might have turned to Takanobu for comfort. It is impossible to set a date to the beginnings of these affairs, although some scholars, without any real evidence, suggest 1177 for her affair with Sukemori.[21]

While these affairs were going on, she was forced for some reason to leave court. She says she did not retire of her own accord (foreword to Poem 123), but the reasons for her withdrawal are unclear. Speculation ranges from official displeasure at her affair with Sukemori, to resentment and jealousy over the liaison on the part of other ladies-in-waiting, to the illness of her mother.[22] There is no doubt, however, that Lady Daibu had left the court before the end of 1178. She writes (foreword to Poem 125) of being away from court and hearing indirectly of the birth of Empress Tokuko's son, Antoku, which occurred in the eleventh month of Jijō 2 (Dec. 22, 1178, in the Western calendar). Since the poem in which she actually tells of her withdrawal from court (Poem 123) is an autumn poem, it is likely that she left early in the autumn of 1178.

Both her love affairs continued after her withdrawal, though there is some difficulty in deciding whether certain poems should be assigned to Takanobu or to Sukemori for this period of her life, and it is no easy task to chart the course of the affairs. The affair with Sukemori appears to have been at

21. *Zenshaku*, p. 41; Tomikura 1942, p. 24.
22. *Zenshaku*, p. 57; Tomikura 1942, pp. 38–39; Nakamura, pp. 140–43.

a very low point in the summer of 1179 (see Poems 158–59), and the affair with Takanobu appears to have been continuing, but with increasing difficulties. On leaving the court, she seems to have gone to live near the eastern edge of the capital, but she moved fairly soon (Poem 162), probably to a place outside the city in the western hills, which she mentions in Poem 167.[23] The move seems to have ended the affair with Takanobu. Sukemori, however, continued to visit her, and the love affair appears to have become more intense. Though she still writes of her loneliness and his neglect, it is obvious that they were drawn closer together than ever at this time, perhaps because of the growing troubles in the world at large. Lady Daibu makes no mention of the problems that now beset the Taira. For this there are two reasons: what concerns her is her own private world of feeling, her love affair and subsequent loss; and the women writers of the Heian period never touched on politics, perhaps from a sense of decorum. It would be remarkable if Lady Daibu had made any references to the political troubles of the times. She later writes of the Taira flight from the capital, of warriors passing through, and of prisoners being paraded through the streets, but only because these things affect her so personally and so deeply and provoke a private, emotional response. She shows no interest in the events of the world in general, and in this her work is very much that of a Heian woman writer.

There were problems enough for the two lovers. Sukemori must have been extremely preoccupied as the Taira position

23. The foreword to Poem 162, which first mentions the move away from the capital and treats it as though it is to be the breaking point in a love affair, could apply to either lover; but most commentators see this as the final poem in the affair with Takanobu, since the affair with Sukemori continues past this point, and the use of the term "Musashi stirrups" (*musashi abumi*) in the foreword is a possible link with poems using the same expression in Takanobu's collection. GSRJ, 12: 59. On this point, as on so many, certainty is impossible.

worsened, and Lady Daibu does seem rather peevish about his absences from her side. It would not have been easy for Sukemori to make frequent journeys out to the western hills, and his legal wife and her family were doubtless none too pleased to see the affair revived. But the two lovers obviously met as and when they could, and the fact that Sukemori pursued the affair at all at this time is proof enough of his feelings for her.

Sometime after her withdrawal from court, Lady Daibu also lost her mother. As usual, an exact date cannot be fixed, but to judge from the position of the poems Lady Daibu wrote on the event, her mother may well have died around 1180, and the death must certainly have occurred during the period when the position of the Taira was steadily worsening.[24] It is likely that this is when she moved outside the city, perhaps to live with her brother, the priest Son-en (dates unknown), who may have been at a temple to the west of the city.[25] Of her everyday life at the time, nothing is known, but with the loss of her mother on top of being cut off from the court, she must have felt quite abandoned and alone. The tone of her poems suggests loneliness and sadness, with some happiness in the continued, if infrequent, visits of Sukemori.

The flight of the Taira from the capital in the autumn of 1183 shattered this relatively peaceful, half-content, half-lonely and melancholy existence. In his last words to her Sukemori had said that she was unlikely to see him again, and she was left to wait in uncertainty for the outcome of the war. At this time her daily life must have been much the same as before.

24. Hon-iden suggests 1179, but this is no more than conjecture. *Zenshaku*, pp. 18–19. Lady Daibu's poems on her mother's death are placed just before those on the death of Retired Emperor Takakura, which occurred in the first month of 1181. But the position of poems in the *Memoirs* is an extremely unreliable way of dating events, and her mother's death could have followed Takakura's.

25. Hon-iden suggests the Zenpōji Temple. *Zenshaku*, p. 62.

She was obviously in touch with friends and relatives, for she made an excursion, which only reminded her that Sukemori was no longer close by her, and she heard all the terrible news of the war: she knew of the Minamoto troops who swarmed into the capital and then left to pursue the Taira westward; she heard of the prisoners and the dead, many of whom were her friends; and she heard of the death of Sukemori's brothers; and finally, in what was only confirmation of what she knew must happen, she heard of Sukemori's death at the battle of Dannoura in the spring of 1185.

At least in the anxious two years of waiting she had had two (perhaps more) messages to keep up her hopes, but with the inescapable certainty of his death, she was prostrated and went through a period of intense depression—her descriptions seem to match the symptoms of clinical depression. Eventually she recovered enough to devote herself to prayers for Sukemori's soul. Her longing drove her to visit places that reminded her of the past, but far from comforting her, they only freshened and intensified her grief as the reality of her loss was brought home to her anew. Like any other person faced with such a loss, she needed to bring back the past and yet to forget it, and all her attempts only made her grief the worse. She seems, in fact, to have sought out painful memories and steeped herself purposely in sorrow, so that she could keep alive her love, though its object was a man now dead.

In her restlessness and her reaching for the past, she went to visit her former mistress, the Retired Empress Kenreimon-in, who after her capture at Dannoura and her return to the capital, had taken the tonsure in the autumn of 1185 and retired to the Jakkōin, a convent at Ōhara some miles north of the capital. The visit impressed deeply on Lady Daibu the changes that had taken place, for the nun she now met seemed a different person from the Empress of the old days. Emperor Takakura had abdicated in 1180 and died in 1181, and his death had perhaps been for Lady Daibu a symbol of the dying of the world she had known. Nothing seemed to remain of the old days, and she herself had little reason to go on as she was. Yet like the fictional Prince who is the hero of *The Tale of Genji*, she could not bring herself to take the tonsure.

In yet another effort to escape her grief, she made a pilgrimage to the temples at Sakamoto on the shore of Lake Biwa. But this too only brought back memories and intensified her sadness, and after a stay of some time at Sakamoto she returned to the capital, probably in the new year 1187, to settle down to a quiet life of memories, attacks of intense grief, correspondence and visits with friends from past days, and endless prayers for the repose of the souls of Sukemori and her mother.

There is no way of knowing where she lived or how she spent her time for the next several years. The poems in her *Memoirs* all seem to be from the years closely following Sukemori's death, and Lady Daibu herself gives no indication of what her life was like in the succeeding years. We can only assume that her poems set the tone for the whole of this period. However, there is an incident in the *Shūgyokushū*, the personal poetry collection of the priest Jien (1155–1225), with enough circumstantial evidence to indicate that it concerns Lady Daibu.[26] It suggests that Lady Daibu lived part of the time with her brother, the priest Son-en, and did not spend all her time in the tearful gloom that enshrouds her *Memoirs* at this point. The passage reads:

On the same snowy morning the Retired Emperor [Goshirakawa] sent to the cell of the priest Jōken requesting some snow with which to build a little snow mountain at his palace. So Jōken raked down the snow from his roof and sent it off. Someone must have seen this, for an unsigned letter was thrown in to him, and on opening it he read:

26. *Ibid.*, pp. 60–61.

Kieyuku o	This is a house where
Oshimu yado dani	Even the slow melting of the snow
Aru mono o	Brings feelings of regret;
Haraitekeri na	Yet now you have swept it all away,
Yuki no uwabuki	The covering of snow upon the thatch.

Thinking the letter was the work of his neighbor, Jitsuryō, he wrote, "This is without doubt the work of Sanmi no Bō, for who, except my neighbor, could have seen me getting the snow down from the roof?" He attached a poem of reply and sent it to the lodging of Enjari [Son-en].

The letter was really the work of Enjari's younger sister, the lady-in-waiting, Lady Daibu.[27]

The date of this episode can be fixed with certainty as the thirteenth of the eleventh month of Bunji 5 (Dec. 22, 1189), and if we accept the strong evidence that the writer of the poem was indeed the Lady Daibu of the *Memoirs*, the incident shows that she was staying with her brother Son-en, possibly at the Hosshōji Temple, and was not averse to some lighter social activities. We are here afforded a brief glimpse of a more cheerful Lady Daibu behind the heroine of the *Memoirs*.

It is almost certain that she did not spend all her time living in temples, and she may only have visited her brother for short periods. But where else and what manner of life she lived cannot be discovered. She may not have been dependent solely on her brother Son-en, for her elder brother Koretsune was a courtier of moderate status and could have provided lodging and support for her, though she makes no mention of him at all in her *Memoirs*. We can only surmise that she lived a peaceful, if melancholy, life of virtual retirement in or close to the capital.

27. Matsushita 1958, p. 66, Poems 5118–21; quoted in *Zenshaku*, pp. 58–59, where Hon-iden argues convincingly that Lady Daibu's brother Son-en was very probably known as Enjari.

The tranquility of the retired existence was broken by her return to court service, an unwelcome turn of events that must have necessitated a considerable readjustment in her life and awakened many slumbering memories. But it had been arranged by influential relatives or friends, and she could not refuse without causing offense.[28] The court she now entered was that of the young Emperor Gotoba (1180–1239), who reigned from 1184 to 1198, and it is clear that she began her service while he was still on the throne. Allowing for the season of some poems that she must have written before Gotoba's abdication, she can have entered court no later than the autumn of 1197, and most probably somewhat earlier. Accurate dating is impossible, but some scholars speculate a time as early as 1191 or 1193, and others opt for 1196.[29]

Lady Daibu makes no mention of what life was like at Gotoba's court, where she must have played the part of an elder lady-in-waiting. She makes no allusions to his political intrigues, to his passion for poetry and the other arts, or to the unusual hobbies, such as the forging of swords, that he pursued after his abdication. She concentrates, as always, on the theme of her loss. Every incident she mentions from this period is one that brings back memories of the past or reminds her of Sukemori's death.

The latest datable incident she writes of is the death of Fujiwara no Sanemune (b. 1149), which occurred on January 1, 1213 (eighth of the twelfth month of Kenryaku 2), and it seems most likely that she was still at court at this time. But how long she remained at court is unknown. One scholar suggests that on the death of Former Empress Kenreimon-in in 1213, she retired to Ōhara to pray for the soul of her erstwhile

28. It is unclear who made the arrangements, but Hon-iden suggests the priest Jien, who was influential at court and was a friend of Lady Daibu's brother Son-en. *Zenshaku,* p. 66.

29. Ōbayashi 1972; Gotō 1971, pp. 17–18; *Zenshaku,* p. 66.

mistress, which is why there are no poems from after the beginning of that year.[30] Popular legend does indeed place Lady Daibu's tomb alongside that of the Former Empress at the Jakkōin, but there is no real evidence to support the theory. Lady Daibu may well have served longer in the court of Retired Emperor Gotoba, perhaps even up to his banishment for plotting against the military government in 1222. How she spent the last years of her life can only be conjectured. She may well have become a nun and lived out her life in quiet religious devotions, but she may also well have spent her last years in the type of retirement that she had been used to before her entry into Gotoba's court. The exchange of poems with Fujiwara no Sadaie that is appended to her *Memoirs* almost certainly dates from 1232, when Sadaie began to collect poems for his imperial anthology, the *Shinchokusenshū*. There is thus little doubt that she lived until at least 1232. But beyond that nothing is known. She fades out with the same obscurity that covers so much of her life. But at some time before 1232 she collected together some of her poems and arranged them into a continuous set of memoirs to tell the story of her love and suffering, and one of her last acts was to ensure the form in which her name would be preserved for posterity.

30. Tomikura 1942, p. 102. However, Hon-iden suggests that Poems 347–48 date from as late as 1229, purely on the grounds that Taira no Chikanaga, the partner in the exchange of poems, did not become *tō no chujō* (Sukemori's last official post) until late 1228, and it was the associations with this post that led to the inclusion of these poems. *Zenshaku* 1974 ed., pp. 269, 278–79.

Poetic Memoirs and Autobiographical
Poetry Collections

Constructed around more than 350 poems that form the climax of each episode and crystallize the emotions and attitudes
of the author for the event described, *The Poetic Memoirs of
Lady Daibu* share an ambiguous status with a large body of
autobiographical and even biographical works that assume
quite different forms: narrative tales, memoirs, diaries, and
poetry collections. All these writings have in common an intense lyricism and the presence of a greater or smaller number
of poems. Though such mixtures of poetry and prose are rare
in Western literature, they were the norm in Heian Japan.
One of the special characteristics of Heian literature is a remarkable affinity between poetry and prose. No work of prose
exists without some poetry in it, and conversely, there is no
collection of poems that does not contain some prose. *The
Poetic Memoirs of Lady Daibu* are typical of many works in
the sense that they may be considered either memoirs or a personal poetry collection, and in fact the Japanese title, *Ken-*

reimon-in Ukyō no Daibu shū, means "The Poetry Collection of Lady Daibu."[31]

This almost symbiotic relationship of poetry and prose stems from the ubiquity of poetry in everyday life. From earliest times, the Japanese considered poetry the natural response to anything in life that moved them, particularly the beauty and pathos of nature and the experience of love. Whether in speech or in writing, poetry was considered the most sensitive, appropriate, and effective means of expression, and was chosen in preference to prose on any occasion of truly deep feeling. To the men and women of the Heian court, with its emphasis on cultivation and sensibility, poetry became an essential part of any social relationship, whether composed to celebrate a love affair, a visit to a friend's house, or a court function. So much was poetry a part of the social fabric that in practical terms it would have been impossible to write about life without resorting to poems.

But the very social nature of poetry, the fact that it was seen as an immediate response to an outside stimulus, meant that every poem had its social or circumstantial context, an understanding of which was often essential for its comprehension. Even where knowledge of the context was not essential, it could often deepen the reader's appreciation of a poem, and when a

31. It is placed among the memoirs by Tamai Kōsuke and Shimada Taizō, but among the personal poetry collections by Kuwabara Hiroshi. Tamai 1965, pp. 375–97; Shimada 1950, pp. 3, 15–16; Kuwabara, p. 33. The Japanese terms are *shikashū* or *ie no shū* for personal poetry collection and *nikki* for memoirs. *Nikki* literally means "day record" and is usually translated "diary" in English, but most Heian *nikki* are a far cry from the typical diaries of English literature, and the term "memoirs" seems closer to their true nature. Lady Daibu's work is often classed as a *nikki* by Japanese scholars, but it is obviously not a "diary" in Western terms. For a discussion of Japanese *nikki* and a useful chart of works that straddle genres, see Miner, pp. 3–20; and for a valuable survey of the problem of genre in works such as Lady Daibu's, see Cranston, pp. 90–125.

poem lacked such information, readers or copiers felt obliged to provide a plausible context. Even the longer poems, which to some extent provided their own context, were often given explanatory titles; but these *chōka*, as the form was called, were hardly produced at all after the eighth century, and the short, five-line *tanka* form, which was the staple of the Heian court, was even more dependent on its context, which was usually supplied in a prose foreword, or *kotobagaki*, whenever poems were gathered into collections or anthologies. The oral provision of such prose contexts was a popular pastime among the ladies of the court, and it was from such activities, known as *utagatari*, or poem-telling, that much prose writing developed, especially in the form of "poem tales," *uta monogatari*, which were a type of poetic biography, often a mixture of fact and fiction.

Another major stimulus to the development of prose was letter writing, an apparently ceaseless activity of Heian courtiers, particularly in the conduct of love affairs. Of course, no letter was complete without at least one poem, and usually it was the poem that expressed the essential point. It was only natural for people to keep their correspondence, and as the letters mounted up, they formed a haphazard collection of mixed poems and prose, to which were usually added all the poems a person had composed at various times or exchanged on social occasions. The poems were usually considered the more important element, for they were the distillation of feeling, the intense expression of emotion that captured an occasion or experience. The rough material of these natural, haphazard collections was often made up into a personal poetry collection in which the prose might be cut to a minimum, left much as it was, or written up artistically as a rich context for the poetry. Sometimes the raw material or the resulting poetry collection was further worked up into memoirs or a diary, an account of a short period in one person's life or an autobiography of a whole lifetime. It was from such raw material as this, the accumulated poems and correspondence of a lifetime, that the memoirs, or personal poetry collection, of Lady Daibu were compiled.

But there is another reason for the compatibility of poetry and prose in Japanese literature. It is by now a cliché to say that the Japanese muse is a lyric muse; but it is a truth. In Heian literature, especially, we search in vain for epic, for tragedy, for the sort of variety that gave to the West its decorum of the separation of styles. There are, to be sure, distinctions in Japanese literature, but they are of a different order from those in the West. In mode all is lyrical—even such a narrative masterpiece as the early eleventh-century romance *The Tale of Genji* might be called a "lyrical novel." Whatever the reasons for such a pervasive lyricism—some inherent preference of the Japanese people, the origins of prose writing in poetry, the use of Chinese as a "classical" written language that could absorb non-lyric creative impulses—the important question here is how it shapes the works of Heian Japanese literature themselves.

Not only is a distinction between prose and poetry virtually impossible in the Japanese literature of the Heian and later periods, but modern Western literary theory has tended to move away from such a distinction and seek other ways of classifying literary types. The theories of Northrop Frye seem particularly useful in reading the "mixed" genres of the Heian period. In his *Anatomy of Criticism* he distinguishes four types of verbal rhythm that belong to Epos, Prose, Drama, and Lyric: it is the last that concerns us here; and the rhythm of the lyric he calls the "rhythm of association."[32] In a later work, *The Well-Tempered Critic*, he distinguishes three basic, or "primary," rhythms, which he calls verse rhythm, prose rhythm, and asso-

32. Frye 1957, pp. 251–81, especially pp. 270ff.

ciative rhythm. He further examines the ways in which these "primary" rhythms can combine to form "secondary" rhythms, giving rise to a spectrum of literary forms. The "primary" associative rhythm, which he considers the dominant rhythm in the lyric, is classed by him as that of ordinary speech. The lyric itself is hence a "secondary" rhythm in which the associative rhythm is more strongly present than the other two rhythms.[33]

It is in this respect that Frye's theories seem so apposite to Heian literature and suggest a reason for the close unity of poetry and prose in the works of the period, for the prose of the Heian courtly writers is essentially that of speech and recitation, rather than that of exposition and narrative description. Even narrative tales and romances developed from and retained the characteristics of recitation. Memoirs and diaries tended even more to use speech rhythms. Using the term free prose for a prose that is influenced by associative rhythm, Frye says: "We find some free prose in personal letters. . . . But the letter is still a form of communication, and free prose is more obvious in diaries, especially diaries kept by people of no great literary pretensions who are not thinking of publication."[34]

In this pursuit of Frye's theories, we should consider also the question of literary pretensions and publication in Heian Japan, for they were certainly unlike those of today. The audience for all literature was restricted to the tiny body of the courtly aristocracy, and even within that circle there were many for whom literature meant relatively little. Poetry was the most widely practiced literary art of all. Poems were "published" by being presented at poetry contests or poetry parties or other social occasions; or by being included in the prestigious imperial anthologies of poetry that were compiled at rare intervals; or by being passed on to one's close acquaintances and fellow

33. Frye 1963, pp. 55–108.
34. *Ibid.*, pp. 81–82.

poets for their criticism. Many personal poetry collections were perhaps made for this last purpose, with the hope that poems might be selected for the great anthologies. Narratives and romances were circulated in manuscript form and were usually read aloud to a group of listeners. The main audience for these and all other forms of literature except poetry tended to be women, ladies of the court and the wives and daughters of courtiers in their own homes. Much of this was a literature written by women for women, though men of literary taste and ability also took great interest in it and themselves wrote diaries and memoirs. Men had always tended to concentrate on writing in Chinese, which was considered the classical language of learning and government and was a requisite for both social and bureaucratic advancement. Japanese prose in the earliest days of its development (the ninth and tenth centuries) was considered an inferior medium and was therefore left largely to women to exploit, though men of literary genius, such as Ki no Tsurayuki (868?–945), had taken an early interest in it. (But, significantly, Tsurayuki had had to write his *Tosa nikki*, the earliest Japanese diary, dating from 936, in the persona of a woman.) The popularity of Japanese prose writing among men increased through the Heian period, but in general the world of Japanese prose was a restricted one inhabited more by female readers than by male.

Memoirs and diaries had an even smaller audience than the narrative forms; they were often shown only to immediate members of the family or close friends. Lady Daibu writes in her conclusion: "Once in a while people would ask me whether I had any such writings, but what I had written was so much my own personal thoughts that I felt embarrassed, and I would copy out just a little to show to them." Her work seems to have circulated among only a few people, and many works of this sort were merely kept with the family papers or copied out and preserved, often through a chance find, by someone with lit-

erary interests. Memoirs and diaries thus had a very restricted
audience. But it was a homogeneous audience that shared beliefs and values closely with the writer, could understand the
slightest hint or allusion, and was above all sympathetic and
highly receptive. It was a private audience, suited to the private world of memoirs and diaries, part of the author's own
private world.

If Heian writers had any sense of a wider "public," it was
likely to have been only with regard to their poems, which were
the legitimate form of public literary activity. Because of this,
personal poetry collections were often used as a public vehicle
for personal views, especially grievances. Many personal poetry
collections of a formal character with relatively little in the
way of prose context contain a series of poems on personal matters, often appended at the end. Examples of these are the
Kudai waka (894) of Ōe no Chisato and the *Sanbokukikashū*
(c. 1128) of Minamoto no Toshiyori (1055–1129), both of which
are extremely formal yet contain intensely personal sections.
The less formal collections are more consistently personal and
tend to merge into memoirs and diaries, often with an apparent, if not real, diminishing of the writer's literary pretensions
and sense of audience. The purely practical considerations of
circulation for private works in the restricted world of the
aristocrats make it difficult to speak of "publishing" or even
to speak of audience and to work out the author's attitude to
these.

But there was a noticeable ambivalence in the attitude of
the writers of memoirs, diaries, and personal poetry collections.
All early literary theories in Japan were basically expressive:
"Art is that which is created when we are unable to suppress
our feelings," wrote Ki no Tsurayuki in the *Tosa nikki*.[35] And
it is true that the creators of these memoirs and diaries were

35. Miner, p. 87.

often writing for the sake of self-expression, to order their own experience and to exorcise their own emotions. "I intend these memoirs for my eyes alone," writes Lady Daibu in the introduction to her work, but her consciousness of her potential readers is clear throughout the work, and she calls out unmistakably for a sympathetic ear. Though works like this form a genuinely private world, the writers clearly desire, however unconsciously, a reader who will understand and sympathize with their experience and feeling, which they believe to be of ultimate human value and significance.

The writers are adopting a pose that is essentially lyrical, for as Frye says, "The lyric is the genre in which the poet turns his back upon his audience."[36] This pose is to be found in many Heian works. In the opening words of such a minor work as *The Personal Poetry Collection of the Priest Anpō* (c. 960), the author writes, "I have written down just a few of those [poems] I remember."[37] But his work is far from being as casual as he implies or as unstructured as it may appear at first glance: it is a collection of selected poems with some sense of order—seasonal groupings, sequences associated by persons, place, time, or theme—not a series of poems jotted down at random just as they came to the author's mind. This pose—and it does not matter whether it is conscious or unconscious—renders the whole work more lyrical and as Frye maintains, encourages the use of the associative rhythm, the speech rhythm that is so closely connected with lyrical writing. The rhythm of Lady Daibu's writing must immediately strike the reader as that of speech rather than that of connected, expository writing, of speech rather than of controlled narrative prose. This is most easily seen in the long prose sections of Part Four, as exemplified in the *kotobagaki* of Poem 206: "At dawn, at dusk, no mat-

36. Frye 1957, p. 271.
37. *Anpō hōshi shū* in *Zoku kokka taikan*, p. 375.

ter what I looked at, no matter what I listened to, how could I cease to think of him even for a moment? How I wanted, just one more time at least, to tell him how I felt! How sad that my wish was unlikely to be granted!" But this associative rhythm is a quality that runs through the whole work and is not easily grasped from one short illustration, just as it is difficult to pin down in short passages the subtle rhythm of a novel by Virginia Woolf. With its associative speech rhythm, Lady Daibu's carefully wrought and artistic prose blends easily with the poems to create one complete lyrical whole, in which the poems are variations in rhythm, high points or "touchstones" in a unified structure.

If the writer is to some extent posing as nonliterary, yet creating a lyrical, literary whole, what of the truthfulness of these memoirs, diaries, and poetry collections? In Japan there has always been an assumption of a very close link between a writer's work and his life, even in novels, much more so in diaries and memoirs. For many Japanese scholars the "truth" or "fiction" of a work is of crucial importance. Some see *The Poetic Memoirs of Lady Daibu* as truly a diary, and hence a sincere, truthful account of her life.[38] But Lady Daibu's work is obviously selective, distorts the events of her life to some extent, and hence is fictionalized. The heroine, Lady Daibu, is a different character in a different world from the Lady Daibu who wrote the work. For that reason some scholars are inclined to call the work an autobiographical novel, a valid enough view, as long as one does not take the term novel too much in a restricted Western sense.

It is certainly true that the artistic, literary memoirs and diaries of Heian Japan tend to use the techniques of the novel rather than those of the conventional Western diary. But such discussions of genre, though interesting in themselves, are be-

38. E.g. Itoga 1961, pp. 35–40; Suzuki Shigeko, p. 20.

side the point, for we are dealing not specifically with diaries or poetry collections, but with literary autobiographies (and sometimes biographies) that are complete lyrical structures. They are to a large extent free of the factual world, even while tied to it: as the seventeenth-century playwright Chikamatsu Monzaemon said of his own works, they float in "the narrow margin between truth and fiction." The genre should be inferred from the work; the work should not be made to fit the Procrustean bed of a diary or a novel or any other preconceived genre. If the reader knows that he is reading memoirs and that they are "poetic," and if he treats the work as a lyrical whole with a lyrical and associative rather than linear and logical structure, he will not have his sense of genre affronted by *The Poetic Memoirs of Lady Daibu* or be disappointed that it does not live up to his own preconceptions about what its genre or structure should be.

Two Western critics have written: "The true autobiographer . . . must select and arrange the events of his life so as to give them a narrative shape and pattern. Even the diarist eliminates from his record countless trivial details. A diarist who makes a second draft of his diary, as Boswell did and as even Pepys may have done, is moving toward fiction already."[39] Lady Daibu's *Memoirs,* and most other works like it, are certainly second drafts, for they constitute a gathering and ordering of existing poems and material and a rewriting of the prose contexts. The original event and the original lyrical impulse lie in the poem or the prose written at the time. The completed memoirs, diaries, or poetry collections are literary reconstructions, re-creations of a world or even creations of a new world, and hence works of art, not records of absolute truth. Works vary, of course, in how far they move away from truth towards fiction, but since so little is known of most writers of Heian memoirs

39. Scholes and Kellogg, p. 258.

and diaries, it is impossible to tell art from truth in their works, and the reader must be content with the character that emerges from the work, without pretending that a given literary creation is identical with its creator. With Lady Daibu, we know there is at least selection in her *Memoirs*, but how far from the truth she wanders, we can never know, even if we do succeed in finding out some of the facts about her life. What we *can* say is that, like any good work of art, the *Memoirs* carry strong conviction and their own sense of sincerity or artistic integrity.

But how, in the end, are we to classify her work? In Japanese terms it is both a *nikki*, diary/memoirs, and a *shikashū*, personal poetry collection. To deny that it is a set of memoirs simply because it has so many poems and is so obviously dependent on them for its structure is to ignore the evidence of other diaries and memoirs. To deny that it is a poetry collection because it is a type of autobiography and contains so much prose is equally to ignore the evidence of other poetry collections, many of which have an (auto)biographical thematic structure and an abundance of prose. Any discussion and classification of Lady Daibu's *Memoirs* involves decisions of the same sort about a large number of similar works.

Many works that are traditionally classified under the heading of *nikki* are replete with poems and could be called poetic memoirs, poetic diaries, or poetic (auto)biographies. Even a work like the *Kagerō Nikki* (c. 975), which is as close to pure prose as one can come in this genre, is so well endowed with poems as to suggest that it developed from some sort of poetry collection.[40] Other works, such as the *Izumi Shikibu nikki* (c. 1004) or the *Ben no Naishi nikki* (1252), seem very similar to Lady Daibu's work in their proportion of poetry to prose, their alternation of poems with long and short prose sections, and

40. Matsuda, p. 47.

their dependence on poems for the expression of their most intense emotion.

There are, of course, differences between the works of this genre. The *Ben no Naishi nikki*, for example, covers the short period between 1246 and 1252, rather than a whole lifetime, and though each episode is centered on a poem or poems, they are far from being the personal outpourings of Lady Daibu's *Memoirs*. There is much less of a personal theme, and the work as a whole is cheerful and bright, consisting entirely of descriptions of life at court. But in form there is much similarity between the two, as there is between these works and a large number of poetic memoirs. Such memoirs include travel diaries, like the *Tosa nikki* and the *Izayoi nikki* (c. 1280), which is the record of a journey between the capital and the military center of government at Kamakura by the nun Abutsu (d. 1283) and is structured around the poems she wrote along the way. *The Poetic Memoirs of Lady Daibu* thus sit very comfortably among the diaries and memoirs that are firmly labeled as such in Japanese and not generally treated as poetry collections, although they may be included in the category of "poetry literature" (*waka bungaku*). No two works in this genre will be exactly alike. They will differ as the individual works in any genre must differ, in theme, treatment, structure, and tone; but for all their variety they are recognizable as a particular genre, just as in English literature the novel, for all its variety, is distinguishable from the short story or the essay.

However, viewing things from the other end of the scale, we need not read far among the personal poetry collections of the Heian period before we encounter some that seem to resemble Lady Daibu's work. Examining these collections is a somewhat more complicated task than with the memoirs or *nikki*, for if there is a large variety of forms among the memoirs or *nikki*, there is a still greater variety among the personal poetry collections. Multiplicity of form has even been cited as one of the particular characteristics of these works.[41] They can be organized in many different ways or simply not organized at all; they may have little accompanying prose or, like Lady Daibu's *Memoirs,* they may have long *kotobagaki* to many of their poems.

It is even difficult to decide whether a given personal poetry collection should be considered in any way autobiographical. Some collections, particularly from Lady Daibu's own day, contain the barest minimum of prose and are personal only in so far as they present the individual poetic style of a particular poet. Of his life they tell us next to nothing. Notable examples are the *Chōshūeisō* of Fujiwara no Toshinari and the collections of Lady Daibu's famous contemporaries Princess Shikishi (d. 1201) and the woman we know only as Toshinari's Daughter (1171?–1254).

But most collections contain both some very personal material and several *kotobagaki* of moderate length. The very name for these works in the Heian period, *ie no shū,* or "house collections," implies that they will embody something of an individual poet's life and family. The earliest collections, especially, show a strong sense of family pride. An outstanding example is the *Kujō daijin shū* by the statesman Fujiwara no Morosuke (908–60), a work that is deeply colored by his sense of his family's position.[42] Collections from the tenth and eleventh centuries tend to show strong personal elements and frequently contain details of a poet's circumstances and how he came to produce certain poems. Posthumous collections were often compiled as much out of interest in a poet's life as in his poetry.

41. *Ibid.,* pp. 147–48.
42. The texts I used for examining personal poetry collections are those found in Wakashi Kenkyūkai, especially vols. 1–3; Kunaichō; and Tamai 1927–31.

Though an increasing number of more formal and impersonal collections appeared, during the twelfth century and after, later poets continued in this tradition. Hence the majority of personal poetry collections tend to have (auto)biographical elements and a strong sense of personal expression, though it is not easy to say at what point a collection earns itself the name of a proper autobiographical collection. Clearly, the autobiographical nature and long prose sections of Lady Daibu's *Memoirs* do not render the work unusual as a poetry collection. It is perhaps more developed or extreme, since few collections can rival her work in thematic unity, structure, and skillful prose; but all collections tend to show some elements of these qualities.

Several collections stand out in their similarity to Lady Daibu's work. The *Ise shū* of Lady Ise (fl. 935) and the *Ichijō sesshō gyoshū* of Fujiwara no Koretada (924–72) begin with sections of thirty-one poems and forty-one poems, respectively, that are virtually independent collections with sufficiently developed themes and enough prose to constitute unified diaries or narratives telling the stories of the poets' love affairs. But both collections lose their narrative structure thereafter, and with it, any resemblance to Lady Daibu's work. Moreover, the opening sections in both are written in the third person. Third-person narration was a common convention in poetry collections—naturally in those compiled by a hand other than the poet's own, but also in those compiled by the poet himself, as the first part of the *Ichijō sesshō gyoshū* is held to have been. Even some so-called diaries, such as the *Izumi Shikibu nikki*, are in the third person. Though such a convention in no way lessens the personal and lyrical qualities of the works, it does create works that are different in tone from Lady Daibu's.

We also find third-person narration in the collection of the priest Zōki (late tenth or early eleventh century?), the *Zōki hōshi shū*, also known as the *Ionushi*, or Master of the Hermitage, a title the poet gives himself. Unlike the two collections mentioned above, this one is organized wholly as a narrative travel diary, giving an account of the priest's wanderings, though it does include a section of miscellaneous poems in the middle of the work. It has long *kotobagaki,* and it has a sense of theme and construction in being centered on two specific trips, but it ends rather inconclusively and does not have the strong personal theme or unified structure of Lady Daibu's *Memoirs.*

The *Zōki hoshi shū* has a short introduction, or prologue, in which the poet briefly sets the scene for his travels. This is a feature it shares with relatively few personal poetry collections, though those that seem to be most strongly autobiographical have similar introductions, and Lady Daibu's work has both an introduction and a conclusion.[43] The presence of an introduction is no guarantee that a work is strongly autobiographical. The early eleventh-century collection *Saishu Sukechikakyō shū* of Ōnakatomi no Sukechika (954–1038) has an introduction that talks of the uses of poetry and how it is written—under the obvious influence of the famous preface to the *Kokinshū,* the first imperial anthology of poetry—and goes on to say how Sukechika is collecting his own poems to leave a record for his daughters. But the collection is hardly autobiographical, let alone a set of memoirs, for it is organized by seasonal categories in the first half and under headings of love and miscellaneous in the second half. Apart from the introduction, it does not contain much prose, even though the *kotobagaki* to some of the love poems have slight narrative elements.

43. Shinoda, pp. 47–48. Shinoda examined 201 personal poetry collections of the Heian period (not counting Lady Daibu's work) and found introductions in only fourteen, conclusions in two, and both in one. Although there may be disagreement about what constitutes an introduction or a conclusion, his findings appear to be basically valid; the incidence of these elements does not seem to be any higher among the collections he did not examine.

The presence of a conclusion or epilogue is no better guarantee of an autobiographical work than an introduction. For example, in his conclusion to *Zenrin-oyōshū*, Fujiwara no Suketaka (mid- to late twelfth century) tells of gathering together his poems and humbly decries their worth, but the collection itself has few and rather short *kotobagaki* and is arranged in categories by season and other formal methods. A similar ending is found in the *Rokujō suri no daibu no shū* of Fujiwara no Akisue (1055–1123), where the poet asserts that there is no doubt a great deal of nonsense in his collection, which consists only of poems hastily copied down. This work is something of a biographical collection, since the prose sections become quite long and diary-like towards the end and deal with the poet's personal reflections, often his regret at his advancing years. But in arrangement the collection is quite miscellaneous; in the early part the *kotobagaki* are few and short, and the poems are taken from such formal exercises as poetry competitions and 100-poem sequences, rather than from the emotional events of Akisue's life.

A rather interesting collection with a very strong personal note but little factual biographical information is the *Yasunori no Musume shū* (c. 993), the work of a poet known only as Yasunori's Daughter. This collection opens with an enormously long introduction, in which the poet writes of her own life and her view of life in general, showing what seems to be a most un-Heian-like concern for human equality. The collection ends with a similar, long conclusion. But the poems in between are almost entirely without prose accompaniment and are arranged according to formal seasonal patterns. The resemblance of this work to Lady Daibu's *Memoirs* is thus very slight.

A work with a much greater superficial resemblance to Lady Daibu's is the *Tonomo shū*, the collection of Lady Tonomo, a court lady about whom almost nothing in known. She was in service with an imperial consort, but it could have been the consort of Emperor Enyū (r. 969–84), Emperor Kazan (r. 984–86), or Emperor Goreizei (r. 1045–68), and so far no conclusive evidence has surfaced to indicate which one of the three it was. She left court service and became a nun shortly after reaching the age of twenty-five. Her collection is divided into two volumes, the first concentrating on court life and love affairs, and the second on her life after becoming a nun. It has a long introduction, a long conclusion, and also a long introductory *kotobagaki* at the beginning of the second volume. In these structural aspects, it bears a remarkable resemblance to Lady Daibu's *Memoirs*. It is even more symmetrically constructed than Lady Daibu's work: each volume contains 65 poems, beginning with a set of twelve, one for each month of the year, followed by one poem on completing religious observances; then come 52 poems exchanged with various people and accompanied by moderately long *kotobagaki* depicting the poet's life as a court lady and as a nun. The whole seems to be chronologically arranged, but there seems to be little connection or association between each poem or group of poems, and there is little sense of development, plot, or theme, in marked contrast to Lady Daibu's work. Furthermore, the poet uses the third person throughout, calling herself "a woman who loved flowers." Despite these marked differences, however, it stands alongside Lady Daibu's *Memoirs* as a notable example of a carefully constructed autobiographical poetry collection.

The two personal poetry collections that most resemble Lady Daibu's are the *Jōjin Ajari no Haha shū* and the *Shijō no Miya Shimotsuke shū*. The first is the collection of a woman known only as Mother of the Holy Priest Jōjin, and is the record of a six-and-a-half-year period, from 1067 to 1073, during which she faces the disappointment and sorrow of learning that her son, with whom she had been hoping to spend the last years of her life, has decided to go on a pilgrimage to China. It begins some years before his departure and ends a year or so after he has left Japan, and the poet writes movingly of a mother's love and grief, and her sense of loneliness and loss. What makes this work so remarkable and so poignant is that the poet is already in her eighties and knows she will die before her son returns. The collection is divided into two volumes, which are dated, and has many long *kotobagaki*, as well as sections where the poems run on without prose interruption. There is no introduction of the sort that Lady Daibu wrote, but the work ends on a note of finality, with a short conclusion in which the poet writes of her hopes for salvation in the life to come. The whole work is unified by her theme of loss, grief, and impending death, but it differs from Lady Daibu's *Memoirs* in covering such a short period of time, being written so close to the events it describes, and having little development or plot. It considerably resembles Lady Daibu's work, however, in its introspection, personal lyricism, and plaintive sense of grief, as well as in its basic form.

The *Shijō no Miya Shimotsuke shū* is like Lady Daibu's collection in being the reminiscences of a whole lifetime and recreating the atmosphere of the poet's younger days and life at court. It is the work of a woman known as Lady Shimotsuke (fl. 1060), who was in service with the consort of Emperor Goreizei. She begins with an introduction in which she tells us that most of her records and poems have been destroyed by fire but she has been persuaded in her old age to write down the odds and ends she can remember—this is either a pose or testimony to an exceptional memory, for her collection contains 211 poems and quite specific descriptions. The collection begins in the appropriate manner, as Lady Daibu's does, with spring, and goes on to recount Lady Shimotsuke's life at court, with the poems and incidents arranged basically in chronological order, but with some sense of association discernible in places between one poem or group of poems and the next. There are many long *kotobagaki*, though none as long as Lady

Daibu's longest, and most of them contain a large proportion of conversation and merely tell a story rather than present a personal attitude or reaction to the events described. All in all, this is a much happier collection than Lady Daibu's and lacks the contrasts and change in way of life that are one of the main themes of Lady Daibu's work. Lady Shimotsuke ends her collection with a short conclusion, remarking that she has written of matters—court life, love affairs—that are not of the most suitable for someone like herself who has renounced the world and become a nun. The collection does not possess such a strong sense of personal expression, of complaint and self-justification, as Lady Daibu's work, but it is well constructed and unified, and is very like Lady Daibu's *Memoirs* in form.

Even in Lady Daibu's own day, when personal poetry collections tended to be more formal and less autobiographical, there were some that resembled her work in both form and nature. The most notable of these is the *Takafusa shū* of Fujiwara no Takafusa (1148–1209), a carefully ordered collection of 100 poems with longish *kotobagaki* that tells the story of a love affair of his youth. There is an introduction to explain how he is reminiscing in old age, and the collection ends on a conclusive note (though not in the form of a proper epilogue), with an appeal to the Buddha to absolve him of his sins.

As this brief survey makes clear, there are a good many autobiographical poetry collections having a greater or lesser resemblance to Lady Daibu's *Memoirs*. The differences between the *Memoirs* and other similar works should remind us that one of the qualities of a real work of literature is its uniqueness, even though it is still a recognizable member of a family or genre. This is certainly true of Lady Daibu's *Memoirs*. No other work is exactly like it, yet it obviously takes its place among the other poetry collections of the age, as well as among the memoirs and diaries. We are still left with the question of how, ultimately, we should classify her work and other works of the same nature: is it a *shikashū* or is it a *nikki,* a poetry collection or diary/memoirs? It is clear that any such decision about Lady Daibu's work implies the same decision for a considerable number of other works. The only answer to this question is that the distinction should not have to be made. All works of this type belong to a continuum: at one end of the scale will be works that tend towards "pure diaries" or "pure memoirs," at the other, "pure poetry collections"; but all are essentially lyric, unified structures with some thematic progression—even poetry collections that are not (auto)biographical have a definite structure and sense of progression that unifies them. Perhaps no term can cover all these works without being too general and vague to be useful or without being a poor fit in some cases, but for Lady Daibu's work, at least, "poetic memoirs" or even "lyrical memoirs" comes as close to describing the work as any short expression can in English.

Structure in
'The Poetic Memoirs of Lady Daibu'

At first sight *The Poetic Memoirs of Lady Daibu* may seem a rather disjointed and even haphazard work, with a disconcerting variety in the length of the *kotobagaki* and even some sections where poem follows poem with no intervening prose, making the reader feel that it is an ill-constructed blend of memoirs and poetry collection. Often there seems to be little connection between one poem, or group of related poems, and the next. Close and sensitive reading, however, reveals a wonderfully unified and flowing structure, based on principles common to all Heian literature.

As discussed in the preceding section, most memoirs and diaries developed from poetry collections of some sort, however haphazard and random, and it is impossible to draw a dividing line between this type of work and other types. Lady Daibu's *Memoirs* were obviously constructed around a collection of poems and have the character of a personal poetry collection, as well as the character of memoirs. It is therefore helpful to examine the types of personal poetry collections that exist.

The simplest and most primitive type is the random collection. In this, the poems with their *kotobagaki*, long or short, are gathered just as they came to hand, with no particular ordering scheme. If the letters and copies of poems and other materials have been piled up in the order in which they were written, the collection is ordered by a chance chronology, which is usually difficult to detect or to see as a pattern. A typical random collection is the *Midō kanpaku shū* of the great Fujiwara statesman Michinaga (966–1028), which like the majority of random collections, consists mostly of poetic exchanges.

The biographical or autobiographical collection is usually a chronological collection, in which the poems have been selected and ordered by the date of composition or by the date of the events to which they relate. The period of time covered may be a whole lifetime or a relatively short interval, such as the course of a love affair.

The purest or most advanced type of collection is what may be termed the classified collection. In this, the poems are arranged, often irrespective of their original context, into the categories that were developed for the imperial anthologies (e.g. spring, autumn, love, parting, travel, laments). The categories themselves follow a set order, and within each category the poems have been arranged to form a flowing whole: seasonal poems follow the changing phenomena of nature; love poems follow the course of an imaginary (or perhaps real) love affair. The collection as a whole is then unified by a type of artistic or artificial chronology and by other methods of association and progression, which became increasingly sophisticated over time.[44] Such personal poetry collections form complete lyrical units, though of a different sort from the chronological or autobiographical collections, and they tend to have little prose,

44. For a full explanation of these methods, see Konishi, Brower, and Miner.

the context for each poem being provided by the poems around it. Some were composed of a series of 100-poem sequences, which were themselves ordered like miniature imperial anthologies. Most of the collections of the major poets of Lady Daibu's day were of this sort. The *Sanbokukikashū* of Minamoto no Toshiyori, a highly polished collection, categorized in the minutest detail, yet retaining personal touches, is an outstanding example of the classified personal poetry collection.

The Poetic Memoirs of Lady Daibu are basically arranged in chronological order. The work moves in due procession through her early life at court, the beginnings of her love affairs, her retirement from court, the flight of the Taira, her experiences following their defeat and the death of her lover, her second period of court service, and finally her exchange with Fujiwara no Sadaie in 1232. But within this general chronological framework there are many lapses from strict order: Poem 73 cannot have been written later than 1169, making it probably the earliest poem in the collection.[45] Poems 332–53 can be dated from the incidents to which they refer and they are presented in reverse chronological order. Other datable poems make it clear that Lady Daibu by no means adhered to the chronological order of her poems. These are probably only a handful among many such departures, but unfortunately, most of the poems are not accurately datable. At any rate, Lady Daibu clearly did not rely on external chronology entirely as her ordering principle. She created an internal chronology in her *Memoirs*, which is no more than to say she created a work of art.

But there is also at work a more insistent and more important structural principle, which matches the lyrical nature of the *Memoirs*. Poems and events are linked by association

45. *Zenshaku*, pp. 19–20.

through person, place, subject, theme, or other subtler means of the sort used in linking formal poetry anthologies. Association moves the reader from poem to poem, event to event, regardless of time. The effect is often like the "stream of consciousness" found in many twentieth-century English "lyrical novels."[46] The resemblance is not a coincidence: it is due to the essential nature of such works.

Although the Japanese text of the *Memoirs* contains no divisions, but is printed as one continuous piece, there are several divisions in the structure.[47] In the first place, the *Memoirs* have a distinct introduction and conclusion, Poems 1 and 357 with their *kotobagaki*, in which Lady Daibu writes of her attitude to her work. These lend to her work a sense of construction and completeness that is lacking in many autobiographical poetry collections.[48] Even works that are more firmly in the realm of prose or are firmly titled *nikki*, such as the *Kagerō nikki* and the *Izumi Shikibu nikki*, tend to fade out rather than end conclusively, though there are, of course, memoirs with definite prologues and epilogues: for example the *Sanuki no Suke nikki* (1108) of a lady-in-waiting called Fujiwara no Nagako. However, the introduction and conclusion of Lady Daibu's *Memoirs* have a similarity of wording and attitude that draws the

46. The term lyrical novel is Ralph Freedman's. Virginia Woolf and James Joyce most immediately bring to mind the associative flow of Japanese memoirs and poetry collections.

47. However, a printed text dating from 1644, the Kan-ei Text, and its derivatives split the work into two volumes between Poems 203 and 204; and modern commentators tend to divide the text into groups of related poems—for instance, Poems 9–11, which are all connected with an excursion to view cherry blossoms—for ease of commentary. Early manuscript versions have no divisions, though one of the earliest manuscripts exists in the form of only the first volume.

48. See note 43, above, on introductions and conclusions in poetry collections.

whole work together and gives it a strong sense of structural wholeness.

There is also an epilogue, Poems 358–59 with their *koto-bagaki*, in the form of the exchange with Sadaie. It is probable that the *Memoirs* had been completed for some time when this exchange took place, but Lady Daibu was so pleased at being recognized as a poet that she could not forbear to add it to her work. It forms an interesting comment on her claims in the introduction and conclusion that she was writing for herself alone. One scholar suggests that the exchange (together with Poems 354–56, which are different in tone from the poems that precede them) was added by a later hand, since it is so much at variance with the rest of the work.[49] Since personal poetry collections were extremely vulnerable to changes by later "editors," this is certainly a possibility, but there is no conclusive evidence for deciding the question. Most scholars accept the epilogue as genuine, while conceding that its presence means the *Memoirs* finally end on a very different note from the conclusion. One reader may feel that this mars the work as a whole, another that it completes the work; but in any case, we can never know whether Lady Daibu herself added the epilogue and gave her work the feeling of happiness and contentment with which it now ends.

In addition to the introduction, conclusion, and epilogue, there are six main parts, which could almost be called chapters. The work can also be divided into two volumes, between Poems 203 and 204. There is some disagreement among Japanese scholars about whether this division should be made. Most argue their case on the basis of the format of manuscripts and the conjectured process and date of compilation, but such external considerations are irrelevant in deciding basic struc-

49. Kusakabe, pp. 32–33.

tural divisions that can be inferred from the work as it exists. The divisions are in the internal structure of the work and independent of external considerations, interesting though these externals may be as problems in their own right.

The first volume up to and including Poem 203 covers Lady Daibu's life as far as the Genpei War, but makes no mention of the war itself; the second volume, beginning with Poem 204, opens with the flight of the Taira from the capital. This is a distinct temporal division between the volumes, marked by the Genpei War. But there is also a qualitative difference between the volumes: the second volume has considerably longer prose sections and tends to be more introspective; the poetry is more personal and less formal, and the tone is much darker than in the first volume. Moreover, the first volume ends with the death of Retired Emperor Takakura, so that it has a certain completeness and finality: the volume begins with Takakura as Emperor, and his death is a fitting symbol for the passing of an age and thus the end of Lady Daibu's early life. There is, too, an echoing between the beginning and the ending of the volume, which gives it a remarkable sense of unity and completion.

Within each volume there is a structural feature that must strike the reader immediately, a long section of poems that run on without prose interruptions. These sections constitute the middle part or chapter of each volume, and the poems in them differ considerably from those in other parts of the collection. All of the poems in other parts are directly related to a specific event, either as Lady Daibu's personal reaction to it, or as part of a poetic exchange, or as a response to the social demands of a particular, identified occasion. But the two long sections consist of poems written not for any specific occasion, but in the first volume, on formal topics (*dai*) that are specified for each poem, and, in the second volume, on the Tanabata Festival, which is virtually a formal topic, since poems on the festival were produced as a matter of course each time it came around.[50] Moreover, Lady Daibu does not specify a particular year for any of these Tanabata poems, so they take on the air of a formal exercise, though with their theme of parted lovers they held personal significance for her.

Some scholars feel these sections mar the *Memoirs*, since the poems are in general of poor quality and seem to have little connection with the rest of the work.[51] But in addition to giving the whole work symmetry and balance by their similarity in length and position in their respective volumes, the group of poems on topics and the group of Tanabata poems function to distinguish Part One from Part Three, and Part Four from Part Six, respectively. They also establish a tone for the middle of each volume and re-create the mood of the part that precedes them, while hinting at the mood of what is to come.

Part One, Poems 2–13, portrays Lady Daibu's early life at court. All is splendor and magnificence; no love affairs have yet appeared to cast a shadow over her enjoyment of life. It is a brief period, reflected in the brevity of the section itself, of complete and perfect happiness, living in close contact with the Empress and Emperor, meeting and flirting with handsome visitors, and indulging in artistic and cultivated activities. The section opens and closes with the Emperor and Empress, and the last incident shows Lady Daibu's familiarity with them both, asserting her participation in court life.

50. The Tanabata Festival and its legend are more appropriately discussed in the Tanabata section itself. For now, the reader need only know that the festival celebrated the reunion of two lovers, the Heavenly Weaving Maid (the star Vega) and the Heavenly Herd Boy (Altair), who were separated by the Milky Way and could meet only once in the course of a year, on the seventh night of the seventh month.

51. For example, "Hyōkai," p. 40; Shinoda, p. 43.

Part Two, Poems 14–53, consists of the poems on topics, the content and function of which are discussed later. Following this, Part Three, Poems 54–203, opens with poems on unhappy love, moves quickly to introduce Lady Daibu's love affairs, recounts the progress of the affairs—interspersed with other events from court life—tells of her retirement from court, and covers various incidents from her days in court and outside up to the early 1180's, ending with the death of Takakura, the final passing of "the old days."

Part Four, Poems 204–70, opens with the flight of the Taira from the capital, her last words with Sukemori, and her parting from him. The horrifying events of the war, culminating in Sukemori's death, follow quickly; then she describes her depression and her attempts to escape from it, her journeys, the things that bring back the past for her, and her devotion to services for the souls of Sukemori and her mother. This section covers her life from 1182 until her entry into the court of Gotoba.

Part Five, Poems 271–321, consists of the Tanabata poems, which are discussed later. Part Six, Poems 322–56, begins with her reentry into court life, but has less to do with her life in Gotoba's court than with her laments about how everything reminds her of the past and of her loss. She tells of the death of several people she knew, and this serves to emphasize the passing of all connected with the old days and to remind her of Sukemori's death. She ends this part with the official celebration of Fujiwara no Toshinari's ninetieth birthday, an auspicious event, lighter in tone than the preceding accounts of death. But this, too, is an opportunity for reminiscence, since Toshinari counts himself part of the old days, and suggests that such times are now past forever.

Thus each part deals with a distinct period of Lady Daibu's life, each with its own atmosphere and theme unified as much by tone as by a sense of time. Parts Three and Four have a temporal movement, but this is less important than the depiction of a mood or a stage in Lady Daibu's life. As with all Heian works, *The Poetic Memoirs of Lady Daibu* are concerned more with arresting moments in the flow of time than with the flow of time itself. It is the emotions of a particular instant or of a static period that are important. Time is seen as a contrast of now and then, not as a process leading logically from one event to another; time is a separator, not a connector. As in other "lyrical novels," time is the accepted force, the accepted continuum; the author therefore seeks to isolate the events in it rather than present them as a connected flow.

Within each section, as a result, the movement of association is the most important structural factor. Often the association of ideas in the author's mind is clear to see: one incident is followed by another involving the same person or someone closely related; the same season continues from one incident to another; an incident is followed by a very similar incident; one example of a lovers' exchange of poems leads to another lovers' exchange; the same images, such as blossoms or maple leaves, appear in two incidents. The more attentively and sensitively a reader reads, the more obvious are the associations, and the fewer breaks there will seem to be as the *Memoirs* trace a path through the remembrances of the writer. The actual associative link may be between two poems, between a poem and a *kotobagaki*, or even between the *kotobagaki* rather than the poems. Sometimes the associations will be of a sort that would have been clear to a Heian reader but are far from obvious to a modern Western reader trained in a different tradition. Often the associations are specifically poetic, those used in the formal imperial anthologies. It is the diversity of associations used, sometimes sophisticated and specifically poetic, sometimes more obvious, natural ones, and the frequency of association by images rather than by people or events that often lead a reader to suppose the work is disjointed and random within its basic chronological framework. But a "stream of consciousness" runs throughout, as it does in Western lyrical novels and in other Heian memoirs and diaries, such as *The Izumi Shikibu nikki* or the *Kagerō nikki*. That a poem from Part Three may pre-date poems from Part One is irrelevant: poems are placed where they are appropriate to the internal structure of the work and follow smoothly from the preceding poems and on to the following poems.

It is impracticable to include here a detailed analysis of the associations in a long sequence of poems, but it is worth ex-amining briefly a short sequence—the first eight poems of Part Three, Poems 54–61, which contain both obvious and obscure links. Poems 54 and 55 are an exchange between Lady Daibu and one of the other ladies-in-waiting about the woman's un-happiness in a love affair. These are followed by a seemingly unrelated poem composed at a chrysanthemum contest (at which chrysanthemums were compared and judged for their beauty) at the mansion of Taira no Shigemori (1138–79). The poems, however, are linked by season: both are autumn, with the changing colors and the autumn rain of Poems 54 and 55 giving way to the chrysanthemum, an autumn flower, of Poem 56. There is also a contrast between the changing of the leaves or the lovers' affections and the unchanging nature of chrysan-themums (which were symbols of longevity), together with the prayer that Shigemori should endure forever unchanged. There follows a poem of congratulations (57), written when Shigemori and his brother Munemori were elevated in the bureaucracy. The next poem (58) was written at the time of a fire in the palace, but this too follows smoothly from the preceding poem by association of person, since Shigemori and his appearance at that time are central to the incident and the poem. Both this poem and the two that follow (59 and 60) are set at the time of the Gosechi Festival in the eleventh month, and the subject of these following poems moves on to Shigemori's brother Munemori and a flirtatious exchange between him and Lady Daibu. Flirtation with Munemori gives way in Poem 61 to the beginning of her love affair with Munemori's nephew (Shigemori's son) Sukemori.

The associative links between poems or incidents are thus smooth and natural even when they are not obvious. Frequently, a change from one person to another, or a change of theme, such as from love to court life, will be achieved by a more distant associative link involving images or rhetoric or the subtler means used in anthologies of poetry. But occasionally the discoverable links between poems are so tenuous that one must question whether they are truly links or one's own inventions. At such times, common sense must guide the reader and prevent excessive ingenuity. There is no doubt that associative linking had become quite subtle by this stage in the history of poetry, and Lady Daibu was not unconscious of the rhetorical play between one poem and another. What may seem farfetched to a modern reader would have been natural to a Heian poet, acutely sensitive to the traditional associations of imagery and to rhetorical play in poetry. To search avidly for links, as in a word puzzle, is to destroy the beauty of the work: the changing patterns of the poetry are to be enjoyed. But there is no doubt that Lady Daibu produced a more unified work than many scholars have allowed.

The poems on topics and the Tanabata poems are not so obviously linked one with another, for there is no immediately discernible flow through either sequence.[52] The poems on topics are not ordered according to the principles governing for-

52. There does often seem to be some simple association of image or season between one poem and the next in the group of poems on topics, continuing sometimes for a space of several poems. Such a sequence is formed by Poems 33–36. But these associative links do not appear to flow through the whole section to unify it.

mal anthologies and sequences, and appear to be a random pattern of seasonal poems mixed with love poems. There is, however, some progression through the sequence, for the first three poems completely match the tone of Part One: they are auspicious spring poems. But the last two poems of the sequence (52 and 53) have the somber tone of Part Three, with all its problems; and scattered throughout are love poems that introduce love in a formalized way in preparation for the personally experienced love of Part Three. The section can be seen as a formalized portrayal of Lady Daibu's court life and love affairs, and a bridge between Parts One and Three.

Attempts have been made to divide the section, by means of its seasonal poems, into eight groups corresponding to the years between 1174, the date of Poem 2, and 1181, the date of Poem 203, which ends Part Three.[53] But this attempt can be faulted on two counts: first, it assumes too direct a relationship between the work and the writer's life, and second, the composition of each proposed group is not very satisfactory as a portrayal of one year. It seems better not to force the section into such a pattern, but to regard it merely as an evocation of the random experience of Lady Daibu's days at court and possibly her retirement—the reference to the secluded mountain village in Poem 51 may be a hint of her retirement from court, and the unseasonable storm in the last poem (53) is unmistakably a metaphor for the war, a meaning derived from the context of the poem in the collection, for it was most probably free of such overtones when it was composed.

Similarly, the section of Tanabata poems has a definite sense of development but no strict pattern. Tanabata poems are, of course, much easier to relate to Lady Daibu's own experience than poems on topics, and as the section progresses, the poems

53. Gotō 1972, pp. 14–17. This article also has a detailed analysis of the discernible patterns in this section.

refer much more explicitly to Lady Daibu's own situation, and the meeting and separation of the two stars are directly compared to Lady Daibu's separation by death from Sukemori.

The early poems of the series seem more conventional, and any tears shed are in sympathy for the Weaver Maid, whereas the tears of the later poems are the tears Lady Daibu sheds for herself. In the later poems the focus seems to turn more and more to Lady Daibu and away from the two heavenly lovers. This suggests that the section portrays the progress of love from her separation from her lover to the complete loss of her lover through death, a reenactment of the events of Part Four up to and including, tonally if not chronologically, Part Six. Certain typical observances of the Tanabata festival recur through this section, and in contrast to the analogous topics section, one can reasonably divide the poems into nine separate groups, each representing the observances of one year. But to see this structure as corresponding to nine years of Lady Daibu's life is to create once again too direct a link between the work and the writer's life.[54] Moreover, the number of poems in each group varies, whereas one would expect a regular seven poems (the prescribed number for the festival) in each group if it had been meant to represent the actual years of Lady Daibu's life. This section functions in the same way as Part Two, to evoke the mood of the years from the Taira flight up to, and perhaps into, her service with Gotoba, and it acts as a bridge between Parts Four and Six.

The *Memoirs* as a whole are unified also by theme, especially in the second volume. The first volume, despite its appearance of patchwork, really concentrates on one essential theme, the love between Lady Daibu and Sukemori in the context of the court and Taira dominance. All events lead to a picture of this

54. Gotō 1971, pp. 17–18. This article analyzes in some detail the possible structure of this section.

life and the more trivial or seemingly unconnected incidents serve to show the glamour of a world that Lady Daibu subsequently lost. In the second volume the concentration on loss, grief, and longing for Sukemori, the darkness of atmosphere, the theme of a continued yet pointless and unwanted existence in a completely changed world, are so consistent as to need no comment.

There is also in the work a type of echoing that brings together the separate parts. The formal symmetry of the work is unusual, with the balancing of the poems on topics and the Tanabata poems, and the pivoting of the work around the junction of the two volumes. The ceremonial court scene of Poem 2 is echoed in the courtly ceremony of Fujiwara no Toshinari's ninetieth birthday.

There seems to be a deliberate use of characters to draw the work together and emphasize the changes between the two volumes. The Taira who appear in such happy circumstances in Part One, Sukemori's brother Koremori (1158–84), his uncle Shigehira (1157–85), the Empress herself, are reintroduced sadly changed in Part Four. Fujiwara no Takafusa, who appears in a blossom-viewing excursion in Part One (Poems 9–11), is shown deep in grief in Part Six (Poems 330–31); and Poems 332 and 333 refer to the death of Fujiwara no Sanemune, who had appeared in such happy circumstances in Part One (Poems 4–7).

Other noticeable echoes are natural objects such as the *hototogisu* (a bird valued for its song), orange trees, and irises; festivals such as the Gosechi Festival; and images such as the moon, which is used as a metaphor for the Emperor and Empress, and then, near the end of the work, as a symbol for all that is past. "Dream" occurs again and again, often in circumstances that seem to require the translation "nightmare," but the essential connotations of the word are insubstantiality and unreality, which the English word nightmare does not convey.

Closely associated with the word is the feeling of things unprecedented, unknown, outside the bounds of normal experience, which recurs frequently in the second volume of the work. "Fate," "destiny," "unexpected," "inescapable," are used again and again like leitmotivs through the work: the blissful "fate" mentioned in Poem 2 changes to the unhappy and unexpected "fate" of the later poems.

In sum, *The Poetic Memoirs of Lady Daibu* are more structured, more whole, than a cursory reading would suggest, and if the unifying principles seem strange to a Western reader, they are not really so very different from those that govern many modern novels. The reader is carried along on a flow of associations that hold the work together from beginning to end, and behind this flow is the author's intense contemplation of her lover, her loss, and her suffering.

Lady Daibu and Her Work

The Poetic Memoirs of Lady Daibu have enjoyed a steady popularity but have never ranked as one of the major works of Heian literature. Nor has Lady Daibu herself ever been considered a writer of the first class. This is due to the restricted and ambiguous nature of the *Memoirs*, which suffer in any comparison with the acknowledged prose masterpieces of the period; her work lacks, for instance, the social observation, penetration, and variety of the *Murasaki Shikibu nikki* (c. 1010) and the complexity and depth of character of the *Kagerō nikki*. Though Lady Daibu was a talented writer of prose—Part Four, the most successful part of the *Memoirs*, certainly reads as a most beautiful and moving account of human loss—the work does not contain enough extended examples for her to be judged beside the great prose writers of her age.

If we judge her work at the other end of the scale, as a collection of poetry, it also fares badly. In fact, as a poetry collection the *Memoirs* are disappointing, for the reader has to put up with a number of dull and rather bad poems. True enough, there are also some extremely good ones, and Lady Daibu was well enough thought of to have twenty-three poems included in imperial anthologies from the *Shinchokusenshū* onwards, but the good poems are relatively few, and she cannot be considered more than a second-class poet.[55] It is instructive to note that Izumi Shikibu (c. 970–1030), the traditionally attributed author of the *Izumi Shikibu nikki*, one of the classics of the Heian period and the exemplar of mixed prose-poetry works, was a first-class poet in her own right, with a large collection of poems in addition to those in her *nikki*. Every Heian writer produced an abundance of poetry in his or her lifetime, and it is intriguing (if profitless) to speculate on what Lady Daibu's unrecorded poetry was like: was much of it better than most of the poetry in her *Memoirs*? It is possible that many excellent poems of hers have been lost because they did not suit the theme of her *Memoirs*. But it is equally possible, and more likely, that the *Memoirs* contain the best of her poetry, and that she was no better a poet than her surviving work suggests.

She certainly seems to have had little reputation as a poet in her own time. None of her poems were chosen for the two imperial anthologies that appeared during her lifetime before the *Shinchokusenshū*; and apart from her possible appearance in the poetry contest at the home of Fujiwara no Shigeie, her probable appearance in a poetry contest sponsored by Retired Empress Takamatsuin (1141–76) in 1175,[56] and her definite par-

55. The poems in imperial anthologies are *Shinchokusenshū*, 11, 197; *Gyokuyōshū*, 61, 67, 154, 196, 205, 251, 258, 261, 266, 268; *Fūgashū*, 56, 71, 73, 215, 217, 239; *Shinsenzaishū*, 232; *Shinshūishū*, 355; *Shingoshūishū*, 35; *Shinzokukokinshū*, 162, 202. Poems by other people in her collection found in imperial anthologies are 70, 72, 147, 153, 221, 354, 356. Poem 146, by Lady Daibu is quoted in the *Gyokuyōshū* in the foreword to Poem 147, a work that is there attributed to Sukemori, but that most scholars now believe to have been written by Takanobu. The numbers given here are those of the poems in the *Memoirs*, not the numbers they have in each anthology.

56. *Takamatsunyōin Shushi Naishinnō no utaawase*. No text of this contest is extant, but circumstantial evidence suggests that Poems 48–50 of

ticipation in an Inari Shrine contest, thought to have been held some time between 1170 and 1175, she does not figure in the extant records of any of the formal and social poetic activities so common in the late twelfth century. Had she had any reputation as a poet, we would expect her name to have been more frequently mentioned. Conceivably her reputation as a poet suffered because of her very high reputation as a calligrapher and musician.[57] Indeed it is quite likely that whenever she was present at a formal occasion she was there in her capacity as a musician and had little opportunity to participate publicly as a poet. If she had been a truly great poet, this would not have hindered her, but she does not seem to have had talent enough to emerge as a poet of the first rank. She can only be called a minor poet.

For all that, her *Memoirs* as a complete work have a special charm and appeal. This is due both to the work itself and to external factors. Her work can never be read without some consciousness of the stirring events that form its background. The *Memoirs* take on a reflected radiance from *The Tale of the Heike*, which gives it an immediate attractiveness and romance. But this reflected radiance takes on the color of the *Memoirs* themselves, for the reader responds immediately and warmly to the humanity, tenderness, and reality with which she imbues the momentous story of the Taira, and to her touchingly human and lifelike portrayal of figures who seem in other contexts larger than life; and the reader, particularly in times of trouble and upheaval, is deeply moved by her description of the sufferings of bereavement and the desolation of war.

The outstanding qualities that Japanese scholars and critics see in the *Memoirs* are sincerity and truthfulness. They see

---

the *Memoirs* were composed for this occasion. Hagitani, 8: 2337–38. (A misprint in this book gives the Retired Empress's name as Maishi.)

57. *Zenshaku*, p. 15.

the work as an artless outpouring of emotion, the unsullied
expression of a pure heart. These are indeed the qualities that
make the work beautiful and moving; but as we have seen, the
Memoirs may or may not describe events as they actually happened, and Lady Daibu's work is far from artless: it is a conscious and artistic literary product, and the degree of truth or
fiction is irrelevant in an appreciation and evaluation of it.
Lady Daibu has achieved a conviction of truth and sincerity,
an apparent simplicity and directness, a vividness and honesty,
that make her *Memoirs* a profoundly moving work of literature and testify to her being an accomplished literary artist.
And yet there is no doubt that the link with known history,
the belief that we are reading descriptions of and reactions to
actual events heightens our interest in and enjoyment of the
work.

The appeal of the work is also due to Lady Daibu's prose
style, and to the way in which the prose and poetry combine.
These are, of course, interrelated, for it is the quality of the
prose that creates the close link with the poetry. Her prose is
fluent, limpid, and gentle-seeming: it has purity, simplicity,
and directness, which match the sense of sincerity in her work,
but are the product of art. She was capable of a sharp observation of her surroundings and displays great skill at describing
detail, qualities that combine with the lyrical portrayal of emotion to strengthen her writing and produce the beautifully evoc-
ative power and the conviction of truth in her work. At its best
her prose rivals that of even the greatest writers of Japan.

She has a fine control of rhythm, which, as mentioned earlier,
is the associative rhythm of speech that combines so well with
poetry. The effect is achieved by certain techniques that are
not unique to her, but can be found in much of the lyrical
prose of the Heian and other periods. All Heian prose tends
towards the natural spoken language and the language of per-

sonal letters. A marked feature of Lady Daibu's prose, a feature that it shares with the associative rhythms of speech and of lyrical poetry, is the repetition of words and sound, a building up of phrases with a sense of climax. A striking example appears early in the *kotobagaki* of Poem 204: "What can I say, what am I to feel? . . . No words, no emotions can do it justice." In the Japanese, the repetition of sound is particularly insistent and is both arresting and fluent at the same time: *tokaku iite mo omoite mo kokoro mo kotoba mo oyobarezu.* Repetition also occurs between poems and prose, linking them closely. Poem 205 contains the line *ikanaru koto o,* "What sort of things," which is an echo of a phrase from the *kotobagaki*: *ikanaru kokochi naran,* "What must he be feeling?" Such effects tend to be lost in translation, but they abound throughout the work, giving Lady Daibu's prose a particular resonance and rhythm.

Lady Daibu also uses many phrases in her prose that are taken directly from or closely influenced by earlier poems and masterpieces of prose. This technique is found in other writers too, and it is always difficult to judge to what extent it is being consciously used, but in the *Memoirs* examples are both frequent and striking. A particularly noticeable example of borrowing from or allusion to an earlier prose work is to be found in the *kotobagaki* of Poem 94: "The sky gradually whitened where it met the rim of the mountains." This is an obvious reference to the very well-known and admired opening paragraph of *The Pillow Book,* by Sei Shōnagon (fl. 990–1000). The use of phrasing from a poem can be seen in the *kotobagaki* of Poem 241, where Lady Daibu writes: "I wondered if this was indeed the same Empress" (*Aranu ka to nomi zo tadoraruru ni*). The Japanese wording is almost identical with the second and third lines of a poem from the personal collection of the ninth-century poet Ono no Komachi: "I wonder if my body

is of this same world" (*Aranu ka to nomi zo | Tadorarure*).[58]
The rhythm of such phrases is often identical with the rhythm
of poetry or only subtly changed so that it will blend into the
prose without losing its distinctiveness: it brings Lady Daibu's
prose closer to the poems and helps to create a link between
the two, as well as enlivening and enriching the prose. Conversely, many of her poems possess a prosiness that enables
them to merge easily into the surrounding prose.

Techniques such as these, together with strong ties of sense
and circumstance, bind her prose, or *kotobagaki*, closely to her
poems and forge the two into one unit. Her prose is in most
cases superior to her poems, but there is no doubt that in the
best instances the combination of the two is far superior to
either element by itself. The prose finds its natural conclusion
as it flows into the poem. At the same time, the effect of the
poem is greatly heightened by the preceding lyrical descriptions, which form an emotional preparation: the poem often
reflects the prose in a concentrated way and acts as a crystalli-
zation of the emotion that fills the prose.

It may be added here that just as the combination of prose
and poem is greater than each individually, so there is a cumu-
lative effect in sections of the work as a whole. Lady Daibu
seems to build up intensity as she moves from one unit of prose
and poem into the next, and this is due to the sustained associative rhythm of the whole work. It is therefore the total effect
of a section and finally of the whole work that gives the *Memoirs* their appeal and their success, that makes them a worth-
while work of art, greater than the constituent parts.

58. *Komachi shū, Zoku kokka taikan* 19656, also *Shinkokinshū* 1404. On
the truly astounding number of possible references or quotations of this
sort in Lady Daibu's work—and for suggestions of probable allusions in
her poems—see Hisamatsu and Kubota, *passim*. There is a detailed discussion of poetic phrases in the prose of Lady Daibu's first volume in Fukuda
1967, pp. 47–52.

The majority of Lady Daibu's poems are in the rather uninspired and conventional style that had been the poetic staple since the early tenth century. It is no coincidence that this style is more obvious in the first volume of the *Memoirs,* for her theme there is court life and her love affairs against a conventional background, subjects that would tend to produce conventional and unremarkable poetry. But even if her poems are not very good, they show a competent grasp of the basic techniques of poetry, for she was certainly not a bad poet. Two poems (107 and 159) will serve to illustrate both this conventional style and the particular rhetorical devices of Japanese court poetry that require explanation for a Western reader. These poems have been selected from among the less trivial of her efforts.

Tabigoromo	Sleeves now left behind
Tachiwakarenishi	By those on the traveling robe
Ato no sode	Of him who is departed,
Moroki namida no	Have they no respite
Tsuyu ya himanaki	From the falling dew of tears?

The first line, *tabigoromo,* "traveling robe," is a pillow word, or *makura kotoba,* a conventional, fixed epithet that could be applied to one or more (of a restricted number of) related words. The conventionality of such words adds luster to a poem and elevates the language, and when skillfully used they have a metaphorical richness that is not weakened by their conventional nature. Very often the pillow word relies on a pivot word, or pun, *kakekotoba,* in order to fit into the poem. Here *tabigoromo* relies on a double meaning in the word it modifies, *tachiwakaru,* which basically means "to depart." However, the first element, *tachi,* means "to cut out (cloth)" and is often modified by the pillow word *tabigoromo,* giving the meaning "cutting out a traveling robe." The pun on *tachi* is associative rather than semantic: it serves only to allow a verbal junction between the pillow word and the rest of the poem, and has no semantic function in the poem as a whole. The use of the pillow word here is meaningful and more than mere decoration, since the poem is about a journey into exile, and the robe is associated with the sleeves that are used later in the poem as a metaphor for the wife who is left behind. Moreover, there is an obvious appropriateness for a time of departure into exile in the image of cutting.

The poem contains several examples of a technique known as *engo*, or word association, since *tabigoromo*, *tachi*, and *sode*, "sleeve," are all words related to clothing. Word association was a common means of adding richness to the short *tanka* form, and often depended on double meanings, as with *tachi* in this poem. The echoes of word association unify a poem and expand it by creating a richness of association and an integrity of imagery that would be impossible by other means in a poem as short as the *tanka*.

A further, common technique is illustrated in the second example, Poem 159:

Oki tsu nami	As waves resound,
Kaereba oto wa	Returning from the open sea,
Seshi mono o	So did he bring me news on his return.
Ikanaru sode no	But now to the haven of whose pillowing sleeves
Ura ni yoruramu	Can he be drawing close?

This poem opens with a device similar to a pillow word, but not fixed and conventional: this is the *jo*, the preface, or rhetorical introduction. Here *oki tsu nami*, "waves from the sea," is added to *kaeru*, "to return," which is the normal expression for the receding of the water from a breaking wave. *Kaeru* is therefore used twice, once with the waves as its subject and once with the lover. When well used, as it is here, the rhetorical introduction adds metaphorical or imagistic richness to the poem, as well as "poetic" decoration. This poem refers to the return of Lady Daibu's lover from the coast, and the sea imagery is entirely suited to the subject. The rhetorical introduction is often linked to the poem by a pun, and is a means of adding richness to a poem with material that is not immediately related to the central theme, but that is often metaphorically or imagistically appropriate. Here the sea imagery is continued in various word associations that depend on puns: *oto*, "sound," can mean "a message" or "the sound of the waves"; *ura* can mean "a bay" and "lining" of a robe (in which meaning it is associated with *sode*, "sleeve"); and *yoru*, "to draw close" is also the normal verb for the approach of a wave. A complex pattern of associations is thus set up, creating a rich texture in the poem.

Pivot words are sometimes essential to the semantic structure of a poem, as well as creating extra associations, and they could greatly expand the scope of the brief *tanka* form. The first poem in the *Memoirs* is a good example of such a poem, but does not need to be quoted here.

Poems of this conventional sort, often depending on wit, abound in the *Memoirs*, especially in Lady Daibu's exchanges with her lovers or other acquaintances. But her better poems are in a different style. One of the remarkable characteristics of Lady Daibu is that she is not at all a poet of her own age.[59] The type of poem quoted above, though produced in abundance throughout the history of the court, is not typical of what is considered the best poetry of the late twelfth century. Occasionally, Lady Daibu did produce poems that could be considered typical of her age, which valued formal poems on pre-set topics and a polished technique, creating poems of

59. For a perceptive and detailed discussion of Lady Daibu's poetry, showing how distinct her style is from the dominant style of her time, see Saiga 1975 and Saiga 1977.

refined, often ethereal beauty, rich descriptive charm, or mysterious symbolism. (See, for example, Poem 80, which is a descriptive poem that almost overloads the senses.) But her best poems bring to mind the style that was popular a hundred years after her own time, the style of the Kyōgoku-Reizei poets, who dominate two later imperial anthologies, the *Gyokuyōshū* (1313) and the *Fūgashū* (1346). It can be no coincidence that of her twenty-three poems in imperial anthologies, seventeen are in these two, and that it was only when Fujiwara no Sadaie was turning to simpler, unadorned styles of poetry in his later years that her poetry was selected for inclusion in an imperial anthology, the *Shinchokusenshū*.

Lady Daibu's poetry resembles that of the Kyōgoku-Reizei poets in being flat, prosaic, unadorned, declarative, and introspective, avoiding images in love poetry, and indulging in intense scrutiny of detail in one's own state of mind or in nature.

Wasuremu to	Think as I will
Omoite mo mata	That I must forget,
Tachikaeri	I change my mind again:
Nagori nakaran	To have no memory of him
Koto zo kanashiki	Would bring true misery.

This poem (226), along with many others in the *Memoirs*, has the same features as those Brower and Miner find in the love poetry of the late classical period: a scrutiny of the moment, an analytical discrimination of seemingly identical states, a choice of moments in which one feeling is about to become another, and a basic subjectivity.[60]

Lady Daibu's poems also share rhetorical techniques with the later poets. She is particularly fond of repeating sounds and words, a device she uses even more than her successors. The most extreme example is Poem 218:

60. Brower and Miner, p. 363.

Omou koto o	Now, as I sorrow
Omoiyaru ni zo	At the sorrow that is yours,
Omoikudaku	Heartrending sorrow
Omoi ni soete	Piles on my own sorrow
Itodo kanashiki	To sink me deeper in my grief.

Such repetition is used to intensify the sense of grief and distraction, and helps to convey the sense of direct outpouring that is characteristic of Lady Daibu. Repetition is even more noticeable in her poems than in her prose. A good example, from Volume One of her *Memoirs*, is this line in Poem 118: *Shimo ni shimo shiku,* "Frost spreads across the frost." She is also fond of rhetorical inversion, new diction or phrasing, and the idiosyncratic use of certain grammatical particles, all of which are also marks of the Kyōgoku-Reizei poets. Rather than quote at length here, a few references can be given to the text. The striking use of the particle *zo* can be noted at the end of line two in the last poem quoted above. Poem 217 is a fine example of inversion; and the first line of Poem 61 and the second line of Poem 314 represent new or unusual phrases.

These considerations add interest to the poetry of Lady Daibu, and we may even wonder whether she was a poetic innovator and why she chose to write in those styles rather than the more accepted styles of her age. The answer to the first question is no. Similar styles to hers are to be found in the work of her contemporaries and some predecessors. But in her adoption of the style she can certainly be called a precursor. The second question is harder to answer. Her best poetry occurs when she is at her most personal, introspective, and subjective, and the Kyōgoku-Reizei style suits such moods. Her experience and her retired way of life must have encouraged introspection and the close scrutiny of objects. She was also, after her retirement from court, away from the public domain of poetry and probably cultivated personal styles rather than the formal and public styles so favored by the leading poets of

the day. It is also likely that her experience was such as could
not be expressed in the conventional poetry of her own age.
Hers was a loss in warfare, which was beyond the experience of
most courtiers of the time, to whom violent death was virtually
unknown. Karaki Junzo has suggested that Lady Daibu is
poised at the junction of two views of transience: in the Heian
period transience was largely an aesthetic concept, a fading
away that was part of the natural progress of the seasons; but
after the Genpei War transience came to mean sudden death,
an untimely loss that could not be adequately expressed in such
aesthetic terms as cherry blossoms.[61] It is significant that Lady
Daibu insists on the uniqueness of her experience: it was an
experience for which Heian aesthetics had not prepared her.

This problem is related to her *Memoirs* as a whole. There is
a marked difference between the two volumes. The first volume has shorter *kotobagaki* and is more like other personal
poetry collections. In the second volume, these introductions
are not only much longer, but also more personal and introspective. This may well be because her experience defied the
conventional form of *tanka* poetry. Both her poetic style and
her use of prose introductions were the product of the experiences she endured. The Kyōgoku-Reizei poets were active
when the medieval ethic had already been established; they
were part of a court that was different in mood from the court
of the late twelfth century. Lady Daibu appears to us as a
figure caught at the very junction of two distinct periods, as
few other courtly writers seem to have been. Her work reflects
the suffering and the ambiguity of her position.

61. Karaki, *Mujō*, especially the chapter "Kenreimon-in Ukyō no Daibu
shū—hakanashi kara mujō e."

The Poetic Memoirs
of
Lady Daibu

1. *Mizuguki*, a poetic word for writing brush, is a pivot word: its first syllable, *mi*, is also read as the stem of the verb *miru*, "to see." *Mizuguki no ato*, literally "traces of the writing brush," is a poetic expression for letters or writings.

VOLUME ONE

Introduction

A personal poetry collection is something written by a poet for posterity. This, however, is far from being that sort of thing. I have merely recorded, just as I happened to remember them, my immediate feelings at those times when something moving, sad, or somehow unforgettable occurred; and I intend these memoirs for my eyes alone.

Ware narade	If not myself,
Tare ka aware to	Who, then, will be moved by pity,
Mizuguki no	As they gaze upon my words,
Ato moshi sue no	Should they be handed down
Yo ni tsutawaraba[1]	To later days?

1. *Kumo no ue,* "above the clouds," is a common expression for the imperial palace or court; it recurs frequently throughout the work.

2. Taira no Shigeko (1142–76), consort of Emperor Goshirakawa and mother of Emperor Takakura. She was the sister-in-law of Kiyomori and hence an aunt of Lady Daibu's mistress, Empress Tokuko. She was thirty-two years old at this time and well past her prime for those days, hence Lady Daibu's special mention of her youthful looks a few sentences later.

3. Taira no Tokiko (?–1185), wife of Kiyomori and mother of Empress Tokuko. At the battle of Dannoura she committed suicide by leaping into the sea, clutching her six-year-old grandson, Emperor Antoku.

4. Several identities have been suggested but none proved for this person.

Part One

While His Majesty Retired Emperor Takakura was still on the throne—it would have been perhaps the fourth year of Jōan [1174]—he visited the apartments of the Empress on the first day of the new year. The two of them were, of course, always imposing, but on that day he in his normal attire and she in full court dress seemed to me quite dazzling, and as I watched from a passageway I felt in my heart:

Kumo no ue ni	Here above the clouds,
Kakaru tsukihi no	I gaze upon the brilliance
Hikari miru	Of such a sun and such a moon,
Mi no chigiri sae	And I can only feel
Ureshi to zo omou[1]	How blissful is this fate of mine.

It must have been during that same spring that Retired Empress Kenshunmon-in[2] spent some time at the palace and visited our quarters. Lady Hachijō,[3] who was also at the palace, paid us a visit at the same time. Hiding behind the Lady of the Wardrobe,[4] I peeped out at them timidly. The Retired Empress looked inexpressibly beautiful and young, wearing a

5. Fujiwara (Saionji) no Sanemune, one of the outstanding lute (*biwa*) players of his day. His full title here is *tō no chūjō*, Captain First Secretary, meaning that he was a captain of the imperial bodyguard and one of the two First Secretaries of the Emperor's Private Office (Kurōdodokoro), one of whom was always a captain of the guards. Sanemune held this post from 1170 to 1176 and later rose to the rank of Grand Minister of the Center (*naidaijin*) in 1205, when he was known as the Ōmiya Grand Minister.

6. Wind amongst the pines is a conventional metaphor for the sound of the zither (*koto*). *Tsurenaki* is a pivot word meaning "having no accompaniment" and "cold, indifferent"; hence the translation "cold and friendless."

gown of several layers shaded from light to dark purple, a top gown of brownish-yellow, a pale pink overrobe, and a green chinese jacket woven with a pattern of butterflies. Used though I was by this time to looking at the Empress, I found her indescribably beautiful in her layered gowns of deep pink, top gown of red, pale green overrobe, and red chinese jacket, all woven with a pattern of cherry blossoms, and with the colors standing out beautifully one against the other. Even the fittings everywhere about the rooms and the costumes of the ladies-in-waiting seemed unusually resplendent, and in my heart I felt:

Haru no hana	Here above the clouds
Aki no tsukiyo o	I feel that
Onaji ori	At the self-same time I view
Miru kokochi suru	The flowers of spring
Kumo no ue kana	And a moonlit autumn night!

First Secretary Sanemune[5] was a constant visitor at the Empress's quarters and used to sing and play the lute with us. Sometimes he would ask me to play my zither too, but I always used to reply that it would only spoil everyone's pleasure.

On one occasion he passed me a message folded up like a letter with just this written on it:

Matsukaze no	Will not the wind amongst the pines
Hibiki mo soenu	Join to my solitary lute
Hitorigoto wa	Its murmuring voice?
Sa nomi tsurenaki	Must I play out to the very end
Ne o ya tsukusamu[6]	Such cold and friendless notes?

I replied:

Yo no tsune no	Were but this wind amongst the pines
Matsukaze naraba	Such as would pass for common in the world,
Ika bakari	Then gladly it would add
Akanu shirabe ni	Notes of its own to melodies
Ne mo kawasamashi	Of which no ear could tire.

7. Fujitsubo, a common name for the Higyōsha, one of the inner halls of the palace compound used as a residence by the Empress or the Emperor's principal consort.

8. The most important public festival of the year for people in the Heian capital. It took place on the last day of the cock in the fourth month and involved gorgeous processions, which were enjoyed by nobility and commoners alike. The term used here is *miare*, which originally meant the preparatory festival on the preceding day—the day of the monkey—but later came to be used as a name for the festival itself. For a detailed description of the festival, see McCullough, pp. 245–47.

9. Taira no Koremori, eldest son of Kiyomori and brother of Lady Daibu's lover, Sukemori. His title, which has been omitted in the translation, is *gon no suke*, Supernumerary Assistant Steward (of the Empress's Household).

10. The usual informal attire for courtiers consisted of *nōshi*, a cloak-like long jacket, and *sashinuki*, a pair of wide trousers rather like a divided skirt that were held in at the ankles by a drawstring. In translating the color of the jacket as dark indigo, I have followed the GSRJ text, as in *Zenshaku*, p. 91, which has *futaai*. Hisamatsu has *futae*, which means a cloth dyed once with one color, then dyed a second time with a pattern. But as Kubota points out, the GSRJ variant, *futaai*, a color very close to indigo, seems more appropriate, since it was a color commonly worn at that season. "Hyōshaku," 2: 163.

11. *Keigo*, ceremonial guard duty that all members of the guards of the rank of captain and below performed during the four days of the Kamo Festival. Koremori was at that time Supernumerary Lieutenant of the Bodyguard of the Right (*ukon no gon no shōshō*).

12. The effect of this poem is much enhanced by two pivot words that give it strong associations with the Kamo Festival. *Au hi*, "meeting day," is identical in written form, though not spoken form (at least as it is pronounced under modern conventions for reading Heian Japanese; it is likely, but not certain, that in Heian times the two words were pronounced the same way), with *aoi*, "heartvine," a small ivy-like, creeping plant that was used as decoration during the Kamo Festival, giving it the popular name *aoi matsuri*. That name is often mistranslated Hollyhock Festival through confusion between this plant, properly known as *futabaaoi*, "twin-leafed heartvine" (*Asarum caulescens* Maxim), and the hollyhock, *tachiaoi* (*Althea rosea*). The *futabaaoi* produces pairs of heart-shaped leaves, hence the translation "heartvine" used by Edward Seidensticker in *The Tale of Genji* and gratefully copied here. *Kakeji*, from *kaku*, "hang," is used in the idiom "to hang one's heart," meaning "to love, long for," and as the verb for hanging up the leaves of heartvine as decorations.

13. This poem repeats the two pivot words in the one above.

This same person came to the Wisteria Hall[7] at the time of the Kamo Festival[8] in the fourth month, and as we were talking together, Koremori[9] passed by. When we called out to him, he stopped, and we told him that we were thinking of getting together soon at one place or another for an informal party. We promised to invite him along.

Then he quickly walked on and stopped a little way off, where we could still see him. His dark-indigo-colored jacket and wide trousers,[10] his browny-green underrobe, and the unlined inner robe worn at that time of the year were not in any way unusual, but the colors stood out particularly well, and equipped as he was for ceremonial guard duty,[11] he looked as beautiful as someone in a picture book. "If I were as good-looking as that," said Sanemune, "I'd really be attached to this life—but that wouldn't be such a good thing after all would it?"

Urayamashi	What envy I feel!
Mi to miru hito no	All who set their eyes on him
Ika bakari	Must find their hearts
Nabete au hi o	Are yearning for a day
Kokoro kakuramu[12]	When they might meet with him.

"That's how you must be feeling just at this moment," he said to me. So I wrote the following poem on the edge of something I had to hand and pushed it towards him from behind my screen:

Nakanaka ni	Not so at all!
Hana no sugata wa	The beauty of the flowers
Yoso ni mite	I view as far beyond my reach;
Au hi to made wa	I have no thought to set my heart as high
Kakaji to zo omou[13]	As on a day when we might meet.

When I produced this, he laughed, saying, "The fact that you resign yourself like that shows how attractive you find him —is your heart really so pure?" It amused me how right he was.

14. The Service of the Eight Lessons, a ceremony lasting four days, in which two books of the *Lotus Sutra* were chanted on each day.

15. A distinction was made between Reigning Empresses (*kisaki*) and Retired Empresses (*nyōin*). There were three types of *kisaki*: the consort of the Emperor, with the title *kōgō* or *chūgū*; the Dowager Empress, *kōtaigōgū*; and the Arch-Dowager Empress, *taikōtaigōgū*. Those present at this ceremony were Empress Tokuko, Dowager Empress Kinshi (1134–1209), and Arch-Dowager Empress Tashi (1140–1201). *Nyōin* were Empresses who had taken holy orders and been granted religious names ending in *in*, usually chosen from the names of the palace gates. The Retired Empresses present during this ceremany were Kōkamon-in (1221–81), Jōzaimon-in (1126–89), and Hachijōin (1136–1211). Lady Sanjō is thought to have been Fujiwara no Sōshi (?–1231), a daughter of the Sanjō Minister, Fujiwara no Kintaka (1103–60). Lady Shirakawa was Taira no Seishi (1156–79), one of Kiyomori's daughters.

16. *Miya no suke*. This is Taira no Shigehira, fifth son of Kiyomori. He was obviously a good friend of Lady Daibu's and is mentioned several times in the *Memoirs*. He commanded the forces that burned down the Tōdaiji Temple in Nara in 1181, and following his capture at the battle of Ichinotani in 1184, he was brought back to the capital, paraded through the streets, and finally handed over to the monks of Nara and executed.

17. *Gon no suke*; Koremori.

18. *Minori*, the Buddhist Law or Dharma, refers to the moral precepts to be followed by believers and to the cosmic law of cause and effect, of death and rebirth. *Minori no hana*, the flower(s) of the Law, is an alternative Japanese reading of the title of the *Lotus Sutra (Hokekyō)*, whose name literally means "Dharma Flower Sutra." The phrase is also a reference to the offerings presented on artificial branches.

19. Fujiwara no Motomichi (1160–1233), an ally of the Taira, who rose to be Chancellor and Regent with Kiyomori's backing. He lost these offices with the downfall of the Taira but survived their defeat and was reappointed to them later. From 1176 to 1179 he simultaneously held the second rank and the post of Captain of the Guards, an unusual combination that earned him the sobriquet Second Rank Captain (*niichūjō*).

20. Fujiwara no Takafusa, a son-in-law of Kiyomori.

A reading of the eight books of the *Lotus Sutra*[14] was held in the palace on behalf of the late Retired Empress Kenshunmon-in, and the Emperor personally copied out the text to be used. On the day of the fifth book the Retired Empresses, the Reigning Empresses, Lady Sanjō, and Lady Shirakawa[15] all presented their offerings, and when various courtiers, who were relations of theirs, brought in these offerings, it was a spectacle both beautiful and moving. I remember that the offerings of our own Empress were carried on two artificial branches by the Assistant Steward of the Empress's Household[16] and the Supernumerary Assistant Steward.[17] The fittings of the rooms that had been occupied by the late Retired Empress had been taken out and placed in the hall used for the ceremony, which made it truly poignant.

Kokonoe ni	These flowers of the Law
Minori no hana no	Whose brilliance shines today
Niou kyō ya	Within the palace walls
Kienishi tsuyu mo	Will surely shed the radiance of their light
Hikari souramu[18]	On one who is now vanished like the dew.

When Lord Konoe was still known as the Second Rank Captain,[19] he invited Lady Shirakawa's ladies-in-waiting to accompany him and other senior courtiers, including Takafusa,[20] Shigehira, Koremori, and Sukemori, on a blossom-viewing excursion. The next day they sent to the Empress's quarters an unusually fine branch of cherry blossom with a note explaining that it was from those who had been out to view the flowers. So I wrote to them:

Sasowarenu	Uninvited—
Usa mo wasurete	Yet our bitterness is now forgotten,
Hitoeda no	For this single branch of blossom
Hana ni zo mezuru	Has captivated all the hearts
Kumo no uebito	Of those who dwell above the clouds.

In reply, Takafusa wrote:

21. Generally thought to be a lady-in-waiting to Takakura, known as Shichijōin Dainagon. She was in fact Kintaka's granddaughter but was adopted as his daughter in order to be sponsored at court, a not uncommon arrangement in those days. Her dates are unknown.

22. *Ne* of *ukine*, "dismal notes," is a pivot word; it can also mean "root" and thus forms a word association with *take*, "bamboo."

Kumo no ue ni	How worthy of our pains
Iro soeyo tote	To pluck that branch of blossom,
Hitoeda o	Thinking we might add
Oritsuru hana no	Some further luster
Kai mo aru kana	To that land above the clouds!

And Sukemori wrote:

Morotomo ni	Then together let us go
Tazunete o miyo	And gaze upon the flowers,
Hitoeda no	If, as you say,
Hana ni kokoro no	This single branch
Ge ni mo utsuraba	Has truly charmed your hearts.

Once on a bright, moonlit night we could hear the Emperor playing most enchantingly on his flute, and I remarked how beautiful it was. So when the Emperor was next on a visit to our quarters, the Empress told him how persistent I had been in my admiration. "What nonsense she talks!" he said, at which I murmured:

Sa mo koso wa	Well may it be
Kazu narazutomo	My worldly rank
Hitosuji ni	Is such as to be ignored!
Kokoro o sae mo	And yet is my heart too
Naki ni nasu kana	So to be set at naught?

Then someone called Lady Dainagon, who was also known as the daughter of the Sanjō Minister,[21] told them what I had said. The Emperor laughed and wrote this poem on the edge of his fan:

Fuetake no	Too well I know
Ukine o koso wa	How dismal are the notes
Omoishire	I blow on my bamboo flute!
Hito no kokoro o	How could it be
Naki ni ya wa nasu[22]	That I set your heart at naught?

1. *Mikawamizu*, the ditches that carried streams of water through the palace compound and past many of the palace buildings, are here used as a metonym for the Emperor and his reign.

2. By convention, the warbler spent the winter secluded deep in a bamboo thicket and sang from the midst of the thicket when spring arrived. The sound of the bird's song was thus one of the signs that spring had really arrived.

Part Two

Among poems written for no occasion in particular:

The first day of spring:

Itsu shi ka to	Before we know it,
Kōri tokeyuku	The ice melts from the palace streams,
Mikawamizu	Which, with this reign, shall flow on
Yukusue tōki	To their far destinations,
Kesa no hatsuharu[1]	This first morn of spring.

Haru kinu to	Who can have told
Tare uguisu ni	The singing warbler
Tsugetsuramu	That the spring has come?
Take no furusu wa	For deep within his thickets of bamboo
Haru mo shiraji o[2]	He will not know the season's change.

The sound of joy in the warbler's song:

Nodoka naru	The joyfulness
Haru ni au yo no	Of this illustrious reign,
Ureshisa wa	Which welcomes such a tranquil spring,
Take no naka naru	Echoes even in the warbler's song
Koe no iro ni mo	Within the bamboo groves.

3. Unless otherwise specified or ruled out by the season under discussion, blossom (*hana*) always meant cherry blossom.

4. An allusion to a story of Chinese origin, which can be found in the Japanese collections *Jikkinshō* (1252) and *Kokonchomonjū* (1254) and appears to have been well known in the Heian period. When a certain woman's husband went to war, she went to the top of a hill to see him off and wait for his return. She stayed there so long that she turned to stone.

5. Based on a poem by the priest Sosei (fl. c. 859–923), *Kokinshū* 273:

Nurete hosu	Soaked by the dew
Yamaji no kiku no	From the chrysanthemums
Tsuyu no ma ni	On the mountain path,
Itsu ka chitose o	When, in the instant ere it dried,
Ware wa heniken	Could I have passed a thousand years?

6. Abalone shells (*awabigai*) were used as a metaphor for one-sided or unrequited love because they were single shells, not bi-valves. Here a reference may be intended to Poem 2798 in the *Manyōshū* (759):

Ise no ama no	I suffer love one-sided
Asa na yū na ni	As abalone shells,
Kazuku tō	Which, so they tell me,
Awabi no kai no	The fishergirls of Ise
Katamoi ni shite	Gather morn and night.

Lady Daibu is probably also alluding to a poem by Fujiwara no Kiyosuke (1104–77), in the *Kiyosuke Ason shū, Zoku kokka taikan* 26255:

Koishisa no	Since I yearn with love
Tagui mo nami ni	That is beyond compare,
Sode nurete	Salt waves soak my sleeves
Hiroiwabinuru	As I find I cannot gather up
Wasuregai kana	The shells of forgetfulness.

Shell of forgetfulness (*wasuregai*) is a term used for an abalone shell or the single half of any bi-valve. That the fourth line is the same in this poem and Lady Daibu's is strong evidence of an intended allusion.

Waiting for the blossoms while looking at the moon:[3]

Haya nioe	"Come quickly into bloom!"
Kokoro o wakete	I urge, as with divided thoughts
Yomosugara	I gaze upon the moon,
Tsuki o miru ni mo	While all night through
Hana o shi zo omou	It is the flowers which fill my mind.

Love in former days:

Aware shirite	Knowing of my grief,
Tare ka tazunen	Will no one come to visit me?
Tsure mo naki	Even though, in suffering
Hito o koiwabi	For love of one so cruel,
Iwa to narutomo[4]	I turn to stone?

Deutzia flowers at an immortal's hermitage:

Tsuyu fukaki	Deep in the dew
Yamaji no kiku o	Along the mountain path,
Tomo to shite	Companions of long-lived chrysanthemums,
U no hana sae ya	The pure white deutzia flowers,
Chiyo mo sakubeki[5]	Shall they too bloom a thousand years?

The shame of unrequited love:

Oki tsu nami	The shame to have it known
Iwa utsu iso no	I suffer from an unrequited love
Awabigai	Impossible as gathering
Hiroiwabinuru	One-sided abalone shells,
Na koso oshikere[6]	Where, from the deep, waves pound the rocky shore!

The moon on a cloudy night:

Kumoriyo o	In reverie the whole night through,
Nagameakashite	I have been gazing at a clouded sky;
Koyoi koso	And now this very night at last
Chisato ni sayuru	I gaze upon a moon whose light
Tsuki o nagamure	Streams clear for a thousand leagues.

7. That is, when the man is not interested enough to visit his mistress, but they each receive occasional messages from or news about the other person.

8. The word she uses, *utsu*, is not fulling in the true sense, which is a process for thickening wool cloth. However, fulling is a conventional translation of the term, which meant to beat cloth on a block with a wooden mallet in order to produce a glossy surface.

9. This poem is generally seen as written from a man's point of view. It was not nearly as common for a woman to write in the persona of a man as it was for a man to write in the persona of a woman. It was often impossible for a woman to discover a man's name, and men could easily use assumed names if they thought they might be rejected or their suit otherwise impeded because of a revelation of their true names. *The Tale of Genji* provides examples of this sort of situation: Yūgao never knew that her lover was Prince Genji; Niou met Ukifune by pretending to be Kaoru. It could also happen that a man did not know the name of the woman he was visiting. Genji, for example, did not know whom he was visiting when he first met Oborozukiyo. *Ukina* is a pivot word meaning both "unhappy, detested name," and "name for fickleness."

Passing at dusk through the flowers on the moor:

Kokoro oba	Leaving my thoughts to linger
Obana ga sode ni	Amongst the beckoning sleeves
Todomeokite	Of pampas grass in bloom,
Koma ni makasuru	I let my horse pick out the path
Nobe no yūgure	Across the moor as twilight falls.

Love when we keep hearing of one another:[7]

Ari to kikare	What torment
Ware mo kikishi mo	That he has news of me,
Tsuraki kana	And I hear tell of him!
Tada hitosuji ni	For then we cannot blot each other
Naki ni nashinade	Utterly from our thoughts.

Deer close to a valley:

Tani fukami	So deep is the valley
Sugi no kozue o	That, amidst the rushing of the wind
Fuku kaze ni	Which blows through the cedar tops,
Aki no ojika zo	I seem to hear the stags of autumn
Koe kawasu naru	Exchange their mournful calls.

Awakening at night to the sound of fulling cloth:[8]

Utsu oto ni	Waking to the thumping of the block,
Nezame no sode zo	I know no cause for sadness
Nuremasaru	In the fulling of the cloth,
Koromo wa nani no	And yet my sleeves, already moist,
Yue to shiranedo	Grow damper still with tears.

Love under an assumed name:

Itowareshi	By changing that detested name,
Ukina o sara ni	Which marked me fickle,
Aratamete	Bringing such unhappiness,
Aimiru shi mo zo	I have at last met with my love,
Tsurasa soikeru[9]	But now I am more wretched still!

10. The call of this small water bird, *Rallus aquaticus indicus*, was thought to resemble the sound of a person knocking at a door.

11. There are no extant records of this poetry contest, nor is it certain which Inari Shrine is meant, though it is likely to be the famous one just outside the capital near the village of Fukakusa.

Evening at a cottage on the heath:

Yū sareba	As evening falls,
Natsuno no kusa no	Across the summer heath the grasses
Katanabiki	Bend beneath the breeze,
Suzumigatera ni	And in the cool it brings
Yasumu tabibito	A traveler rests.

Every night the sound of the water rail:

Arehatete	So tumbledown is my poor hut
Sasu koto mo naki	There is no bolt or bar
Maki no to o	Upon the pinewood door:
Nani to yo karezu	Why then night after night
Tataku kuina zo[10]	Comes the knocking of the water rail?

When a lover has arranged to meet two ladies on the same night:

Tanomeokishi	This night when he had promised
Koyoi wa ika ni	He would come to visit me,
Mataremashi	How long would I have waited
Tokorotagae no	Had I not seen his letter,
Fumi mizariseba	Sent to me, but meant for her!

From the Poetry Contest at the Inari Shrine:[11]

A warbler at morn in the shrine precincts:

Marone shite	After a night within the shrine,
Kaeru ashita no	This morning I set out for home,
Shime no uchi ni	And how it stirs my heart
Kokoro o somuru	To hear the warbler sing
Uguisu no koe	Within these sacred grounds.

12. The name *asagao* was earlier applied to two common flowers: first to the campanula, then to rose of sharon (*hibiscus syriacus*, not *hypericum*, which is also known as rose of sharon in some places). But in the Heian period the term seems to have applied to the morning glory or possibly to the convolvulus.

13. Young horses were turned loose in spring to graze on the fresh greenery. The word *nozawa*, used here and translated simply as fields actually means fields with expanses of shallow water: "water meadows" seems too agricultural, and "marsh" too wet, boggy, and sad.

14. The geese are leaving Japan and returning to what was considered their home in Siberia for the summer. The poem is based on a famous one by Lady Ise, *Kokinshū* 31:

Harugasumi	The geese that fly away,
Tatsu o misutete	Abandoning the sight
Yuku kari wa	Of the rising mists of spring,
Hana naki sato ni	Are they accustomed to a life
Sumi ya naraeru	In hamlets where no flowers bloom?

Blossom amongst the pines at evening:

Irihi sasu	Can the cherry have come into bloom
Mine no sakura ya	High on the mountain tops,
Sakinuramu	Caught in the rays of the setting sun?
Matsu no taema ni	Streams unending of white cloud
Taenu shirakumo	Float in the gaps between the pines.

Love in the middle of the day:

Chigiriokishi	The promised time
Hodo wa chikaku ya	Is surely close at hand
Narinuramu	When we shall meet?
Shiorenikeri na	For already it is wilted!
Asagao no hana[12]	The short-lived morning glory!

Spring rain in the depths of night:

Fukuru yo no	Deep in the night I wake,
Nezame sabishiki	And in my loneliness
Sode no ue o	I find my sleeves are soaked,
Oto ni mo nurasu	Just by the sound
Haru no ame kana	Of the soft spring rain.

Colts in the distant fields at springtime:[13]

Haruka naru	Left to run wild
Nozawa ni aruru	On the distant fields of spring,
Hanaregoma	The colts must come to know
Kaesa ya michi no	How far their way is,
Hodo mo shiruramu	When they turn for home.

Wild geese returning north through the dark sky:

Hana o koso	All thought of blossoms
Omoi mo suteme	Well may they give up!
Ariake no	But why do the geese,
Tsuki o mo matade	As they journey home, not even wait
Kaeru kari ga ne[14]	For the crescent moon of dawn?

15. *Yobukodori* is a pivot word meaning "cuckoo" and "bird that calls." Here the first part, *yobu*, is read together with *tare o* in the preceding line, giving "whom does he call?"

16. Sugata Lake, near the city of Nara, was renowned for its irises (*kakitsubata: Iris laevigata*). Sugata contains a play on the place-name and its meaning of "form."

17. The point of the poem lies in a play on the name Narabi no Oka, a hill in the western part of the capital, which also means "side-by-side hill." *Hitori sumire*, "a single violet," contains the phrase *hitori sumi*, "living alone."

18. Ide, not far from the capital, was renowned for its kerria.

A cuckoo just before the dawn:

Yo o nokosu	Waking while yet the night is dark,
Nezame ni tare o	I hear a cuckoo sing.
Yobukodori	Yet who can he be calling to?
Hito mo kotaenu	For no one makes reply
Shinonome no sora[15]	Across the sky in the early dawn.

Seedling beds in the mountains:

Yamazato wa	In this mountain village
Kadota no oda no	Where the seedlings grow
Nawashiro ni	In small rice fields before the gate,
Yagate kakei no	They draw the water as it comes,
Mizu makasetsutsu	Straight from the bamboo pipe.

Irises at an ancient lake:

Asenikeru	These irises that show
Sugata no ike no	Such faded outward form
Kakitsubata	Beside the waters of Sugata Lake,
Iku mukashi o ka	From what distant ages
Hedatekinuran[16]	Can they have flourished here?

Violets at a famous beauty spot:

Obotsukana	How strange it is!
Narabi no oka no	"Side-by-Side Hill"
Na nomi shite	Is a name and nothing more:
Hitori sumire no	A solitary violet blooms
Hana zo tsuyukeki[17]	Soaked with its tears of dew.

Kerria blooming here and there:

Waga yado no	About my house the kerria
Yaeyamabuki no	Glows in the setting sun:
Yūbae ni	I can only feel I look upon
Ide no watari mo	The sights at Ide,
Miru kokochi shite[18]	Famous for its flowers.

19. Probably based on a Chinese poem by Ono no Takamura (802–52), *Wakan rōeishū* 12:

> Tzu ch'en nen chüeh jen ch'üan shou
> Pi yü han lu chui t'o nang

* * *

> Purple dust of young fern: a man clenching his fist.
> Green jade of a cold reed: a gimlet emerging from a bag.

20. Takasago, in modern Takasago City, Hyogo Prefecture, was famous for its cherry blossoms. The visual image intended here is probably both cherry trees in full bloom on the hills about the harbor and scattered blossoms floating on the sea.

21. Yogo Lake is in Shiga Prefecture, north of Lake Biwa. It looks as if the topic (*dai*) for this poem has been lost, since the topic for the preceding poem does not fit, and all poems in this section, apart from Poem 14, which goes with 13, have their own topics.

A spring evening on a sea voyage:

Ikari orosu	The anchor falls into the depths,
Namima ni shizumu	The setting sun
Irihi koso	Sinks down beneath the waves—
Kureyuku haru no	Such is the cast of evening
Sugata narikere	At the close of spring.

Snow lingering near a waterfall:

Kōri koso	The ice has learned of spring's return,
Haru o shirikere	Freeing the torrent
Taki tsu se no	Of the waterfall,
Atari no yuki wa	And yet about the stream
Nao zo nokoreru	The winter's snow is lingering on.

Young fern shoots:

Murasaki no	No more do they seem
Chiri bakari shite	Than a scattering of purple dust:
Onozukara	Young shoots of fern,
Tokorodokoro ni	Which, by some power of their own,
Moyuru sawarabi[19]	Burst forth in every place.

Cherry blossoms at an anchorage:

Takasago no	As I gaze upon the spring
O no e no haru o	That crowns the mountain tops
Nagamureba	Of Takasago Bay,
Hana koso fune no	The boat itself floats
Tomari narikere[20]	Anchored in the blossoms.

Tomobune mo	Companions on their voyage,
Kogihanareyuku	The boats now sound
Koe su nari	As though they row apart:
Kasumi fukitoke	Blow, blow away this mist,
Yogo no urakaze[21]	O breeze on the bays of Yogo Lake!

22. Based on episode 63 in the *Tales of Ise*, in which the hero, Narihira, takes pity on an old woman and makes love to her. One day, when she goes to his house, he catches sight of her peeping in, and pretending not to know she is there, he recites the following poem:

Momotose ni	The lady with thinning hair—
Hitotose taranu	But a year short
Tsukumogami	Of a hundred—
Ware o kourashi	Must be longing for me,
Omokage ni miyu	For I seem to see her face.

Translation from McCullough, p. 110. Both poems rely on the belief that a person would see the image of a beloved who was thinking of him or her.

23. Mount Obasute, in the Yamashina district of modern Nagano Prefecture, was famous as a place for moon-viewing. *Kai* is a pivot word: it means both "valley" and "result, effect."

24. *Moji no seki*, the name of a barrier or check point for travelers in what is now Fukuoka Prefecture, is here a pivot word with the second meaning "barrier of words." *Moji*, "words," combines with *tamazusa*, a poetic word for "letter," in the previous line to make "a barrier for the words of our letters."

Blossoms scattering on a robe:

Sasoitsuru	The wind, it seems,
Kaze wa kozue o	Has passed in invitation
Suginu nari	Among the topmost boughs,
Hana wa tamoto ni	For on my sleeve the blossoms
Chirikakaritsuru	Have come scattering down.

Love for an old woman:

Tsukumogami	Aged and gray-haired,
Koinu hito ni mo	The image of a woman
Inishie wa	Appeared in days of old
Omokage ni sae	To one who felt no love for her—
Miekeru mono o[22]	Why does no image come to me?

Plants in the rain:

Sugite yuku	Hard-hearted is the one
Hito wa tsurashi na	Who passes coldly by,
Hanasusuki	While waving pampas grasses
Maneku masode ni	Beckon with their sleeves,
Ame wa furikite	On which the rains begin to fall.

The moon owes its brightness to the location:

Na ni takaki	Is it but the effect
Obasuteyama no	Of looking from the valley
Kai nare ya	Of well-renowned Mount Obasute?
Tsuki no hikari no	Why should the moon appear
Koto ni miyuramu[23]	So exceptionally bright?

Love separated by a barrier:

Koiwabite	Even the letters that I write
Kaku tamazusa no	In anguish at love's separation
Moji no seki	Are halted on their way:
Itsuka koyubeki	When shall our fate allow us
Chigiri naruramu[24]	To cross the barrier of words?

25. *Saibara*, a type of folk poem set to music and sung as a popular song at the Heian court.

26. *Azumaya* means an arbor or a small hut open at the sides, and was the title of a popular song of the *saibara* type. *Karegare* is a pivot word; it means both "few, far apart," and "withered." In its second meaning it forms a word association with *wasuregusa*, "lilies of forgetfulness," which are day lilies (*Hemerocallis aurantiaca* Bak.). Day lilies occur frequently in Heian poetry, especially in love poems, where the literal meaning of their name can be exploited.

First snow at a mountain hut:

Haru no hana	A sight to match
Aki no tsuki ni mo	The beauty of spring blossoms
Otoranu wa	Or the autumn moon:
Miyama no sato no	In this secluded mountain village
Yuki no akebono	Snow brightens in the dawn.

Love expressed by referring to a popular song:[25]

Mishi hito wa	He who once loved me—
Karegare ni naru	How few his visits now,
Azumaya ni	While round the withered arbor
Shigeri nomi suru	Where we met
Wasuregusa kana[26]	Only the lilies of forgetfulness grow rank.

Waiting for blossoms at a mountain hut:

Yamazato no	In this village of the mountain depths
Hana osoge naru	The cherry flowers bloom late,
Kozue yori	But the storm waits not,
Matanu arashi no	It sweeps amongst the tree tops
Oto zo monouki	With dismal and unwelcome sound.

1. Kinhira (1158–93) was a poet of some renown in his day. Here his title is given as Captain (*chūjō*).

2. The *ha* of *koto no ha*, "words," also means "leaves," which associates it with *shiguru*, "to rain," *iro*, "hue," and *fukage naru*, "deep."

3. In the background is the image of the leaves turning darker colors beneath the rain. It was believed that the autumn rains turned the leaves red.

4. Taira no Shigemori, eldest son of Kiyomori and father of Lady Daibu's lover, Sukemori.

5. Heian courtiers could organize a contest around practically anything, it seems. Here teams of the left and the right produced chrysanthemums, often with poems attached, and the side with the finest flowers and poems won the day.

Part Three

A lady in the Empress's service was being ardently wooed by Fujiwara no Kinhira.[1] She complained time and again that this brought nothing but unhappiness, so early in the autumn I sent her a poem:

Aki kite wa	With autumn's coming
Itodo ikani ka	How much more thickly they must fall,
Shigururamu	The chill tears of this season's rains,
Iro fukage naru	Adding their deepening colors
Hito no koto no ha[2]	To the dark hue of your words.

She replied:

Toki wakanu	No season to these constant tears,
Sode no shigure ni	Which deepen the color of my sleeves;
Aki soite	But can you know
Ikabakari naru	To what dark tints they turn,
Iro to ka wa shiru[3]	Now autumn adds its melancholy rain?

Composed on behalf of another person when the Komatsu Grand Minister[4] held a chrysanthemum contest.[5]

6. He became Commander of the Bodyguard of the Right (*ukon no taishō*) in 1174 and of the Left (*sakon no taishō*, the senior position) three years after; later in 1177 he became Minister of the Center (*naidaijin*).

7. Taira no Munemori, second son of Kiyomori. He became Commander of the Bodyguard of the Right when Shigemori became Commander of the Left.

8. Mount Mikasa was often used as a metaphor for the imperial bodyguard, *konoefu*, since there were three ranks of senior guards officer, and the name Mikasa literally means "three hats." The element *mi*, "three," can also be read as an honorific prefix, which gives the meaning "imperial hat." This meaning can be extended to "imperial protection," and with the pun on *mi* it becomes "threefold imperial protection" and hence "imperial bodyguard."

9. Celebrations that were held in conjunction with the Harvest Festival (*niinamematsuri*) each year in the eleventh month, from the second day of the ox to the second day of the dragon, a period of four days. The fire that is described here is probably the one known to have occurred on the twentieth day of the eleventh month of Angen 1 (Jan. 3, 1176). *Zenshaku*, p. 127.

10. Nanden, an alternative name for the Great Hall of State (Shishinden), which was situated at the south of the inner palace compound, facing the main gate. The large square in front of the building would make an ideal gathering place at such a time.

Utsushiuuru	May both this flower
Yado no aruji mo	And the master of this house
Kono hana mo	Where it has found new root
Tomo ni oisenu	See autumn after autumn
Aki zo kasanen	Untouched by age.

When this same Grand Minister came to offer his thanks on becoming joint Grand Minister and Commander of the Guards,[6] he was accompanied by his brother, the Guards Commander of the Right.[7] Their power seemed so prodigious that I wrote:

Itodoshiku	More and still more the blossoms of success
Sakisou hana no	Burst forth upon the treetops,
Kozue kana	Where together these two branches stand
Mikasa no yama ni	On the heights of Mount Mikasa,
Eda o tsuranete[8]	Threefold guardian of our Lord.

One year a fire broke out near the palace at the time of the Gosechi Celebrations,[9] and in view of the imminent danger, sedan chairs were made ready for us at the South Hall.[10] From the commanders downwards, the members of the guards looked very striking, each dressed in his own style; and I shall never forget how even amidst the general uproar, I could not help thinking that this was a sight I would hardly see in the outside world. Word came that Her Majesty was to leave in a hand-drawn carriage. The Komatsu Grand Minister made a particularly vivid impression when, as a guards commander, he came to the Empress's quarters wearing a quiver of arrows over his ordinary clothes.

Kumo no ue wa	Here above the clouds,
Moyuru keburi ni	Even the sight of people
Tachisawagu	Scrambling in chaos
Hito no keshiki mo	Through the fire and smoke,
Me ni tomaru kana	How it entrances me!

11. On the second day of the Gosechi Celebrations, the day of the tiger, a presentation of combs formed part of the ceremony, and from this grew the custom of sending combs to friends or lovers during the time of the celebrations.

12. *Usuyō*, here and throughout translated as "thin paper," was a type of *tori no ko* paper, one of the best varieties. *Usuyō* was normally used for letters and came in various colors, each suitable for a particular season.

13. In this poem and the next there is a play on the word *yosu* (*yosuru, yosekeru*), which means both "to express as, put into the guise of, compare to," and "to come near." *Kurenai*, "scarlet," was closely associated with passion and was often used to describe the tears of blood that were shed by thwarted lovers.

14. Hisamatsu retains *arufushigi koto*, "something unthinkable," the grammatically strange expression found in his base manuscript, but the translation follows the emendation to *arumajiki koto*, "something that should not happen," as suggested by Murai Jun, Kubota Jun, and Hisatoku Takafumi. *Hyōkai*, pp. 66–67, "Hyōshaku," 5: 161–62; Hisatoku 1968, p. 21. The GSRJ text has *arumaji no koto*, a grammatical variant with the same meaning as *arumajiki koto*. *Zenshaku*, p. 132.

These days Taira no Munemori seems to be called the Lord of Yashima, but while he still went by the title of Counsellor, I once asked him for a comb.[11] Having promised to let me have one, he insisted on giving me a quite magnificent comb decorated with a picture of a small boat thrusting its way through reeds. It had been pushed into a piece of thin scarlet paper,[12] on which he had written:

Ashiwake no	See how my heart,
Sawaru obune ni	Dyed deepest scarlet in its passion
Kurenai no	As it draws itself to yours,
Fukaki kokoro o	Resembles this small boat
Yosuru to o shire[13]	Which pushes through obstructing reeds.

I replied on thin white paper:

Ashi wakete	That your heart may be compared
Kokoro yosekeru	To this tiny boat
Obune to mo	Pushing through the reeds
Kurenai fukaki	The depth of scarlet in your words
Iro nite zo shiru	Tells to me full well.

I used to be amused by the various love affairs I saw around me or heard about, though I myself had no thought of following everybody else in such behavior. But among the many men who used to mingle with us at all times of the day and night, just like other ladies-in-waiting, there was one in particular who made approaches to me, though after seeing and hearing of other people's unhappy affairs I felt I ought not to let anything of that sort happen to me.[14] Destiny, however, is not to be avoided, and in spite of my resolve, I also came to know love's miseries.

Once, while this affair was causing me a great deal of heartache, I was at my home, lost in thought and gazing westward into the distance. The light of the evening sun was fading on

15. Since people slept on the floor, the expression "beneath the pillow" leads one to assume that the crickets are chirping underneath the flooring. *Aki* is frequently a pivot word meaning both "autumn" and "being sated, tired of." This double meaning, together with the mention of the pillow, gives the poem distinct overtones of love.

16. Two nights, the fifteenth of the eighth month and the thirteenth of the ninth month, were supposed to be the best times to view the moon.

the treetops, and this filled me with melancholy. Then the sky darkened and the fitful winter rain began to fall. As I looked out at this, I felt:

Yūhi utsuru	Caught in the last rays
Kozue no iro no	Of the setting sun, the treetops
Shigururu ni	Darken in the chilling rain:
Kokoro mo yagate	So too my heart is dimmed
Kakikurasu kana	And clouded over in its misery.

The crickets had been chirping near the Empress's quarters, but at the close of autumn their cries came to an end; and then I heard them still chirping in other places:

Toko naruru	Abandoning the place
Makura no shita o	Beneath the pillow
Furisutete	Of their long accustomed bed,
Aki oba shitau	The crickets now cry out their lingering regret
Kirigirisu kana[15]	For the passing autumn of indifference.

Once when I was even more depressed than usual, I was looking out at the plumes of pampas grass laden with dew:

Tsuyu no oku	Dew falls
Obana ga sode o	On the sleeves of pampas grass,
Nagamureba	And as I gaze,
Tagū namida zo	Tears to keep it company
Yagate koboruru	At once well up and fall.

Mono omoe	How this sight seems
Nageku to nareru	Its very self to grieve
Nagame kana	And bid my thoughts be sad—
Tanomenu aki no	The fickle autumn
Yūgure no sora	And its evening sky.

One night when the moon was bright:[16]

114

17. The text has *tachibana*, which could refer to either the blossom or the fruit of the orange tree. Orange blossom is usually *hanatachibana* or *tachibana no hana*, and in the GSRJ text the word *mitsu*, "three," follows *tachibana*, clearly indicating three oranges. This would be echoed in the *mitsu*, meaning "I have looked," in the poem. Moreover, the fruit is an autumn phenomenon and would harmonize with the season of the preceding poems, whereas the blossom is a summer phenomenon and would involve a large seasonal jump. Some commentators refrain from committing themselves on this question, but Murai and Hon-iden have no doubt that the fruit is intended. See *Hyōkai*, pp. 49–50; and *Zenshaku*, p. 136. For further support of this view, see the following note.

18. Based on an anonymous poem, *Kokinshū* 139:

Satsuki matsu	As I smell the fragrance
Hanatachibana no	Of orange trees that wait to bloom
Ka o kageba	Till the Month of Rains,
Mukashi no hito no	There comes to me again that fragrance
Sode no ka zo suru	Which clung to the sleeves of a person from my past.

Any reference to the orange tree would call to mind this very famous poem, and the rules of allusion often required a change in the precise circumstances or images. Therefore the interpretation of *tachibana* in Lady Daibu's poem as fruit does not rule out an allusion to the earlier poem. There is, moreover, a similar occasion in *The Tale of Genji*, when a present of oranges calls forth a poem on the scent of orange blossom. While Genji is talking to Tamakazura, the daughter of his former mistress Yūgao, who is now dead, he notices a strong resemblance between mother and daughter. Some fruit happens to have been brought in as a present. "Handling an orange that lay amongst the fruit on the lid of the box, Genji said:

Tachibana no	When I compare you
Kaorishi sode ni	With that one whose sleeves once bore
Yosoureba	Fragrance of orange blossom,
Kawareru mi to mo	I cannot make myself believe
Omoenu kana	This is a different person I behold."

Abe Akio et al., 3: 77. There is also a possible reference in the first line of Lady Daibu's poem to a Chinese story found in the *Wu chih* and *Meng ch'iu*, in which a man called Lu Chi is presented with some oranges and clasps them to his breast. Hisamatsu and Kubota, p. 34. This reference would support the argument for a present of fruit rather than blossom.

19. This translation follows the GSRJ text, used by Hon-iden, in which this passage begins *kakehanareieba*, "When I speak at a distance." Hisamatsu, following the Kyūshū Daigaku Text, has *kakehanareiku wa*, "When I go away," which would make the sentence read: "To be away from him was not wholly unhappy, but when he was close by me . . ." By far the

Na ni takaki	Not only those two nights
Futayo no hoka mo	That are renowned for viewing;
Aki wa tada	But constant the whole season through
Itsumo migakeru	Is autumn, in the color
Tsuki no iro kana	Of its burnished moon.

In reply to someone who sent some oranges[17] for me to look at:

Kokoro arite	Not with deep feeling
Mitsu to wa nashi ni	Did I look upon these oranges,
Tachibana no	Yet for no reason I can know,
Nioi o ayana	Their rich fragrance
Sode ni shimetsuru[18]	Has sunk deep into my sleeve.

Now when I look back on it, the affair was not totally unhappy, but right at the time, when I was in the middle of it, I felt mortified and resentful, and was frequently depressed.[19] Meanwhile, with the turning of the year, the spring appeared almost before I noticed it, filling me with envy. As I heard a warbler calling:

Mono omoeba	In the turmoil of my thoughts
Kokoro no haru mo	My heart knows none
Shiranu mi ni	Of the peace of spring:
Nani uguisu no	Why has the warbler come?
Tsuge ni kitsuramu	What words can he have for me?

To ni kaku ni	Wherever I turn,
Kokoro o sarazu	My heart will not be rid
Omou koto mo	Of these wretched thoughts.
Sate mo to omoeba	The more I think, 'Enough, let be!'
Sara ni koso omoe[20]	The more they press upon my mind.

majority of manuscripts have the same reading as the GSRJ text. See Ikari 1969, p. 361. The variant seems to have arisen because the *kana* symbols for *(h)e* and *ku*, the penultimate syllables in the two variant expressions, are easily mistaken for each other—*kakehanarei(h)eba* was mistakenly copied as *kakehanareiku wa*, or possibly vice versa. Kubota admits that linguistic objections can be raised, whichever version one chooses. "Hyō-shaku," 6: 161. Hon-iden interprets *kakehanareieba* in terms of viewpoint, to read: "When it is viewed with detachment." *Zenshaku*, 1974 ed., pp. 70–71. But since the preceding and succeeding poems imply being parted by time, Murai's interpretation is to be preferred. *Hyōkai*, pp. 50–51.

20. There are differing interpretations of the fourth line: "When I think I shall give up such thoughts" (*Zenshaku*, p. 137); "Things will remain as they are," i.e. I shall not be abandoned (*Hyōkai*, p. 51). The translation here follows Kubota, who takes *sate* to mean "[to be] as it is." "Hyōshaku," 6: 162. This is certainly the usual meaning of the expression.

21. This is generally believed to be Yukiie, the middle brother, for the eldest, Koretsune, lived until 1227, and the third brother, Son-en, was clearly alive after the death of Sukemori. The *Amida Sutra*, one of the three main sutras of the Pure Land Sect, extols the blessings of rebirth in the paradise of the Pure Land and is most suitable as an aid to salvation for the dead.

22. The soul was thought to wander beyond the grave for forty-nine days between this life and the next. Acts of devotion by relations were particularly important during that period in helping the soul towards paradise.

23. Lady Kojijū (c. 1120–1200) was a well-known poet of the Ki family.

24. The wit of the poem depends on the pivot word *kaze*, which means both "wind" and a "cold." Between this poem and the next, the GSRJ text has the following additional poem: "On viewing cherry blossom:

Kazu naranu	Unworthy and wretched
Uki mi mo hito ni	Though I am, in this at least
Otoranu wa	I equal others:
Hana miru haru no	My heart in springtime
Kokoro narikeri	As I view the cherry flowers."

This poem is also included in (among others) the Yoshimizu Jinja text, which Ikari believes to have been an early draft of the first volume. His view is that the poem was part of the preceding exchange with Kojijū but was later omitted so as to keep the balance of a simple two-poem exchange. Ikari 1964, p. 5. Another likely reason for the exclusion of this poem is that with its reference to Lady Daibu's wretchedness (*uki mi*), it suggested the tone of later events too strongly. If this is the case, it indicates the care taken in selecting and ordering the material in the work.

25. Princess Shikishi (?–1201), one of the outstanding poets of her day. She was priestess (*saiin*) at the Kamo Shrine, 1159–69.

26. Identity unknown.

I was copying out the *Amida Sutra* for my elder brother, who had died:[21]

Mayoubeki	Before him, perchance,
Yami mo ya kanete	It will dispel the darkness
Harenuramu	Where he well might wander lost—
Kakioku moji no	The brilliance of the Law,
Nori no hikari ni[22]	Whose syllables I copy down.

The ladies-in-waiting to the Emperor and Empress went out together in a great number of carriages to view the cherry blossoms. They were escorted by middle-rank courtiers and high court nobles who were personal attendants of the Emperor. I did not go with them, since I was unwell, so they sent me a branch of cherry blossom with a poem attached to it, written on thin scarlet paper. It was by Lady Kojijū.[23]

Sasowarenu	Though it hurts me
Kokoro no hodo wa	That your feelings should be such
Tsurakeredo	As not to come with us,
Hitori mirubeki	Surely the beauty of these blossoms
Hana no iro ka wa	Should not be viewed by us alone?

This was all due to my having a cold, so in reply I sent:

Kaze o itou	I knew it would not do
Hana no atari wa	If I approached the blossoms,
Ikaga tote	Which detest cold winds;
Yosonagara koso	But though I was not with you
Omoiyaritsure[24]	I mused upon them from afar.

During the time that the Ōinomikado Priestess[25] was still officiating and living at the priestess's palace, Lady Chūjo,[26] one of her ladies-in-waiting, broke off and sent me a branch of blossoms, which she said were "cherry blossoms from within the sacred fence":

27. This poem has strong overtones of love, particularly in the use of the expression *mi o kudaku* (*mi o mo kudakazu*), "torment oneself," which normally referred to love and is rather strong for cherry blossoms. "Hyō-shaku," 7: 172–73.

28. Kiyotsune (1163?–83), was the third son of Taira no Shigemori, here given the title of Captain (*chūjō*).

29. Still to be found in modern Ōsaka. At that time it was next to a beach celebrated for its beauty.

Shime no uchi wa	Within these sacred precincts
Mi o mo kudakazu	My heart remains untroubled;
Sakurabana	All feelings of regret
Oshimu kokoro o	At the inconstancy of cherry blossoms
Kami ni makasete[27]	I leave unto the gods.

My reply:

Shime no hoka mo	Outside the sacred precincts, too,
Hana to shi iwan	Would that we might trust
Hana wa mina	Unto the gods
Kami ni makasete	All blossoms worthy of the name,
Chirasazumogana	That they might never fall.

I heard that this Lady Chūjo was having an affair with Taira no Kiyotsune,[28] but before long it came to my ears that he had transferred his affections to another lady in service at the same palace. So while I was sending a letter, I also wrote:

Sode no tsuyu ya	How falls the dew of tears
Ikaga koboruru	Upon your sleeve,
Ashigaki o	Now that you have seen the wind
Fukiwataru naru	Blow without lingering
Kaze no keshiki ni	Past the frail reed fence?

Her reply:

Fukiwataru	Seeing the wind blow by me,
Kaze ni tsukete mo	How I reproach myself
Sode no tsuyu	That ever the dew began
Midaresomenishi	To fall with my tangled thoughts
Koto zo kuyashiki	Upon my sleeve.

While the man who was causing me so much heartache was still a courtier of middle rank, he went with his father, the Grand Minister, on a pilgrimage to Sumiyoshi Shrine.[29] On his return he sent me the following poem, written on thin blue paper and attached to some "lilies of forgetfulness," which were

30. The poem uses the general term *kusa*, "plants," rather than the specific term *wasuregusa*, "lilies of forgetfulness" (day lilies), but the coast at Sumiyoshi was famous for its day lilies, and there is thus no need for them to be mentioned by name in the poem; in any case they would be instantly recognized on the tray. The poem depends on two pivot words: *ura mite*, "seeing the bay," can also mean "resenting"; and *kai*, "shells," also means "reward, effect." Thus the first two lines can be read: "Though I see the bay, there are no sea shells. Though I am bitter, there is no point in it." There is an allusion to a poem by Ki no Tsurayuki, *Kokinshū* 1111:

Michi shiraba	But knew I the way,
Tsumi ni mo yukamu	I would go and gather love's
Sumi no e no	Lilies of forgetfulness,
Kishi ni ou chō	Which, it is said, grow on the shore
Koiwasuregusa	Along the Bay of Sumi.

31. The Japanese name for this scarlet color was *momiji*, "red leaves." The paper is thus appropriate for autumn.

32. This poem uses the same pivot words as the preceding one.

33. Fujiwara no Sōshi (?–1231), consort of Emperor Goshirakawa.

34. Picture Island (Ejima) was an island near Awaji Isle in the Inland Sea. The first element in the name, *e*, "picture," functions as a pivot word to give *e ni tomeshi*, "held in the picture."

35. The *hototogisu*, a small bird of the cuckoo family (*Cuculus poliocephalus*), was famous for its beautiful song. It first sang in the hills, where its song was considered to be at its freshest, and appeared in the city somewhat later, usually in the fifth month, when the song was thought to have passed its best. In any case, the song was eagerly awaited.

placed on a tray modeled into a beach scene and containing assorted shells:

Ura mite mo	Gazing at the bay brings me no shells,
Kai shi nakereba	Nor does my bitterness avail;
Sumi no e ni	So I have been in search
Ou chō kusa o	Of lilies of forgetfulness, which,
Tazunete zo miru[30]	It is said, grow by the Bay of Sumi.

Since the season was autumn, I sent a reply on thin scarlet paper:[31]

Sumi no e no	Forgetfulness, which grows
Kusa oba hito no	With lilies from the Bay of Sumi,
Kokoro nite	Lies within your heart, not mine;
Ware zo kai naki	I am the one who should resent
Mi o uraminuru[32]	A love with no reward.

The Arch-Dowager Empress[33] sent some attractive paintings to the Empress, and among them were a few on which someone had made my father write commentaries as calligraphy exercises. I was extremely moved at seeing them:

Megurikite	Seeing them now surround me
Miru ni tamoto o	Brings tears to soak my sleeves—
Nurasu kana	In Picture Island,
Ejima ni tomeshi	Held there and enduring,
Mizuguki no ato[34]	The traces of his hand!

Around the fourth month, while I was staying in a mountain village with someone I knew well, the *hototogisu* was constantly singing:

Miyakobito	There in the capital
Matsuran mono o	They must be waiting still
Hototogisu	To hear the *hototogisu*'s song,
Nakifurushitsuru	But here it has been sung to staleness
Miyamabe no sato[35]	In this village deep within the hills.

36. Taira no Tokitada (1127–87), brother of Kiyomori's wife, Tokiko, and of Retired Empress Kenshunmon-in.

37. This plant is in fact a sweet flag (*Acorum calamus* var. *angustatus*), the Japanese *shōbu*, which was also known as *ayame* in Heian times. In view of the unfamiliarity of the name sweet flag and the resemblance of the plant's roots and leaves (but not flowers) to those of an iris, I have used this conventional translation. These irises and various pomanders were used as decorations and given as presents on the fifth day of the fifth month, which was a festival known as *tango no sechie*. Iris leaves and roots were hung in buildings and thrust under the eaves, and were also worn in one's hair or on one's clothes (see Poem 85 below).

38. *Hiki*, part of the verb *hikikurabu* (*hikikurabureba*), "to compare," can also mean "pulling," and as such it forms an association with *ne*, "root."

39. *Hikeru* is a pivot word to be used with *tameshi*, "example," as "to draw an example," and with *ne*, "root," as "to pull up."

40. *Itsu ka* is a pivot word meaning both "which day" and "fifth day (of the month)."

The scent of orange blossom came wafting with the wind, which blew just as the rain was stopping:

Tachibana no	The fragrance
Hana koso itodo	Of the orange blossom
Kaoru nare	Now grows stronger still:
Kazemaze ni furu	Mingling with the wind,
Ame no yūgure	The rain falls through the dusk.

On the fifth day of the fifth month we received from Tokitada,[36] Supernumerary Steward of the Empress's Household, a box lid with a picture of a pomander lacquered on it. It had been lined with thin iris-colored paper, on which there lay an unusually long iris root,[37] and it was accompanied by a poem written on the same type of paper:

Kimi ga yo ni	When we compare it
Hikikurabureba	With Your Majesty's enduring reign,
Ayamegusa	Even this iris root,
Nagashi chō ne mo	Which men may well describe as long,
Akazu zo arikeru[38]	Hardly deserves to be so called.

Our reply was on thin paper the color of orange blossom:

Kokorozashi	Well does this iris show
Fukaku zo miyuru	Your deep regard for us,
Ayamegusa	For you have pulled so long a root
Nagaki tameshi ni	To stand as an example
Hikeru ne nareba[39]	Of our long-enduring reign.

To someone who sent me an iris root while I was secluded in my house owing to a bereavement:

Ayame fuku	While I was yet unaware
Tsukihi mo omoi	That now is the time
Wakanu ma ni	To deck our eaves with irises,
Kyō o itsu ka to	You have made known to me
Kimi zo shirasuru[40]	What very day this is.

41. A member of the Fujiwara family; almost nothing is known of her. On Narichika, see note 62, below, p. 134.

42. *Fukaki*, "deep," is to be read both with *omoi*, "feelings," and with *e*, "inlet." *E* itself also has a second meaning, "connection, friendship," so that *omoi fukaki e* means "a friendship of deep feeling," while *fukaki e* means "a deep inlet" or "deep in the inlet."

43. *Uki* is a pivot word meaning both "mud" and "grief." *Ne* is a pivot word meaning both "root" and "cries, sobs."

44. *Ashide*, a way of writing a message on paper on which a picture had been painted. The writing was cleverly blended in with reeds and water plants so as to appear part of the painting.

I was acquainted with Narichika's daughter,[41] who was the wife of Koremori, and this poem came from her together with a pomander:

Kimi ni omoi	Deep is my feeling for you,
Fukaki e ni koso	So I pulled this iris root
Hikitsuredo	From deep within the bay,
Ayame no kusa no	But still too shallow did it grow
Ne koso asakere[42]	To show my true regard!

My reply:

Hiku hito no	Well it becomes me that I wear
Nasake mo fukaki	On my sleeve this iris root,
E ni ouru	Which grew so deep within the bay,
Ayame zo sode ni	Showing how deep was the affection
Kakete kai aru	Of the one who plucked it thence!

Written for practice when I was using my inkstone:

Aware nari	How piteous when I think of them,
Mi no uki ni nomi	Their roots caught in the mud,
Ne o tomete	As my sobs are caught in grief—
Tamoto ni kakaru	Irises worn on people's sleeves,
Ayame to omoeba[43]	As I wear tears on mine.

Towards the end of autumn Retired Empress Kenshunmon-in came to the palace and stayed for quite some time in the Empress's quarters. She was to return to her own palace on the last day of the ninth month, and on the preceding day a servant was sent in to us with a poem written on thin crepe paper in such a way as to look like reeds in a painting.[44] It was folded formally in a long strip and wrapped in thin crimson paper:

Kaeriyuku	Since we must part from you
Aki ni sakidatsu	Before the autumn even
Nagori koso	Takes its final leave,
Oshimu kokoro no	Our hearts are overflowing
Kagiri narikere	With yearning and regret.

45. Taira no Tomomori (1152–85), fourth son of Kiyomori.
46. Tadanori (1144–84) was the younger brother of Kiyomori; also known
as a poet.

Our reply was written on thin chrysanthemum-colored paper, white on the front and green on the back; but we had no idea who had sent us the first poem, so we had ours delivered by Tomomori,[45] who was then visiting the ladies-in-waiting. The day was indeed one to bring feelings of regret, since the late-autumn rain was falling steadily, and there was a melancholy air to it; yet we wrote:

Tachikaeru	How can you feel regret
Nagori o nani to	At parting from us now,
Oshimuran	When you are living in a world
Chitose no aki no	That shall enjoy
Nodoka naru yo ni	A thousand years of tranquil autumns?

From the wife of Koremori there came this poem written on thin blue paper and attached to a spray of red maple leaves:

Kimiyue wa	For your sake
Oshiki nokiba no	I grudge not in the least
Momiji o mo	To break a spray
Oshikarade koso	Of the precious crimson maple
Kaku taoritsure	That grows about my eaves.

My reply was on thin crimson paper:

Wareyue ni	That for my sake
Kimi ga orikeru	You broke off these scarlet leaves
Momiji koso	Adds, in my sight,
Nabete no iro ni	Yet deeper color
Iro soete mire	To their normal hue.

Lord Tadanori[46] sent me an unusually fine branch of red maple leaves, with a message to say he had been viewing them on the western hills, and with this poem attached to it:

47. *Fukaki*, "deep," refers both to *omoi*, "feelings," and to *miyama*, "mountain depths." *Ori* is a pivot word meaning both "season" and "breaking (off leaves)." The same words are used with double meanings in the poem of reply.

48. Presumably the same woman mentioned in the prose introduction to Poem 3.

49. Unidentified, but obviously one of the ladies-in-waiting who served with Lady Daibu.

50. The *ha* of *koto no ha*, "words," means "leaves," which forms word associations with *kaze*, "wind," and *chirasu* (*chirasan*), "scatter."

51. One of Kiyomori's mansions, an imposing place occupying six blocks in the south part of the city just west of the central Suzaku Avenue, which split the city into eastern and western halves. "Hyōshaku," 10: 165–66.

52. Identified in the text only by his title, *gon no suke*, Supernumerary Assistant Steward (of the Empress's Household).

53. Taira no Tsunemasa (?–1184), a nephew of Kiyomori's.

54. Kiyomori's son-in-law Fujiwara no Takafusa, mentioned in Part One.

Kimi ni omoi	By this I tell you of the season
Fukaki miyama no	And how deep my feelings are,
Momiji oba	For while there was some respite
Arashi no hima ni	From the storm deep in the hills,
Ori zo shirasuru[47]	I broke off these maple leaves.

My reply:

Obotsukana	What does this mean?
Ori koso shirane	I see no season here for you!
Tare ni omoi	For whom can you intend
Fukaki miyama no	As sign of your profound regard
Momiji naruramu	These crimson leaves from deep within the hills?

The Lady of the Wardrobe[48] had been rather a long time away from the palace at her own home. Lady Ben[49] went to see her and on returning brought me a message asking why I had not taken the opportunity of sending a letter. So I wrote:

Naozari ni	Far from neglectful
Omoi shi mo senu	Are my thoughts of you:
Koto no ha o	How could I let the words
Kaze no tayori ni	That tell of them
Ikaga chirasan[50]	Scatter as tidings on the breeze?

One spring the Empress was on a visit to the mansion in the western part of the eighth ward.[51] She was, of course, accompanied by her usual retinue; and her brothers and nephews were also on duty, so that there were several people constantly in attendance. On a bright, moonlit night when the cherry trees were in full bloom, Koremori[52] said, "Are we to let such a night pass away without enjoying it?" and began to sing verses and play his flute, while Tsunemasa[53] played the lute, and the ladies behind their curtains also joined in with their zithers. Just as we were having this delightful concert, Takafusa[54] came from the palace with a letter from the Emperor. We summoned him in without delay, and when we had exhausted our stock of mu-

sic, we chatted of past and present and gazed at the scene until dawn. The blossoms that were still clinging to the branches and those that were scattering down were equally beautiful, and they blended mistily into the moonlight. The sky gradually whitened where it met the rim of the mountains, and though always a deeply moving sight, it was then inexpressibly beautiful. Takafusa had received the Empress's reply and was on his way out when I remarked, "You can't leave just like that!" Unfolding one end of my fan, I wrote the following poem on it and had it passed across to him:

Kaku made no	Had we not reached the limits
Nasake tsukusade	Of elegance and beauty,
Ōkata ni	But merely seen the moon and blossoms
Hana to tsuki to o	In an ordinary way, it would be hard—
Tada mimashi dani	But of tonight, what can we say?

To my embarrassment he sang my poem out loud, then called for an inkstone and insisted that everyone there should write something—no matter what—and he himself wrote the following poem on his own fan:

Katagata ni	In all we have done
Wasurarumajiki	This night is such
Koyoi oba	As we shall not soon forget;
Tare mo kokoro ni	Treasure it, each one of you,
Todomete omoe	Keep it within your hearts!

"What about someone who can't compose poems?" demanded Koremori. But, of course, he was made to produce one:

Kokoro tomu	Even if we were told
Na omoiide so to	Not to remember it
Iwan dani	Or keep it in our hearts,
Koyoi o ikaga	How could we easily
Yasuku wasuren	Forget this night?

55. In the original manuscript this introduction to Poems 98 and 99 continues without a break from the preceding paragraph, and so, these poems could conceivably have been composed on the same occasion as the preceding four; however, most scholars are of the opinion that they were not. The poems are given in reverse order from the topics.

56. *Sumu* (*sumubeki*) is a pivot word meaning "to be clear" and "to dwell"; hence the poem hints that the person for whom it is intended shall live for a thousand years.

57. This poem is unified by word associations: *ha*, "leaves" (through the double meaning of *ha* in *koto no ha*), *oku*, "to settle" (here translated "laden"), and *tsuyu*, "dew."

Lord Tsunemasa recited:

Ureshiku mo	What joy to be numbered
Koyoi no tomo no	In this company tonight!
Kazu ni irite	It shall become our chance
Shinobare shinobu	To be remembered fondly
Tsuma to narubeki	And to have our own fond memories.

At this everyone laughed at him and told him how conceited he was to be thinking that he was going to be specially remembered. "When did I ever say such a thing?" he protested. It was most engaging.

Someone also asked me to write poems on "Love Under the Moon" and "Celebration Under the Moon":[55]

Chiyo no aki	Shall not the brilliance
Sumubeki sora no	Of this night serve as an example
Tsuki mo nao	Even of a moon that is to shine
Koyoi no kage ya	Clear and tranquil in the sky
Tameshi naruramu[56]	Across the autumns of a thousand ages.

Tsure mo naki	He who has been so cruel
Hito zo nasake mo	Shows me this kindness after all!
Shirasekeru	Were they not soaked with tears,
Nurezu wa sode ni	How could I have seen
Tsuki o mimashi ya	The moon reflected on my sleeves?

In reply to a relation of mine who sent a message of sympathy when I was unwell:

Nasake oku	Heavy with sympathy,
Koto no hagoto ni	Like leaves that are laden with the dew,
Mi ni shimite	Your every word goes to my heart,
Namida no tsuyu zo	And thicker than ever now
Itodo koboruru[57]	The dew of tears spills down.

58. Shigemori died on the first of the eighth month of Jijō 3 (Sept. 3, 1179).

59. Three images lie behind the darkened color of the sleeves: the somber hue of robes of mourning, sleeves darkened by the dampness of tears falling on them, and leaves being turned red by the rain.

60. The unswept sleeping place is a common image for loneliness or the loss of someone dear.

61. Dates unknown. She was a daughter of the poet Fujiwara no Toshinari and thus possibly closely connected with Lady Daibu.

62. Fujiwara no Narichika (b. 1138), one of the conspirators in the Shishigatani Plot against the Taira family in 1177. He was exiled and killed the same year.

Sent in condolence to a person who was in mourning:

Aware to mo	I would you might know
Omoishiranan	The distress that I too feel:
Kimi yue ni	For your sake
Yoso no nageki no	It falls thick about me,
Tsuyu mo fukaki o	Dew of a grief that is not mine.

Following the death of the Komatsu Grand Minister, I sent these poems to his widow sometime in the tenth month:[58]

Kakikurasu	My thoughts are with you
Yoru no ame ni mo	As rain falls through the nights
Iro kawaru	Clouded with blackness,
Sode no shigure o	And the wintry drops add yet more color
Omoi koso yare[59]	To your sleeves already dark.

Tomaruramu	My thoughts are with you
Furuki makura ni	As the dust lies thick
Chiri wa ite	On his old pillow,
Harawanu toko o	Where it surely still remains
Omoi koso yare[60]	On a bed that is unswept.

Her replies:

Otozururu	My nightly visitor is now
Shigure wa sode ni	The winter rain,
Arasoite	Which vies upon my sleeve
Nakunaku akasu	With tears of my long vigil—
Yowa zo kanashiki	The depths of night bring me such misery!

Migakikoshi	Piled high, the dust lies
Tama no yodoko ni	On that bed of ours, which once
Chiri tsumite	We kept as bright as a polished gem,
Furuki makura o	And there lies his pillow as of old—
Miru zo kanashiki	To see it brings such misery!

Sent to Lady Kyōgoku[61] after her husband, Counsellor Narichika,[62] had been banished to a faraway place:

63. *Tachi* in *tachiwakaru*, "to depart," can also be read as "to cut out (cloth)" and is therefore associated with the pillow word *tabigoromo*, "traveling robe," and *sode*, "sleeves."

64. *Shinobu* means "to long for," but it is also a commonly used abbreviation of *shinobugusa*, "grasses of longing," a type of evergreen fern, *Polipodium lineare*, that grows on trees, the eaves of buildings, and in shady places. In this sense it is closely associated with *areyuku yado*, "house which falls into decay."

65. *Rinji no matsuri*, a term that could apply to a variety of secondary festivals, but commonly, as here, referred to the second and less important Kamo Festival, which was held on the last day of the cock in the eleventh month. This particular festival took place on the twenty-sixth day of the eleventh month of Angen 1, and since the seventeenth day was Dec. 31, 1175, in the Western calendar, the exact date was Jan. 9, 1176.

66. *Kaeridachi no mikagura*, dances performed by the messengers and dancers at the end of the festival, when they returned first to the palace for the dances and a banquet and finally to the Kamo Shrine.

67. "Asakura" (Morning Storehouse) is the name of a song belonging to the sacred music (*kagura*) that was performed at the festival. It was often used as a rhetorical introduction to *kaesugaesu*, "over and over," either because the refrain of the song was repeated many times or because *kaesu*, "return," was a technical term for the type of accompaniment used with that song. Here it may be seen as a meaningful introduction, since it is closely connected with the occasion of the poem.

The flowers used for decoration were artificial ones, attached to the headwear of the participants, wisteria for the messengers and cherry blossoms for the dancers. *Ori*, "time, occasion," also has the meaning "break" and is thus associated with flowers.

Ika bakari	Now of all times
Makura no shita mo	How thick the frost must lie
Kōruramu	Beneath your pillow,
Nabete no sode mo	When even sleeves of those who have no grief
Sayuru konogoro	Freeze with the season's cold!

Tabigoromo	Sleeves now left behind
Tachiwakarenishi	By those on the traveling robe
Ato no sode	Of him who is departed,
Moroki namida no	Have they no respite
Tsuyu ya himanaki[63]	From the falling dew of tears?

Her reply:

Toko no ue mo	On my bed, on my sleeves,
Sode mo namida no	There are icicles of tears,
Tsurara nite	As all night through
Akasu omoi no	I lie awake with thoughts
Yaru kata mo nashi	From which there can be no escape.

Hi ni soete	Think with pity of this house,
Areyuku yado o	Which falls into decay
Omoiyare	With the passing of the days,
Hito o shinobu no	As I grow wasted by the dew
Tsuyu ni yatsurete[64]	Falling from the grasses of my longing.

At the time of the Second Kamo Festival[65] in the winter of the first year of Angen [1175], I was unable to accompany the Empress to her quarters in the Emperor's apartments because of a defilement. I was so downcast at missing the "Sacred Dances of the Return,"[66] which I had so much wanted to see, that I left this poem in the Empress's writing box, written on a scrap of thin paper:

Asakura ya	Over and over, like the melodies
Kaesugaesu zo	Of the "Morning Storehouse" song,
Uramitsuru	I feel resentment at myself—
Kazashi no hana no	How could I be unaware this is the season
Ori shiranu mi o[67]	For the flowers that decorate the dance!

68. The main mansion of Kiyomori. It was situated just outside the city proper, on a level with the sixth ward and east of the Kamo River, which formed the eastern boundary of the city at this point.

69. A hall set well back in the inner palace and used as quarters for imperial consorts and ladies-in-waiting.

70. There is the usual double meaning in *sumu*, "to be clear," and "to dwell."

71. Fujiwara no Kanemitsu (1144–96). He was a Private Secretary (*kurōdo*) from 1168 to 1179.

72. Edible berries of the *muku* tree, *Aphananthe aspera*, a member of the elm family. The berries are similar to litchi fruit. The leaves of the tree were used for cleaning and polishing.

73. Unidentified.

74. The six paths are the six realms in which living beings continue to be reborn according to their karma: the realms of hell, hungry demons, beasts, evil spirits, human beings, and heavenly spirits. *Muku* (on which see note 72 above) is echoed in the word *mukui*, "reward."

A lady-in-waiting who was spending time in her own home sent a message that she would like to see some of the scarlet maple leaves from in front of the Wisteria Hall. They had all fallen, however, so I sent her a branch of artificial leaves with this poem attached:

Fuku kaze mo	Such is this age
Eda ni nodokeki	That even rushing winds
Miyo nareba	Are tranquil in the boughs:
Chiranu momiji no	Gaze, then, upon the colors
Iro o koso mire	Of maple leaves that shall not fall.

The Empress returned to the palace after spending some time at the Rokuhara Mansion.[68] The moon was beautiful that night, and one of the ladies who had accompanied us in our carriages went with several of us to gaze at it from near the Tōkaden Hall.[69] She left us just before dawn, and that morning she wrote saying that she had completely left her heart behind with the moon of the previous evening, so I replied:

Kumo no ue o	The moon you speak of
Isogiidenishi	Let you part in haste
Tsuki nareba	From the realm above the clouds;
Hoka ni kokoro wa	So I know full well
Sumu to shiriniki[70]	Your heart is lodged elsewhere!

At the time that Counsellor Kanemitsu[71] was a private secretary to the Emperor, he sent us a package containing six *muku* berries.[72] When Lady Harima[73] asked me what she should reply, I wrote:

Mutsu no michi o	Our hearts reject
Itou kokoro no	The six paths of rebirth,
Mukui ni wa	And this is our reward:
Hotoke no kuni ni	How shall we fail
Yukazarame ya wa[74]	To reach the Buddha's realm?

75. A reference to a poem by Taira no Kanemori (d. 990), *Shūishū* 1151:

Yamazato wa	In this mountain village
Yuki furitsumite	Snow lies thickly piled,
Michi mo nashi	And the path is covered:
Kyō komu hito o	How lovingly I shall look
Aware to wa mimu	On the person who will come today.

76. *Tsumoru* (*tsumorihatete*), "gathering, piling up," is associated with *yuki*, "snow."

One morning at my own home, as the snow lay thick, I was looking out at the unkempt garden and distractedly murmuring the lines "The person who will come today,"[75] when Sukemori appeared, unannounced, through the garden gate. I was dressed in a pale green gown with a thin pink overrobe, but he was clad in a hunting cloak of brownish weave over a crimson robe, with trousers of woven purple, drawn in at the ankles. He looked so much smarter than I did, so splendid, that I can never forget it. Though the years and months have gone by, it seems so recent in my heart that the pain still haunts me:

Toshitsuki no	Though the months and years
Tsumorihatete mo	Have piled up in between,
Sono ori no	That one occasion,
Yuki no ashita wa	That morning in the snow,
Nao zo koishiki[76]	I cherish still.

Once, when we were staying in a mountain village, we got up and went out in the dawn while the moon still lingered in the sky. Seeing a morning glory blooming on the fence just in front, I thought how sad it was that it should flourish for so short a while. I feel as though it had only just happened, and I keep thinking how the flower itself must have thought that man was indeed just as short-lived, and how our own lives have been no ordinary example of impermanence:

Mi no ue o	Only could it have been
Ge ni shirade koso	Through ignorance
Asagao no	Of how my own life would be
Hana o hodo naki	That I could call the morning glory
Mono to iikeme	A thing of transience.

Ariake no	Unforgettable!
Tsuki ni asagao	That time I gazed
Mishi ori mo	At the morning glory,
Wasuregataki o	With the dawn moon in the sky—
Ikade wasuren	But would I had some way to forget!

77. This can only be her brother Son-en.

78. Some commentators see a pivot word in the second *shimo* of line four, since it can be read as "frost" and as two emphatic particles, *shi* and *mo*. It is likely, however, that no pivot is intended, and that *shimo* is to be read only as "frost" to give an uncomplicated visual image.

My elder brother, on whom I was particularly dependent, was a priest.[77] Once, while he was on retreat in the recesses of Mount Hiei, it snowed, and I wrote:

Ika bakari	How deep is the snow
Yamaji no yuki no	On the mountain paths
Fukakaran	At such a time,
Miyako no sora mo	When even in the capital
Kakikurasu koro	The sky is darkened over?

Visiting the Kamo Shrine on a winter night when the moon was bright:

Kamigaki ya	Within the holy fence,
Matsu no arashi mo	Amongst the pines the storm
Oto saete	Sounds clear and cold;
Shimo ni shimo shiku	Frost spreads across the frost,
Fuyu no yo no tsuki[78]	The moon of a winter's night.

There was a time when his feelings for me were not all I could have wished for, and I longed to change everything back to the old days before we had ever met:

Tsune yori mo	More than ever
Omokage ni tatsu	His image clings to me
Yūbe kana	In the evening's dusk,
Ima ya kagiri to	Just when I think that this
Omoi naru ni mo	Shall be the end of our affair.

Yoshi saraba	No sooner do I think
Sate yamabaya to	"Very well, let it be so!
Omou yori	Would I might end it now!"
Kokoroyowasa no	Than I feel myself once more
Mata masaru kana	Succumb to the weakness of my heart.

One moonlit night I was sitting by the edge of the veranda, lost in thought and turning the same questions over and over in my mind, while up above it looked as though the scattered banks of clouds would soon be gone from the sky:

79. *Kakaru,* "to weigh (upon the heart)," can also mean "hang, float"; hence it is associated with *kumo,* "clouds."

80. *Aki no miyama,* "deep in the autumn hills," contains *aki no miya,* "autumn palace," which was a term for the Empress or her quarters. *Sumu* is as usual a pivot word. There are four associated words in this poem: *yami ni kurasasu,* "be made to live in darkness"; *aki,* "autumn"; *tsuki,* "moon"; and *sumu,* "to dwell, be clear."

Miru mama ni	Just as I gaze,
Kumo wa hareyuku	The clouds disperse,
Tsuki kage mo	But even the brilliance of the moon
Kokoro ni kakaru	Does not touch me,
Hitoyue ni nao[79]	Because of him who weighs upon my heart.

After he had not been to see me for a very long time, I woke up late one night, thinking over the problems of our affair. Unwittingly, I must have shed tears, for when I looked the next morning, the light blue paper cover of the pillow was dreadfully faded:

Utsurika mo	The scent he left behind
Otsuru namida ni	Is washed away
Susugarete	By my falling tears;
Katami ni subeki	Not even the color now is left
Iro dani mo nashi	For me to keep as a memento.

Against my own real wishes I had given up court service, and sometime afterwards I was spending the whole night as I usually did, gazing vacantly at the moon. I began to think of the Empress's face, which I had never tired of looking at, and I realized in amazement just how my days had passed of late. Then my eyes were dimmed with tears:

Koiwaburu	Tormented by its longing
Kokoro o yami ni	My heart is forced
Kurasasete	To live in darkness;
Aki no miyama ni	But surely deep in the autumn hills
Tsuki wa sumuran[80]	The moon is shining clear?

Just around that time I noticed my zither covered in dust. I was deeply affected as I thought how the days and months had passed since I had last played it. I longed terribly for the times when I had been constantly playing it and joining in concert with the flutes of those who served by Her Majesty's side:

146

81. *Koto* is a pivot word meaning both "thing, fact (of doing)," and "zither." *Oriori*, "time after time," can also mean "breaking and breaking" and is thus associated with *take*, "bamboo."

82. The future Emperor Antoku (acceded 1180, died 1185). The birth occurred on the twelfth of the eleventh month of Jijō 2 (Dec. 22, 1178), and the child was named Crown Prince just over one month later, so this poem was probably written early in 1179.

83. *Haru no miyako*, "palace of the spring," is a term for the Crown Prince's palace. It is, of course, an appropriate expression for the season of the poem, since spring began with the first month of the year in Heian Japan.

84. "Niwabi," a song from the repertoire of sacred music (*kagura*).

85. Fujiwara no Yasumichi (1147–1210), here given the title Captain (*chūjō*), a noted flautist of his day.

86. Here given as Naishidokoro (Office of Palace Attendants), which was an alternative name for the building. The sacred mirror was enshrined in this hall, and each year in the twelfth month a performance of sacred music was held there.

87. *Ne* is a pivot word meaning both "sound (of flutes)" and "cry, sob."

Oriori no	Time after time they played,
Sono fuetake no	But now the sound of the flutes is broken
Oto taete	Like the joint of a bamboo stem:
Susabishi koto no	Times I beguiled myself upon my zither
Yukue shirarezu[81]	Have fled and left no trace.

I was spending my days with tears as my companions when I heard that the Empress had safely given birth to a child.[82] Then news came that the baby was a boy and was to be made Crown Prince. I could only continue my wretched thoughts:

Kumo no yoso ni	To hear it from beyond the clouds
Kiku zo kanashiki	Is misery indeed:
Mukashi naraba	Had it been times of old,
Tachimajiramashi	I would myself have mingled there
Haru no miyako o[83]	In the palace of the spring.

When I heard the sound of flutes next door playing the song "Garden Fires,"[84] the first thing that came to mind was the wonderful playing of Koremori and Yasumichi[85] each year during the sacred music at the Unmei Hall:[86]

Kiku kara ni	When I hear these notes,
Itodo mukashi no	I yearn more strongly still
Koishikute	For those times past;
Niwabi no fue no	To the sound of flutes in "Garden Fires"
Ne ni zo naku naru[87]	I add the sounds of weeping.

There was a person going far away under sentence of banishment from the court, and on hearing that he had spent the previous night at a certain place, I sent this poem to a relative of his:

Fushinarenu	Making his unaccustomed bed
Noji no shinohara	On the road through the grassy plain—
Ika naramu	What can it be like?
Omoiyaru dani	Merely to imagine it
Tsuyukeki mono o	Brings forth the dew.

88. There is a comic pun on the word *tsuki*, which means "moon" and "bowl"; hence lines two and three could be read: "The moon has lodged itself within the moon."

89. *Hitoe* can mean both "simply, completely," and "single layer." It is in the second sense that it is introduced by *natsugoromo*, "summer robe," a rhetorical introduction without much significance.

An acquaintance of mine who was a nun said she would visit me, but no word came from her, so:

Tanometsutsu	Though she had made me trust her
Konu itsuwari no	She does not come to me,
Tsumoru kana	And her lies pile up and up—
Makoto no michi ni	Even a person
Irishi hito sae	Who has entered on the Path of Truth!

Next to the brazier in my room was a bowl of water, and the moon shining into it was reflected in a most entrancing way:

Mezurashi ya	How strange, how rare!
Tsuki ni tsuki koso	The moon has lodged itself
Yadorikere	Within this bowl!
Kumoi no sora yo	You clouds far in the sky
Tachi na kakushi so[88]	Do not rise up to shroud it.

There was someone from whom I had promised not to hold back any secrets, but now that I had unexpectedly brought these miseries on myself, it was not very easy, after all, to tell her exactly how things stood. I felt, however, that she was likely to hear of it somehow, so I wrote to her:

Natsugoromo	I would not have you think
Hitoe ni tanomu	That I have drawn apart from you,
Kai mo naku	Or that it was in vain
Hedatekeri to wa	To trust me as simply
Omowazaranamu[89]	As the single layer of a summer robe.

Saki no yo no	You, after all,
Chigiri ni makuru	Must surely know
Narai o mo	It is the common lot
Kimi wa sasuga ni	To surrender to our destinies,
Omoishiruramu	Wrought in our earlier lives.

At the beginning I really did not feel ours was a normal sort of love affair, and I was extremely embarrassed about it. De-

90. *Chirasu*, "scatter," forms a word association with the *ha*, "leaves," of *koto no ha*, "words." The name Mount Shinobu contains a pivot word: *shinobu* can mean "to keep secret," "to endure," and "to long for." This might have been one of two Mount Shinobus: the mountain in old Iwashiro Province, (modern Fukushima) or the one in old Mutsu Province (modern Aomori Prefecture).

91. This seems to be an apt description of Fujiwara no Takanobu, to judge from other sources. Perhaps his behavior is unexpected because he is in a place where he ought to have been curbing his amorous tendencies; if it is the nun's house, then he should be on his best behavior out of respect for her holy orders.

92. The phrase "when the moon was close to full" has been added for clarity. In the lunar calendar the full moon usually occurred on or about the fifteenth of the month, so the light should have been quite bright by the tenth. The Japanese wording of this passage is vague and ambiguous, and it is difficult to be sure of what is going on. The GSRJ text omits the words *hito no* ("other people") and lends itself to a possible interpretation "He must have sensed that I was close by." This does not seem to suit Takanobu's concern for not being seen, and Kubota, for instance, is inclined to reject this interpretation. "Hyōshaku," 13: 155.

93. The Japanese does not specifically say the message was sent afterwards, but in view of the intermediary used to deliver the message and the wording of Lady Daibu's second poem of reply, it is not likely to have been delivered on the same night. *Ibid.* There is an extra sentence in the text at this point: "That man was Imperial Advisor and Captain So-and-So." But this is generally considered to be a comment by a later copyist, and I have omitted it from the translation. Hon-iden discusses this extra sentence in some detail. *Zenshaku*, 1974 ed., pp. 122–24.

jectedly, I could only think how dreadful it would be if the affair should become known to the ladies I mixed with all the time, or, even worse, to any of the men. So I found myself writing in my calligraphy practice:

Chirasu na yo	Do not scatter them abroad,
Chirasaba ikaga	For if you do,
Tsurakaran	How bitter it would be—
Shinobu no yama ni	These words of longing that we keep
Shinobu koto no ha[90]	As secret as hidden Mount Shinobu.

Koiji ni wa	Though I had thought
Mayoiiraji to	That I would not lose myself
Omoishi o	Upon the paths of love,
Uki chigiri mo	Thither I have been drawn
Hikarenuru kana	By my wretched destiny.

Ikuyo shi mo	My only consolation
Araji to omou	Is to think that I
Kata ni nomi	Have but few years to live;
Nagusamuredomo	And yet this comfort
Nao zo kanashiki	Makes me sadder still.

Sometime prior to that I had been approached by a man who was rumored to be more versed in love than most men of the world. This happened in an unexpected place, where he had just been talking with a certain rather elegant nun, and the night was already far advanced.[91] He must have sensed that there were other people close by, for he whispered to me, even though it was the tenth of the fourth month, when the moon was close to full, that the moonlight was rather dim and no one was likely to see what we were about.[92] Afterwards, he sent someone with this message:[93]

Omoiwaku	No way have I
Kata mo nagisa ni	To understand my feelings!
Yoru nami no	But must my tears fall heavily as this

94. *Nagisa*, "shore," is a pivot word. In the old orthography (and probably pronunciation too) it contains the word *naki*, "there is not, I have not." Hence there are two clauses: *kata mo naki*, "I have no way," and *nagisa ni yoru nami*, "waves that approach the shore." *Nagisa* forms word associations with *nami*, "waves," *nurasu* (*nurasubeshi*), "drench," and *sode*, "sleeves"—the last because sleeves were traditionally in a state of perpetual dampness from one's tears, which are salty. The same pivot words and word associations are to be found in the reply.

95. *Ama* is a pivot word meaning "nun" or "fishergirl," and in the second meaning is associated with the *nagisa*, "shore," of the previous poem. It is introduced in its second meaning by the expression *moshio kumu*, "to gather seaweed (for salt making)." There is a double meaning to *yosu* (*yosete*), which can be transitive, "to bring (one's heart) near" or intransitive, "to come near (of waves)." The word *kudaku*, "break," can be used, as in English, for hearts or waves. All these words are associated with each other. The following poem of reply takes up the images of this one.

96. Her affair with Sukemori, which she often calls "unexpected."

97. The sea imagery of the previous poems continues. *Takumo* is seaweed that has been gathered into a pile, doused with sea water and left to dry, then burned so the salt that has been evaporated out will be left in the ashes. The smoke from the fires was a common image in poetry. The word is associated with *urayamashi*, "jealous," through a pun on *ura*, which means "bay." *Nabiku* (*uchinabikiken*), "to incline," has strong overtones of love, and this image of smoke and salt fires was by this time commonplace in poetry.

Ito kaku sode o	And drench my sleeves,
Nurasubeshi ya wa[94]	Like waves that drench the shore?

To this I replied:

Omoiwakade	If you do not know your thoughts,
Nani to nagisa no	And these your waves of tears
Nami naraba	Fall on one or another shore,
Nururamu sode no	There can be little cause
Yue mo araji o	For the drenching of your sleeves.

Moshio kumu	I have perceived that, like the waves
Ama no sode ni zo	Which rush from the deep and soak the sleeves
Oki tsu nami	Of girls who gather weed upon the shore,
Kokoro o yosete	Your heart is breaking, drawn towards
Kudaku to wa mishi[95]	The pillowing sleeves of that same nun!

He then replied:

Kimi ni nomi	The waves of my love
Wakite kokoro no	Are strongly drawn to you alone;
Yoru nami wa	They do not fall
Ama no isoya ni	Or linger on that shore
Tachi mo tomarazu	By the home of nun or fishergirl.

Though it began as a lighthearted affair, his attentions became very serious. My only thought, however, was that it should never develop into the usual kind of relationship, and I remained firm. But he soon heard details of this other unexpected liaison of mine[96] and hinted to me what he knew:

Urayamashi	Now I am jealous!
Ika naru kaze no	To whose charms
Nasake nite	Are you inclining,
Takumo no keburi	Like the smoke from salt fires
Uchinabikiken[97]	Slanting to the wind?

98. It was common for the woman to claim that her lover's cruelty was causing her to vanish or waste away (*kienubeki* from the verb *kiyu*, "vanish"). Murai interprets this *kiyu* as applying to the affair with Sukemori implying to Takanobu that it is about to end. *Hyōkai*, pp. 97–98. But that is not the usual use of the verb in love poems.

99. This poem contains the same pivot words as Poem 6. See Part One, note 12.

100. *Morokazura* is an alternative name for heartvine. It is here used for irony, since the first half of the word, *moro*, means "together." There is probably an allusion to a poem by Fujiwara no Michinaga (966–1028), *Goshūishū* 1109:

Morokazura	Though the leaves upon the heartvine
Futabanagara mo	May be split in twain,
Kimi ni kaku	We have met like this today;
Aoi ya kami no	And like the vine that decorates your brow,
Shirushi naruramu	This surely is a sign of favor from the gods.

The ironic reversal of the meaning of the original makes this a skillful use of allusion.

My reply:

Kienubeki	I am like the last faint trace
Keburi no sue wa	Of smoke about to vanish:
Urakaze ni	I incline not to one side,
Nabiki mo sezute	But drift upon the wind
Tadayou mono o[98]	That blows across the shore.

Again, on the same subject:

Aware nomi	All of your deepest love
Fukaku kakubeki	You ought to give to me,
Ware o okite	Yet you are casting me aside:
Tare ni kokoro o	With whom can it be
Kawasu naruramu	That you now exchange your heart?

My reply:

Hito wakazu	Love perchance I know,
Aware o kawasu	Yet I will not reveal it
Adabito ni	To one so fickle,
Nasake shirite mo	Who will exchange his love
Mieji to zo omou	Heedless of whom it is with!

From the same person on the day of the festival:

Yukusue o	Our future lives
Kami ni kakete mo	I pledge unto the gods in prayer;
Inoru kana	And may the heartvine
Aoi chō na o	Truly show its name
Aramashi ni shite[99]	In this, a day of meeting.

My reply:

Morokazura	Pray though you may
Sono na o kakete	And pledge yourself upon the names
Inorutomo	Of heartvine and of "meeting day,"
Kami no kokoro ni	I think not that the gods will look on you,
Ukeji to zo omou[100]	With favor in their hearts.

101. The name Ōsaka is a well-worn pivot word, since it means "hill of meeting." Ōsaka was famous for its barrier, which was not far from the Capital, south of present-day Ōtsu city on the road to the east. All travelers going back and forth between the capital and the eastern part of Japan had to pass through it.

In this way my whole life was changed, and at a time when I was especially overcome with thoughts of regret:

Koenureba	Once crossed,
Kuyashikarikeru	The barrier of the hill of meeting
Ōsaka o	Brings nothing but regret.
Naniyue ni ka wa	Oh, why did I begin
Fumihajimekemu[101]	To turn my steps this way?

He would send his carriage, and I used to go to his mansion. But then I heard that he was about to make final arrangements for taking a wife. Around that very time I caught sight of an inkstone, and drawing it towards me, I wrote this poem, fixing it to the pillow I had come to know so well:

Tare ga ka ni	Whoever it may be
Omoiutsuru to	Whose fragrance draws his thoughts away,
Wasuru na yo	Do not forget me,
Yo na yo na nareshi	You at least, O pillow,
Makura bakari wa	That I have known night after night!

He immediately sent a message to say he had seen my poem after I had left:

Kokoro ni mo	The fragrance of your memory
Sode ni mo tomaru	Lies on my sleeve and in my heart.
Utsurika o	Should you, then,
Makura ni nomi ya	Make your vows of love
Chigiri okubeki	To no one but this pillow?

Once as we lay in bed together we had listened to a *hototo-gisu*, and now, during this period, as I woke up alone in bed I heard one pass overhead with its call sounding quite unchanged. That morning in response to a letter from him I wrote:

102. The first two lines refer to the famous poem on orange blossom quoted in note 18, above, p. 114, and of course the next poem makes it clear that this was the intended allusion. The last three lines refer to an episode found in a Chinese story in the *Chin shu* and reproduced in the *Karamonogatari*, a Japanese tale collection of the thirteenth century or earlier (but the story was circulating long before it was incorporated into that collection). A certain Chinese man, Pang An-Jen, was so attractive that when he went through the streets in his carriage, young ladies threw oranges into it. The original Chinese story merely mentions fruit, but the Japanese version specifies oranges—in fact, branches from orange trees, presumably laden with fruit. For the original Chinese, see Hisamatsu and Kubota, p. 69; and for the *Karamonogatari* version, see *Zenshaku*, pp. 196–97. For the associative transfer of thought from oranges to orange blossom, see Poem 66 and the accompanying notes 17 and 18. Takanobu is probably being deliberately provocative here rather than impossibly conceited. This is the last of the poems definitely attributable to Takanobu, but most scholars believe that Poems 152–54 also apply to him, because of their proximity to the other poems relating to him and because of the flow of the collection.

Morotomo ni	Unaltered
Koto kataraishi	From that morning
Akebono ni	When we two together
Kawarazaritsuru	Lay with our loving words—
Hototogisu kana	The *hototogisu*'s call.

In his reply he said that he too had been recalling that occasion and similar things, which I thought most unlikely to be true:

Omoiidete	Ah, the *hototogisu*!
Nezameshi toko no	It came to tell you
Aware o mo	Of my tender feelings,
Yukite tsugekeru	As I lay sleepless on my bed,
Hototogisu kana	Lost in thoughts of you.

On another occasion after there had been no word from him for some time, he sent me an ardent letter. When I replied, I felt for some reason extremely agitated, and I took a spray of orange blossom that I saw close by, wrapped it up, and sent it to him. He could not understand my meaning, he said in reply:

Mukashi omou	Does this mean fragrance
Nioi ka nani zo	Bringing memories of old?
Oguruma ni	Or is it something else?
Ireshi tagui no	No paragon am I, like him whose carriage
Waga mi naranu ni[102]	Was filled with branches from the orange tree!

My reply:

Wabitsutsu wa	It was in my dejection
Kasaneshi sode no	That I broke off this orange blossom,
Utsurika ni	For it brought to mind
Omoiyosoete	The scent with which my sleeves were steeped,
Orishi tachibana	When they were piled on yours in sleep.

160

103. This refers to the belief that a person's heart or soul could leave his body and visit his beloved. Supposedly, if one's beloved was thinking of one, he or she would appear in one's dream, and if the beloved did not appear, then one's love was not returned.

104. It was considered unlucky to marry in either the fifth month or the ninth month.

After a long break in our relationship, he thought of me again and sent his carriage. I kept on thinking that I would rather leave things as they were, but I was weak-willed and went to him. As he saw me alighting from the carriage, he greeted me with, "Why, you're still alive, then!" When I heard that, I suddenly felt deep inside me:

Arikeri to	When he says to me
Yū ni tsurasa no	"Why, you're still alive!"
Masaru kana	My wretchedness grows worse—
Naki ni nashitsutsu	After he has let the days go past
Sugushitsuru hodo	And paid me not the least regard!

He was continually appearing in my dreams, and I remarked to him how strange that was, since his heart was surely not coming to visit me.[103] He replied:

Kayoikeru	My heart does visit you;
Kokoro no hodo wa	How deep its feelings are
Yoru o kasane	Judge from your own dreams,
Miyuramu yume ni	Where I appear
Omoiawase yo	Night after night.

My reply:

Ge ni mo sono	Oh yes, indeed!
Kokoro no hodo ya	The state of your heart
Mietsuramu	May be perceived—
Yume ni mo tsuraki	For you look cruel
Keshiki naritsuru	Even in my dreams!

A man who was courting a certain person's daughter had promised to put off the marriage until the end of the fifth month, but he grew impatient and secretly went to see her.[104] I therefore sent this poem on behalf of another person:

Minazuki o	Until the month of no rains
Mate to chigirishi	You promised you would wait,

162

105. "Month of no rains" is here chosen as a more pleasant translation of *minazuki* than "sixth month." The "correctness" of this translation is a matter of debate. See Ikeda, pp. 439–40, for a discussion of the original meaning of *minazuki*. *Wakakusa*, "young grass," the metaphor for the young lady, forms a word association with *musubu*, "to bind up."

106. The Kumano Shrine, on the coast of present-day Kii Peninsula, well to the south of the capital. This visit took place in 1179.

107. There is the usual pivot on *urami*, "to resent" and "to see the bay." The "lily" here is the *hamayū* (*Crinum asiaticum lycoris*), a plant that grows near the sea and looks rather like a lily. It has many layers of leaves growing from one stem and is therefore used as a rhetorical introduction to *kasanu* (*kasenen*), "to mount up, pile up." It forms word associations with *ura*, "bay," and the name Kumano. The poem alludes to and cleverly reverses the sense of one by the priest Dōmyō (fl. c. 1000), *Goshūishū* 886:

Wasuru na yo	Do not forget me!
Wasuru to kikeba	If I hear you have forgotten me,
Mikumano no	Then deep as the many-layered leaves
Ura no hamayū	Of lilies at the Bay of Kumano
Urami kasanemu	Shall my resentment grow.

108. Another name for the Bay of Sumi mentioned in Poems 76 and 77.

Wakakusa o	And yet you have already
Musubisomenu to	Bound up the young grass!
Kiku wa makoto ka[105]	So I hear: can it be true?

At a time when my mind was filled with nothing but the most pointless regrets, I kept wishing that things were different. But the very uselessness of wishing that just made me miserable:

Omoikaesu	Would that I knew a path
Michi o shirabaya	Where I might turn back my thoughts
Koi no yama	Amidst love's mountains,
Hayama shigeyama	Now that I have pushed my way from the foothills
Wakeirishi mi ni	To the thickly tangled depths.

From somewhere the sound of sutra-reading came faintly to my ears and made me feel keenly the poignant sadness of this world:

Mayoiirishi	Just as I feel
Koiji kuyashiki	The bitterness of love's path,
Ori shi mo	Where I wander lost—
Susumegao naru	It seems to summon me,
Nori no koe kana	The Voice of the Holy Law.

I heard that Sukemori had visited Kumano[106] with his father, the Grand Minister, but even after he returned, there was no word from him for quite some time, and I felt:

Wasuru to wa	Even were I to hear
Kikutomo ikaga	He has forgotten me,
Mikumano no	How could I feel resentment mounting up,
Ura no hamayū	Like the many-layered lily leaves
Urami kasanen[107]	Seen around the Bay of Kumano?

It embarrassed me to feel that way. I recalled how in the previous year he had visited me immediately on his return from Naniwa Bay:[108]

109. There is considerable ingenuity in this poem. Sode no Ura, literally Bay of Sleeves, is the name of a place in northern Japan often celebrated in poetry. There are word associations between *ura*, "bay," *kaeru* (*kaereba*), "return," *yoru*, "to draw close," and *oki tsu nami*, "waves from the open sea"; and between *sode*, "sleeves," and *ura* in its second meaning of "lining." For a full discussion of the pivot words in this poem, see the Introduction, pp. 70–71.

110. *Nageki*, "laments," acts as a pivot word; its last syllable, *ki*, means "trees." *Shigeki*, "dense," thus modifies both "trees" and "laments."

111. A reference to Episode 13 in *Tales of Ise*. The term *musashi abumi*, "Musashi stirrups," is used by a lady in a poem in which she says she would rather not hear from her unfaithful lover and yet would be upset if she did not. For details, see McCullough, pp. 78–79, 206–7. The appearance of this expression in Takanobu's poetry collection tends to support the opinion that this poem applies to him rather than to Sukemori, but it is hardly conclusive evidence. GSRJ, 12: 59.

Oki tsu nami	As waves resound,
Kaereba oto wa	Returning from the open sea,
Seshi mono o	So did he bring me news on his return.
Ikanaru sode no	But now to the haven of whose pillowing sleeves
Ura ni yoruramu[109]	Can he be drawing close?

The prospect from my room was of evergreen trees so dark that they resembled a dense forest; even the sky was scarcely visible, and the view brought me no consolation:

Nagamubeki	So dense are the trees
Sora mo sadaka ni	That I can hardly see the sky
Mienu made	In which might be my comfort.
Shigeki nageki mo	Dense too are my laments,
Kanashikarikeri[110]	Which bring such misery.

To the east the upper slopes of the mountain behind the Chōrakuji Temple were visible in the distance. It was distressing enough just to see the grave markers on the summit of the mountain, where a friend of mine had been buried; but as I gazed out, the sky darkened and the mountain faded from sight in the lowering clouds, and I was overcome with sadness:

Nagameizuru	Even the treetops
Sonata no yama no	On that far mountain
Kozue sae	Where I fix my troubled gaze,
Tada to mo sureba	Why of a sudden
Kakikumoruramu	Do they cloud over darkly?

Even after retiring from the palace I was still visited from time to time by a man, and even though I was not wholly in love with him, I went on in a state that may best be described as the indifference of "Musashi stirrups";[111] indeed the affair only became more dreary, and I felt our relationship was no longer at all what it had been. To see how his feelings really were, I moved away, and as I was putting my private papers

112. *Nagaru (nagarete)*, "to go on forever," can also mean "to flow," and it thus forms a word association with *mizu*, "water," in *mizuguki*, "letters." *Kaki* in *kakitaenubeki*, "will be no more," can be read as an emphatic prefix and as the stem of the verb "to write," in which sense it is associated with *mizuguki*.

113. *Fukikau kaze no*, "the wind blowing hither and thither," is used as a rhetorical introduction to *oto*, "sound," which here has the primary meaning of "sound of a message," but was the normal term for the sound of the wind.

114. Jōzaimon-in was the consort of Retired Emperor Toba (r. 1107-23) and foster mother of Emperor Goshirakawa.

115. *Toyo no akari*, a celebration held in the palace on the day following the Harvest Festival, the second day of the dragon in the eleventh month.

116. A member of the Fujiwara family, ?-1184.

117. Taira no Michimori (?-1184), eldest son of Taira no Norimori (1129-85), younger brother of Kiyomori.

118. *Someshi*, when used with *kokoro*, "heart," means "to fall in love, set one's heart on," but it also means "to dye" and forms a word association with *momiji*, "red leaves." The same words and associations appear in the poem of reply (*momijiba, someken*).

in order I wrote this poem on the edge of a letter in which he had said over and over again that his love would not weaken through all eternity:

Nagarete to	For all time, he said
Tanomeshi koto mo	And made me trust in him:
Mizuguki no	But now the sadness
Kakitaenubeki	Of these letters—the last traces
Ato no kanashisa[112]	That soon will be no more.

Someone in service with the Empress was always exchanging letters with me, and she once asked me how things were with Sukemori at that time. So while I was replying to her I wrote:

Kumo no ue o	Hither and thither blows the wind,
Yoso ni narinishi	But it carries not a sound
Uki mi ni wa	To one as wretched as myself,
Fukikau kaze no	Cut off now
Oto mo kikoezu[113]	From that land above the clouds.

It must have been sometime in the Jijō period [1177–1181] when some ladies-in-waiting to Retired Empress Jōzaimon-in[114] came with just two carriages to the palace to see the sights during the Feast of Abounding Light.[115] They were all very attractive, but one of them, known as Lady Kosaishō,[116] was exceptionally striking, even in such details as the way her hair cascaded from her brow with two locks falling across her cheeks. I had heard that someone who had had his heart set on her for years had lost her to Lord Michimori[117] and had been very upset about it. It seemed to me he had good reason for feeling as he did, so I wrote to him:

Sa koso ge ni	In truth you must have been
Kimi nagekurame	So deeply grieved—
Kokoro someshi	Having someone else break off
Yama no momiji o	That branch of red mountain maple leaves
Hito ni orarete[118]	On which your heart was set!

119. Michimori was killed in the battle of Ichinotani in 1184.

120. In Chinese and Japanese legend, on the seventh night of the seventh month the Herd Boy (the star Altair) could cross the River of Heaven (the Milky Way) to meet his mistress, the Weaving Maid (the star Vega). This was celebrated in the Tanabata Festival. For further details on the legend and the festival, see Part Five, note 1.

His reply:

Nani ka ge ni	Why, in truth, why
Hito no orikeru	Did I begin to let my love
Momijiba o	Transfer itself
Kokoro utsushite	To scarlet maple leaves,
Omoisomeken	Which another now has plucked?

At the time of that exchange I thought her affair with Michi-mori was only a lighthearted thing, and yet for love of him she drowned herself after his death.[119] It was an unparalleled tragedy, which would never have happened if only she had been attracted to the person who was longing for her from afar. What can one say of such an unprecedented bond of fate?

My life in general was unsettled, and I was, moreover, brooding constantly on the unhappiness deep in my heart. At that time, autumn was gradually drawing on. Even if I had not been in such a state, the sound of the wind would have pierced my soul, and consequently, I was so sunk in melancholy reverie that I simply cannot describe it. As I watched the sky where the two stars have their lover's meeting, I was weighed down with sadness:[120]

Tsukuzuku to	I have spent my days
Nagamesugushite	Sunk in deepest reverie,
Hoshiai no	And tonight brings me no change,
Sora o kawarazu	As I gaze out at the sky
Nagametsuru kana	And the love tryst of the stars.

While I was living out towards the western hills, he went for a long time without sending word, relying perhaps on the excuse that he had no time to spare. Some withered blossom there suddenly made me think:

170

121. *Tama maku*, "curved like jewels," is a common epithet for *kuzu*, "ivy."
Some scholars believe that *maku* is the verb "to scatter," and that the expression means "scattering jewels" (i.e. of dew). But the use of the expression in contemporary sources shows that the intended meaning of *maku*
was "to curve, roll." "Hyōshaku," 15: 176.

Towarenu wa　　　　　Though I do not count
Ikuka zo to dani　　　　How many days have passed
Kazoenu ni　　　　　　Since he last came to visit me,
Hana no sugata zo　　　This blossom has a face
Shirasegao naru　　　　That tells me well enough.

This blossom was a branch he had broken off and brought
with him when he had visited me about ten days earlier; as he
was leaving he had thrust it into the bamboo blind.

Aware ni mo　　　　　I can but be
Tsuraku mo mono zo　　Touched by its poignance,
Omowaruru　　　　　　Filled by it with pain—
Nogarezarikeru　　　　Destiny that is not to be escaped
Yoyo no chigiri ni　　　From one world to the next.

Ivy was growing over the fence in front of the house, and
the bamboo grass bent to the breeze:

Yamazato wa　　　　　Curved like jewels, the ivy leaves
Tama maku kuzu no　　In this mountain village
Ura miete　　　　　　Show their undersides, as I show bitterness—
Kozasa ga hara ni　　　Across the plains of bamboo grass now blow
Aki no hatsukaze[121]　　First autumn winds of his indifference.

One moonlit night, unable as usual to hold back my memories:

Omokage o　　　　　　As I gaze out,
Kokoro ni komete　　　Keeping his image
Nagamureba　　　　　Locked within my heart,
Shinobigataku mo　　　The moon, so clear, so tranquil,
Sumeru tsuki kana　　　Is impossible to bear.

With the onset of winter the chill rains had swept furiously
across the reeds in the withered fields, and the sodden colors
were depressing. But even in advance of spring the fresh green
of new buds could be seen here and there low down on the

122. Minamoto no Masayori (1127–87). Nothing is known of his daughter.

bushes, and the dew had settled over all, reminding me of autumn:

Shimo sayuru	The frost lies crisp
Kareno no ogi no	On the withered fields;
Tsuyu no iro	And on the reeds the color of the dew—
Aki no nagori o	Does it yearn, with me,
Tomo ni shinobu ya	For the autumn past?

For no particular reason, I was dusting the sleeping mat in the room where we slept, and I could think only of him:

Yū sareba	As evening falls,
Aramashigoto no	I see the image of the one
Omokage ni	Whose visit I am longing for,
Makura no chiri o	And so I sweep away the dust
Uchiharaitsutsu	That lies upon our pillow.

Akugaruru	Filled with yearning,
Kokoro wa hito ni	My heart is surely gone
Soinuramu	To be with him I love;
Mi no usa nomi zo	Only the misery in me
Yaru kata mo naki	Has nowhere to escape.

Counsellor Masayori's daughter,[122] who was in service with the Empress and known as Lady Suke, was a most amiable person and an amusing talker. We used to talk about all sorts of things, and when she once took herself off for a long time to take a hot-spring cure at a mountain village, I sent her these poems along with some message or other:

Mashiba fuku	The moon that filters
Neya no itama ni	Through the cracks in the wooden walls
Moru tsuki o	Of your bedroom thatched with brushwood,
Shimo to ya harau	Do you wipe it, thinking it is frost,
Aki no yamazato	In that autumnal mountain village?

Mezurashiku
Waga omoiyaru
Shika no ne o
Aku made kiku ya
Aki no yamazato

The calling of the deer,
Which I imagine
As something rare,
Do you listen till you tire of it
In that autumnal mountain village?

Itodoshiku
Tsuyu ya okisou
Kakikurashi
Ame furu koro no
Aki no yamazato

Does dew of your own making
Join, in yet heavier streams,
With the rain that falls
From the darkened sky
In that autumnal mountain village?

Urayamashi
Hodaki kirikube
Ika bakari
Miyu wakasuramu
Aki no yamazato

How I wish that I were there!
What quantities of water they must heat,
Chopping the firewood,
Feeding it to the flames,
In that autumnal mountain village!

Shii hirou
Shizu mo michi ni ya
Mayouran
Kiri tachikomuru
Aki no yamazato

Even the peasant,
Gathering acorns there,
Must miss his path,
As mist shrouds all
In that autumnal mountain village.

Kuri mo emi
Okashikaruran to
Omou ni mo
Ide ya yukashi ya
Aki no yamazato

When I think
How enchanting it must be,
As chestnuts burst forth from their shells,
How I would like to see them too,
In that autumnal mountain village!

Kokorozashi
Nashi wa saritomo
Waga tame ni
Aruramu mono o
Aki no yamazato

There is nothing for a gift,
You well may say.
Yet just for me
There must be something
In that autumnal mountain village.

Konogoro wa
Kōji tachibana
Narimajiri

Just at this time
The orange and the tangerine
Will be ripening all at once,

Ko no ha momizu ya	While the maple leaves turn scarlet
Aki no yamazato	In that autumnal mountain village.
Uzura fusu	Used to the clacking of bird scarers
Kadota no naruko	In the rice fields by your gate,
Hikinarete	Where quails lie hidden,
Kaeriuki ni ya	You will be loath to think of your return,
Aki no yamazato	In that autumnal mountain village.
Kaerikite	When you return,
Sono miru bakari	You will have to tell me
Kataranan	Of everything you saw
Yukashikaritsuru	That has piqued my curiosity
Aki no yamazato	In that autumnal mountain village.

The replies were also frivolous, and over the years I have forgotten them.

In the middle of winter, a relative of mine who was upset at being passed over in the autumn appointments sent me this poem, along with a chrysanthemum he had plucked from a clump of frost-withered flowers because it had begun to show a little fresh bloom:

Shimogare no	Seeing this chrysanthemum
Shitae ni sakeru	Blooming amidst
Kiku mireba	Frost-withered lower stalks,
Waga yukusue mo	I feel more confident
Tanomoshiki kana	Of my own future path.

I replied:

Hana to ieba	When we speak of flowers,
Utsurou iro mo	Their fading colors
Ada naru o	Are short-lived,
Kimi ga nioi wa	But the luster of your glory
Hisashikarubeshi	Shall long endure.

123. *Oshiake no* is a pivot word with three meanings: it goes with *nagori* of the previous line to form *nagori oshi*, "feel regret"; it can mean "pushing open (the door)"; and it means "the early dawn."

I was on particularly good terms with one of the Empress's personal attendants, a lady-in-waiting of high rank. My lover's brother was on duty at the palace more often than usual, for he was not only a relative of the Empress, but also an officer of her Household; and he secretly began an affair with this lady. There did not appear to be any lack of affection on either side, but as is the way of the world, the woman seemed to have become very anxious about it. I did not know for sure, but I thought she might be right, so I just sent these poems to the man to find out how he felt:

Yoso nite mo	To a mere spectator even
Chigiri aware ni	She seems to be
Miru hito o	So much in love:
Tsuraki me miseba	Were you to show unkindness,
Ika ni ukuran	How unhappy I would be.

Tachikaeru	Though it may utter
Nagori koso to wa	No words of regret,
Iwazutomo	When you leave at dawn,
Makura mo ika ni	How anxiously her pillow, even,
Kimi o matsuran	Must wait for you to come.

Okite yuku	As you rise and leave her,
Hito no nagori ya	Does she feel regret?
Oshiake no	White through the open door
Tsukikage shiroshi	Is the moonlight of the early dawn,
Michishiba no tsuyu[123]	And on the grasses of the path the dew.

"What confounded meddling!" he replied. "Anyway, I'm no hand at things like this—I haven't got the words for it."

Waga omoi	You guess away
Hito no kokoro o	At what I feel
Oshihakari	And what is in her heart:
Nani to samazama	What are they about,
Kimi nagekuramu	All these complaints of yours?

124. This alludes to an anonymous poem, *Kokinshū* 647:

Ubatama no
Yami no utsutsu wa
Sadaka naru
Yume ni ikura mo
Masarazarikeri

The reality of meeting
In a darkness black as jet
Cannot compare
By far with meeting in a dream
Where all is clear and distinct.

Makura ni mo	Both to her pillow
Hito ni mo kokoro o	And to her
Omoitsukete	You attribute your own thoughts,
Nagori yo nani to	Then you make up talk
Kimi zo iinasu	Of such things as regrets!

Akegata no	As I set out on my way,
Tsuki o tamoto ni	I catch the moonlight of the dawn
Yadoshitsutsu	On the broad width of my sleeves—
Kaesa no sode wa	They are the ones
Ware zo tsuyukeki	That are laden with the dew!

We had attended the Empress on her way over to the Emperor's rooms one night, and after our return some of us sat talking. The fire gradually died down, but we raked up the glowing embers in the brazier, and four of us who got on well together decided to confess to each other our inmost hearts and hold nothing back. Yet we were not able to discuss openly the various secret sorrows that we each kept locked inside us. I realized this because of the feelings in my own heart, and I was deeply moved:

Omou dochi	All with the same thought,
Yowa no uzumibi	We rake up the dying embers
Kakiokoshi	In the depths of night,
Yami no utsutsu ni	And in the darkness that is our reality
Madoi o zo suru[124]	We sit together in this group.

Tare mo sono	Though we none of us
Kokoro no soko wa	Can talk of the many things
Kazukazu ni	That lie deep within our hearts,
Iihatenedomo	How clear it still is,
Shiruku zo arikeru	All that is left unsaid.

While I was pondering these things, Shigehira appeared, explaining that he had been on duty in the palace. As usual he told us all sorts of amusing things, some of them comical and some of them serious. I and the other ladies all laughed enor-

125. *Nuresomu* (*nuresomeshi*), "become wet," is associated with *tsuyu*, "dew," as is *sode*, "sleeves," through the conventional identity of dew and tears.

mously. But he ended up telling horror stories, and we found ourselves literally sweating with fright. "We're not going to listen!" we said. "Some other time!" But he went on telling them regardless, so in the end we lay down and pulled the bedding up over our heads so that we could not hear him. Then deep inside I felt:

Adagoto ni	Just for the fun of it
Tada yū hito no	He tells these stories;
Monogatari	But even that
Sore dani kokoro	Has thrown my heart
Madoinuru kana	Into such wild distress!

Oni o ge ni	Such is my terror
Minu dani itaku	That I do not have to see
Osoroshiki ni	Demons with my own eyes!
Nochi no yo o koso	The world to come is one
Omoishirinure	That I now already know.

Shigehira was always joking with me and used to ask why I rejected someone from the same family as Sukemori. He would tell me I ought to think of him as the same person, so I wrote to him:

Nuresomeshi	When already I have made
Sode dani aru o	My sleeves so drenched,
Onaji no no	Why should I walk, as I have before,
Tsuyu oba sa nomi	Amongst the dew drops
Ikaga wakubeki[125]	Of that selfsame field?

We always used to have pleasant conversations, and when he said that we should try to preserve our friendship as it was forever, I said:

Wasureji no	If this were a world
Chigiri tagawanu	That did not contradict
Yo nariseba	Our pledges never to forget,
Tanomi ya semashi	Then I would trust in it,
Kimi ga hitokoto	This word of yours.

126. *Komorisō*, a priest who remained secluded in a chapel of mourning praying for the salvation of the dead person throughout the forty-nine days that the soul was supposed to spend wandering between one life and the next.

127. His full name and title were Ashō no Bō Inzei. His dates and family name are unknown.

I kept thinking over and over again about the same problem and constantly wishing that I could really forget Sukemori in my heart of hearts. But it was in vain:

Saru koto no	Trying not to wonder even
Arishika to dani	If all these things
Omowaji o	Have happened to me,
Omoiketedomo	I make myself forget, and yet
Ketarezarikeri	They will not be blotted out.

Once, when we were talking about nothing in particular, I unthinkingly said something I should not have, and he often used to harp on it. Now, long afterwards, it causes me great unhappiness to think of it:

Nani to naku	Every word of mine
Koto no hagoto ni	That held no special meaning
Mimi tomete	He dwelt on in his mind,
Uramishi koto mo	And then reproached me in his bitterness—
Wasurarenu kana	This I never can forget!

My mother had become a nun before she died, and her faith being particularly strong, she had left instructions with people on what should be done after her death. She died early in the fifth month, and from then on, I lived day and night with no sense of purpose in anything I did. But when the forty-ninth day arrived, I took out the robes and the stole that she had worn and presented them to the priest who had been saying prayers for her soul[126] and to the holy priest Ashō.[127] Even the creases in the robes were exactly as when she had worn them, and her image appeared to me still more vividly. In this re-awakened grief:

Kinarekeru	Often she wore these robes,
Koromo no sode no	And even in the folds
Orime made	Upon the sleeves
Tada sono hito o	I feel I see her
Miru kokochi shite	In the flesh itself.

128. On the fourteenth day of the first month of Jijō 5 (Jan. 30, 1181).

129. There is a word association between *kumo*, "clouds," and *tsuki no hikari*, "light of the moon." It is interesting to find Lady Daibu using the moon as a metaphor for the Emperor in this poem and as a metaphor for the Empress in the next one, where the Emperor becomes the sun.

This sensation only made me all the more depressed and wretched:

Aware chō	What shall become of me?
Hito mo naki yo ni	I am left behind
Nokoriite	In a world
Ika ni narubeki	Where there is no one
Waga mi naruramu	Who will look on me with tenderness

When I heard that Retired Emperor Takakura had passed away,[128] I remembered countless things from the time when I had been so used to seeing him; and though his death was a matter in which I could not be directly involved, I was immeasurably affected by it. When someone commented that in all things he had truly been too good for these degenerate days, I wrote:

Kumo no ue ni	How grieved I am to hear
Yukusue tōku	That the light has vanished
Mishi tsuki no	From that moon which once
Hikari kienu to	I thought would shine forever
Kiku zo kanashiki[129]	In that land above the clouds.

I was saddened to think what the Empress must have been feeling in her heart:

Kage narabe	The sun that used to shine
Teru hi no hikari	Beside the moon
Kakuretsutsu	Has veiled its radiance;
Hitori ya tsuki no	Surely the moon in its solitude
Kakikumoruramu	Is overcast with grief.

1. *Kurōdo no tō*, one of the two First Secretaries to the Emperor's Private Office (Kurōdodokoro). Since Sukemori was also a Captain of the Guards at this time, he must have been Captain First Secretary (*tō no chūjō*). He was appointed to the post on the twentieth of the first month of Jūei 2 (Feb. 14, 1183). The Taira fled the capital on the twenty-fifth of the seventh month of that year (Aug. 14), so he must have been extremely busy trying to keep up with his new duties while coping with the deteriorating position of his family during his last six months in the capital.

2. Generally taken to be a reference to the difficulties caused by Sukemori's legal wife and her family, as well as the inadvisability of being linked to the Taira when the war was obviously going badly for them.

VOLUME TWO

Part Four

Such was the upheaval in our world at the time of Jūei and Genryaku [1182–85] that whatever I may call it—dream, illusion, tragedy—no words can possibly describe it. It was so confused that I cannot even say exactly what occurred, and in fact right up till now I have repressed all thought of it. What can I say, what am I to feel about that autumn when I heard that those whom I knew were soon to be leaving the capital? No words, no emotions can do it justice. None of us had known when it might happen, and faced with the actual event, we were all stunned, those of us who saw it with our own eyes and those who heard about it from afar. We could only feel that it was just some indescribable dream.

At that time, when all was in uproar and such disquieting rumors were reaching us, Sukemori was a First Secretary to the Emperor[1] and seemed to have little time away from his duties. Moreover, those about me insisted that it was a hopeless, even scandalous affair,[2] so we became more cautious than we had been earlier, and it was with a great deal of hesitation that we met.

On these occasions he would tell me, just as though it were a normal thing to say:

"These troubles have now reached the point where there can be no doubt that I, too, shall number among the dead. Then, surely, you will spare me just a little pity? Though you may not feel much for me, yet out of regard for the many years that we have been together, do not fail to pray that I may find light on the dark path that awaits me. Even if, perchance, my life is spared for a while longer, I am resolved in my heart not to think of myself as the person I once was. For if I once begin to feel emotion, to think with longing of time past, or to yearn for a particular person, there would never be an end to it.

"I cannot know how weak my spirit might be in spite of my determination, so I have renounced all attachments to this world. I have made up my mind not to send you even the briefest of messages from whatever distant shore I find myself upon. Don't think, however, that my love for you is weak merely because I send no word. In all that concerns this world I have come to think of myself as one already dead. And yet, in spite of all, my former feelings will surely overcome me—to my intense regret!"

As I listened to him I knew how right he was, but what could I say? Tears were my only reply.

At the beginning of autumn news came at last of that dream within a dream—the flight from the capital. To what can I compare my feelings? Of course, there was not one person of sensibility who did not talk of and reflect upon this tragedy. But for me, among all the people that I knew, there was no friend to whom I could open my heart. So I spoke of it to no one, I brooded constantly, and when my feelings were more than my heart could bear, I could only turn to the Buddha and spend my days in tears.

Our lives, however, must go on for their allotted span; we

3. The original text has *uchitachitaru* ("setting out"). The translation follows the suggested emendation of most commentators to *ukitachitaru* ("straggling").

cannot end them as we wish; and even my desire to enter holy orders was frustrated, since I could not flee the house by myself. How much it pained me that I had to go on living as I was!

Mata tameshi	Now that I have seen
Tagui mo shiranu	Such miseries that I cannot know
Uki koto o	Their like or their example,
Mite mo sate aru	A hateful destiny is this
Mi zo utomashiki	That keeps me living as of yore!

My anxiety was indescribable as I watched the autumn draw on, and I felt more than ever that I could no longer endure this life. One bright, moonlit night as I gazed out, musing on the sadness of the scene—the sky, the shapes of the clouds, the sound of the wind—I could think only of what Sukemori must be feeling, as he journeyed to his unknown destination beneath a traveler's sky. I was overcome with tears of despair:

Izuku nite	In what far place,
Ikanaru koto o	With thoughts of what sad things,
Omoitsutsu	Will he be gazing
Koyoi no tsuki ni	At the moon this night
Sode shiboruramu	And wringing out his tear-drenched sleeves?

At dawn, at dusk, no matter what I looked at, no matter what I listened to, how could I cease to think of him even for a moment? How I wanted, just one more time at least, to tell him how I felt! How sad that my wish was unlikely to be granted! It was too frightful for words to hear of him straggling[a] from place to place:

Iwabaya to	Many, so many
Omou koto nomi	Are the things
Ōkaru mo	I wish I could say to him.
Sate munashiku ya	And now am I to die like this,
Tsui ni hatenamu	My longings vain and unfulfilled?

4. These were the Minamoto forces under the command of Minamoto no Yoshitsune (1159–89), pursuing the Taira to the west.

5. *Nami kaze*, "waves and winds," forms a word association with *tadayoite*, "drifting"; *kaze*, "wind," is also associated with *sora*, which can mean "sky" but here means "feeling" or "mind." Hon-iden and Hisamatsu interpret this *sora* to mean "time," but Kubota shows several examples to demonstrate that "feeling" was a common meaning, particularly in combination with *yasuki*, "peaceful," and usually with a negative verb, as in this case. *Zenshaku*, p. 244; Hisamatsu, p. 467; "Hyōshaku," 19: 168.

6. The Japanese is *tsurenasa*, which Hon-iden and Hisamatsu interpret in its common meaning of "cruel," i.e. "the cruelty of life." *Zenshaku*, p. 245; Hisamatsu, p. 467. But a standard meaning of the word is "unchanged despite one's hopes." Ōno et al., p. 875. Kubota, "Hyōshaku," 19: 169–70, cites examples of this use. The interpretation "unchanged" does seem more appropriate for the poem here and for the text in general.

7. Of 1184.

Large numbers of fierce warriors were leaving the capital for the west.[4] Whenever I heard any rumors, I wondered in agitation what news would come next, and when. One night after I had cried myself to sleep with these gloomy thoughts, Sukemori appeared to me in a dream. He was as I had always seen him, wearing informal court dress. He gazed into the distance as though lost in thought, while the wind raged violently about him. I awoke with a throbbing heart; I cannot even begin to describe my feelings. I wondered if he really was at that very moment exactly as he had appeared in my dream:

Nami kaze no	Adrift in the turmoil
Araki sawagi ni	Of wild winds and waves,
Tadayoite	He is surely
Sa koso wa yasuki	Just as I saw him now,
Sora nakarurame[5]	No peace for his troubled mind.

Perhaps because I was so distraught, I fell ill with a fever for some time. I felt so wretched that I wanted to die:

Uki ue no	Before I hear
Nao uki koto o	Of yet more misery
Kikanu saki ni	To add to the misery I know,
Kono yo no hoka ni	Would that I might become
Nari mo shinabaya	No longer of this world!

So I desired, but it was not to be; and as my life went on unchanged[6] I felt crushed with grief:

Ararubeki	Though I do not feel
Kokochi mo senu ni	That I can go on living,
Nao kiede	Still I do not die.
Kyō made furu zo	What misery it brings
Kanashikarikeru	To have survived until this day!

The following spring[7] a relative of mine invited me to accompany her on a pilgrimage. I was in no mood for any activity, but this outing had a religious intent, so I roused myself

8. Following the defeat of the Taira at the battle of Ichinotani, on the seventh of the second month of Jūei 3 (March 20, 1184).

9. See Part One, note 16.

from my depression and went with her. On our way back she pointed out a place where the plum blossoms were unusually fine. She then entered the grounds, so of course I followed her, and the blossoms did indeed look far lovelier than the ordinary.

I listened as my companion talked with the hermit who owned the place. "Every year," he said, " a certain person used to come and ask to have the place roped off, so that he could enjoy the blossoms without being disturbed. But this year he hasn't come. What a shame, for now they will have bloomed and scattered all for nothing!"

My companion must have asked who the person was, for he distinctly mentioned Sukemori's name, and at that my heart was thrown into a turmoil of painful emotions:

Omou koto	All that I feel,
Kokoro no mama ni	Everything in my heart;
Katarawamu	I shall confess to you,
Narekeru hito o	O blossoms, if you too
Hana mo shinobaba	But long for him I loved.

Among the ghastly and terrifying rumors I heard that spring came the painful and unspeakable news that great numbers of my close friends had been killed, and that their heads were being paraded through the streets of the capital.[8] To hear people naming the dead was the most dreadful thing I had ever known:

Aware sareba	Alas! Alas!
Kore wa makoto ka	Can it be true?
Nao mo tada	I ask myself.
Yume ni ya aran	Or can it after all
To koso oboyure	Be no more than a dream?

When I heard that Captain Shigehira[9] had been taken prisoner and had been brought back to the capital for a while, I thought dejectedly of how among all those I had known he had

10. See Part One, note 9. According to some accounts, Koremori drowned himself in the sea off Kumano, near Nachi, on the twenty-eighth of the third month of Jūei 3 (May 10, 1184).

11. A celebration of Retired Emperor Goshirakawa's fiftieth birthday (by Japanese reckoning), held in his main residence, the Hōjūji Palace, on the fourth to the sixth of the third month of Angen 2 (April 14–16, 1176).

12. "Seigaiha," one of the most famous of the courtly dances (*gagaku*).

13. An allusion to the "The Festival of Autumn Leaves" chapter ("Momiji no ga") of *The Tale of Genji*, in which Prince Genji performs the same dance with prodigious success.

14. A quotation from "The Flower Festival" chapter ("Hana no en") of *Genji*.

been especially close to me. He would say such amusing things, and even in the most trivial matters he used to be so considerate towards other people. He was indeed an exceptional person: what could he have done in a previous life to bring this upon himself? Those who saw him said that his countenance was unchanged, and they could not bear to look at him. I cannot describe how painful, how grievous it was to hear this:

Asa yū ni	By day, by night,
Minaresugushishi	How often we would meet
Sono mukashi	In those days now long ago:
Kakarubeshi to wa	Never did I imagine
Omoite mo mizu	That it would come to this.

Over and over I imagined what was in his heart:

Mada shinanu	While yet not dead,
Kono yo no uchi ni	Still of this world,
Mi o kaete	But in how changed a state!
Nanigokochi shite	With what thoughts in your heart
Akekurasuramu	Do you pass your days, your nights?

People were deeply distressed to hear that Koremori had drowned himself at Kumano.[10] Whenever I meet anyone these days, I can only think what truly superior figures the Taira were. But Koremori was exceptional to a degree, both in appearance and in thoughtfulness; indeed among all the people I have ever known, of old or in recent times, no one can compare with him. Who could fail to praise him whenever he appeared?

At the celebration in the Hōjūji Palace,[11] when Koremori danced "The Blue Waves of the Sea,"[12] people remarked that they could not help being reminded of the Shining Prince Genji.[13] I even heard them say that "the beauty of the cherry blossom itself must be eclipsed."[14] Of course, I was bound to have fond recollections of him as he had been on such occa-

15. After his performance of "The Blue Waves of the Sea," Koremori was known as the Cherry and Plum Blossom Lieutenant.

16. *Mi* is a pivot word acting as a prefix to the place-name Kumano, with the meaning "holy," and as the stem of the verb *miru*, "to see," here used in the idiom *me o miru*, "to meet with an experience."

17. Kiyotsune, the youngest of the three, drowned himself in the tenth month of Jūei 2 (1183).

sions, but I knew him so well that, distressed though I was at the deaths of all my friends who had perished, his death was a particularly heavy blow.

"Think of me as you do of Sukemori," he would say to me from time to time. "Oh, but I do!," I would reply. Then he would say, "That's what you say, but I'm not so sure!" I cannot describe the many pangs of grief that these memories aroused:

Haru no hana no	The vision of that face,
Iro ni yosoeshi	Which was once compared
Omokage no	To the beauty of spring blossoms,
Munashiki nami no	Is withered now
Shita ni kuchinuru[15]	Beneath the empty waves.

Kanashiku mo	How wretched the dismal fate
Kakaru uki me o	That he has met!
Mikumano no	Under the waves that wind
Urawa no nami ni	About the bay of holy Kumano
Mi o shizumekeru[16]	He has laid himself forever.

The news of Koremori's death particularly affected me because of my anxiety for his brother Sukemori. Naturally the news was distressing in itself. But when it was widely rumored that Koremori and his brother Kiyotsune had sought their own deaths,[17] I could imagine how much more depressed Sukemori must have felt, alone as he now was. However, because of what he had said to me before leaving the capital, or perhaps for some other reason, he sent me not a single word. In the winter of the year he had left the capital, there had been the briefest of messages. All he had said was: "As I told you, I regard myself as no longer of this world, and I trust that everyone will think of me that way. Please pray for the good of my soul in the life to come."

I knew of no one through whom I could send a letter, nor was it possible for me to send a messenger of my own, so even

18. *Moshiogusa*, "salt weed," is the same as *takumo* (which Lady Daibu uses earlier), seaweed that was gathered into piles and burnt for the extraction of salt. It functions as a rhetorical introduction to *kakiatsumu*, "gather into words," since *kaki* is a pivot word meaning "to write" or "to rake," and *moshiogusa kakiatsumu* means "to rake together the salt weed." *Moshiogusa* forms a word association with *midaru (midarete)*, "be tangled," and it can also read as a pivot word, since *moshi* is orthographically the same as *moji*, "letters, writing."

19. The effect of the original, with its repetition of *omou/omoi*, "thoughts, sorrows," at the beginning of four lines, is no less strange, though more mellifluous, than the translation. It is a device for conveying her grief and distraction. The last two lines of the preceding poem are noteworthy as an example of the repetition of sounds.

20. This interpretation of *mameyaka* ("proper") follows Kubota. "Hyō-shaku," 20: 170.

though I was indescribably anxious about him, there was no way for me to tell him what I felt. But shortly after I had heard of his brother's fate, I found a dependable person who could be trusted to deliver a message safely. Among other things, I mentioned that I had not really intended to write to him in this way but could not resist the chance:

Samazama ni	This way, that way,
Kokoro midarete	My heart is torn.
Moshiogusa	No hope in the least have I
Kakiatsumubeki	That I can gather into words
Kokochi dani sezu[18]	The tangled salt weed of my thoughts.

Onaji yo to	How wretched it is
Nao omou koso	To think that this is still
Kanashikere	The same world as before,
Aru ga aru ni mo	A world where life itself
Aranu kono yo ni	No longer counts as life.

I spoke also of his brothers:

Omou koto o	Now, as I sorrow
Omoiyaru ni zo	At the sorrow that is yours,
Omoikudaku	Heartrending sorrow
Omoi ni soete	Piles on my own sorrow
Itodo kanashiki[19]	To sink me deeper in my grief.

In reply to this Sukemori wrote that in spite of all he had said, he was pleased to receive my letter. "I cannot tell whether my fate will overtake me today or tomorrow," he wrote, "and I now have a feeling of utter resignation. Only this once will I send you a proper letter."[20]

Omoitojime	My feelings I have stifled,
Omoikirite mo	My thoughts cut off,
Tachikaeri	And yet it all returns;
Sasuga ni omou	Many, many are the memories
Koto zo ōkaru	That fill my mind.

21. Sukemori perished—possibly he drowned himself—in the Taira defeat at Dannoura on the twenty-fourth of the third month of Jūei 4 (May 6, 1185).

Ima wa subete	No more now
Nani no nasake mo	Will I look upon,
Aware o mo	No more listen to
Mi mo seji kiki mo	Compassion, words of tenderness—
Seji to koso omoe	In this I am resolved!

He talked of those who had gone before him:

Aru hodo ga	This is wretchedness—
Aru ni mo aranu	To see such tragedy,
Uchi ni nao	While I yet live
Kaku uki koto o	In the midst of life
Miru zo kanashiki	That is not life at all.

Less than ever can I convey the emotions I felt on reading this.

In the spring of the following year [1185] I finally heard that he was in truth no longer of this world.[21] How can I possibly convey what I felt then. I had already known that it would come to this, and yet I felt completely dazed. I was utterly unable to hold back my tears. But I was upset at the idea of having people witness my despair, so I told them I did not feel well, and I spent the whole day lying on my bed. I drew the covers up over my head and abandoned myself to my tears. Try though I might to drive away all memories of him, his image stubbornly clung to me, and I felt I could hear his every word. My body itself was in torment, and I can never describe all the anguish I suffered. People are distressed and say how sad it is, even when they hear of someone dying at his natural and expected time; to what, then, I wondered over and over again, could I compare this grief of mine:

Nabete yo no	Whoever called them sad,
Hakanaki koto o	This world's ordinary,
Kanashi to wa	This world's natural deaths,
Kakaru yume minu	Must have been one who never knew
Hito ya iiken	A nightmare such as this.

22. The translation follows the punctuation and interpretation favored by Kubota, rather than Hisamatsu. *Ibid.*, 21: 164–65.

23. The Japanese *utsushigokoro* has given rise to various and often ingenious interpretations. Kubota once again cuts the Gordian knot, and the translation follows his interpretation. *Ibid.*, p. 165.

Eventually, someone sent me a letter saying "How dreadful this must be for you." I felt, however, that it was done merely out of courtesy:

Kanashi to mo	If only, oh, if only
Mata aware to mo	We could use some
Yo no tsune ni	Common, ordinary words,
Yūbeki koto ni	And call this
Araba koso arame	Pitiable or sad!

In this state I let the days and nights go by, shutting myself off from the normal life of the world, even while I was still living in it.[22] However, feelings of reality[23] intruded upon me, and then the more I turned things over in my mind, the more my unhappiness grew. I was not the only one to have endured such a short-lived and heartbreaking love affair. There were many people, both known and unknown to me, who had lived through the same nightmare in their relationships with the Taira family, but at the time I felt that my experience was utterly without parallel. Natural deaths at their natural hour had brought about many separations in the past and even in my own day, I reflected, but such a bitter parting as mine could never have happened to anyone else.

It was only natural that I should think this way. My mind had been so filled with thoughts of Sukemori that I could not forget him. If only, if only I could make myself forget, I kept on thinking. But it was not to be, and in my unhappiness I wrote:

Tameshi naki	Cruel, cruel,
Kakaru wakare ni	That despite this parting,
Nao tomaru	Such that we shall never see its like,
Omokage bakari	The specter of his face
Mi ni sou zo uki	Clings to me yet!

24. *Tachikaeri*, "change my mind," is associated with *nagori*, "memory."
25. One of Japan's most popular bodhisattvas and an ever-present source of help in attaining salvation for beings in all realms of existence. He was commonly believed to manifest himself in six forms corresponding to the six paths (on which see Part Three, note 74).

Ikade ima wa	Would I had a heart
Kai naki koto o	That could forget
Nagekazute	And cease from its lament
Mono wasure suru	At things that,
Kokoro ni mogana	Now, nothing can ever change.

Wasuremu to	Think as I will
Omoite mo mata	That I must forget,
Tachikaeri	I change my mind again:
Nagori nakaran	To have no memory of him
Koto zo kanashiki[24]	Would bring true misery.

I kept my feelings locked away in my heart, feelings that were too much even for tears. But what use was it all, I miserably pondered, even though he had told me to pray without fail for his salvation after death—and indeed he must have met his end in a far from tranquil state of mind. There were, of course, people who had managed to survive and who could pray for him, but those who were related to him had to avoid the public eye in all things and could do nothing freely. I realized that I alone was the one to do it, and it so upset me that I roused myself from my depression.

I picked out old letters, remade them into fresh paper, and wrote out sutras on them. Some I took and smoothed out just as they were. But the old writing was still visible, and it so embarrassed me that I pasted things on the back to hide it. With my own hand I drew the six forms of Jizō[25] in black ink and went through various observances, though I could not do them properly and performed them only in the secrecy of my own mind. I had to be careful of letting other people see me, so I told no one except those who were very close to me. But to perform these ministrations alone and secretly within my own breast was an unbearable sadness:

26. The same priest performed these services after her mother's death. Part Three, note 127.

27. This *darani*, a spell or formula, was especially effective in removing obstacles to salvation.

28. The style at this point is reminiscent of the part of "The Enchanter" chapter ("maboroshi") of *The Tale of Genji*, where Genji is sorting out his correspondence after the death of his wife, Murasaki. Lady Daibu's quotation from *Genji* a few lines below is from this same section. See Abe Akio et al., 4: 534.

Sukuu naru	Trusting in the vow
Chikai tanomite	That promises salvation,
Utsushioku o	I copy out these images:
Kanarazu mutsu no	Fail him not, therefore, in your guidance
Michi shirube seyo	On the six paths of the dead.

Thus I tearfully offered up my prayers from the depths of my heart, and I requested the holy priest Ashō to dedicate my offerings.[26] The old letters had, after all, accumulated in large numbers, and I used them to write out the Sonshō *darani*[27] and a great many other things. Halfheartedly I tried not to look at them, but my eyes were drawn to them all the same, his handwriting, the very words of his letters: even at some less tragic time, such reminders of past days would inevitably have brought forth tears, but now the world went dark before my eyes and my mind was numbed.[28] It was too dreadful for words. To read there what had happened on this or that occasion and see his reply to letters I had written him made me feel that I was dragging back the past. I therefore disposed of them all in the same way and left not a single one. As I did this, I found myself recalling that scene from *The Tale of Genji* where the Prince says: "It does no good to gaze upon them." How cruel it seemed that this scene should spring to mind just then, for it set me wondering what my reasons were for doing as I did:

Kanashisa no	These traces of his hand
Itodo moyōsu	Do but provoke in me
Mizuguki no	Yet greater wretchedness:
Ato wa nakanaka	Rather I wish
Kiene to zo omou	That they would fade away.

Ka bakari no	I hate this thread of life,
Omoi ni taete	Which I draw on and on,
Tsure mo naku	So lacking in all feeling
Nao nagarauru	That I am able to endure
Tama no o mo ushi	Such miseries as these.

29. An allusion to an anonymous poem, *Manyōshū* 1995:

Minazuki no	In this month of no rains
Tsuchi sae sakete	The sun beats down
Teru hi mo	As though to split the earth itself,
Waga sode hime ya	Yet will my sleeves never be dry,
Kimi ni awazu shite	While I cannot meet with you?

30. *Higurashi* is a pivot word meaning both "cicada" and "the whole day through."

31. This poem takes up the implications of the previous poem. If Lady Daibu's salvation is in doubt, it would be better to vanish completely from the phenomenal world, rather than simply die, only to be reborn and continue (leave her traces) in the unending cycle of misery. In the Heian period *uki yo* had connotations of both misery and transience.

The room where I spent my days during the late summer had doors that opened out onto a valley, and one day as I gazed down into it, the leaves of the bamboo seemed to have curled and shriveled in the fierce sunshine. It looked hot enough to "split the earth itself,"[29] and yet, I wondered, would my sleeves still not dry. I found myself once again overcome with tears.

In the dense growth of the treetops the cicadas shrilled the whole day through so loud as to be irritating; but since they too were crying, I thought of them as my companions in sorrow:

Koto towamu	Something I would ask you—
Nare mo ya mono o	Do you too have your griefs,
Omouramu	That you should cry with me
Morotomo ni naku	The whole day through,
Natsu no higurashi[30]	Cicadas of the summer?

Having no other source of comfort, I turned to the Buddha. After all, I had had faith in him ever since my childhood. But there were so many things to convince me that my fate had always been wretched, and now I had such sorrows as had never been heard of. What had I done to deserve this, I wondered, and I began to resent even the gods and buddhas:

Saritomo to	In spite of all
Tanomu hotoke mo	I have trusted in the Buddha.
Megumaneba	But he withholds his blessings,
Nochi no yo made o	So now I have these miseries of doubt
Omou kanashisa	About the life to come.

Yukue naku	If that be so,
Waga mi mo saraba	Would that my body too could join my heart
Akugaren	And wander with no destination,
Ato todomubeki	For I would leave no traces of myself
Uki yo naranu ni[31]	In this brief world of misery.

32. "A plain of reeds" (*asaji ga hara*) was often used in poems as a description of dilapidated mansions. "A tangle of wormwood" (*yomogi ga soma*) is taken from a poem by Sone no Yoshitada (fl. c. 985), *Goshūishū* 273:

Nake ya nake	Cry, cry on,
Yomogi ga soma no	You crickets hiding
Kirigirisu	In the tangled wormwood,
Sugiyuku aki wa	For the autumn drawing to its close
Ge ni zo kanashiki	Is truly cause for sorrow.

This poem is also to be found in Yoshitada's personal collection, *Sotanshū* (242), where the fourth line reads *kureyuku aki wa*, which produces no difference in meaning.

33. "Violet hempweed" is translator's license for *fujibakama* (*Eupatorium strechadosmum*), which is closely related to boneset, thoroughwort, and hemp agrimony, none of which sit comfortably in a translation. "An autumn field rich with the cries of insects" (*mushi no ne shigeki nobe*) is a quotation from a poem by Miharu no Arisuke (fl. c. 900), written on visiting the dilapidated home of a person who had died some time before, *Kokinshū* 853:

Kimi ga ueshi	The single clump of pampas grass
Hitomurasusuki	That you once planted
Mushi no ne no	Has now become
Shigeki nobe to mo	An autumn field
Narinikeru kana	Rich with the cries of insects.

34. There is a word association between *tsuyu*, "dew," and *nohara*, "wild moors."

There was a charming place in the northern hills that had been owned by that person who was now dead. We were always making our way there to see the cherry blossoms at their height or the beauty of the autumn fields, and everyone had at some time seen the place. I heard that it had become the property of a certain hermit, and since he was a relative of mine, I went in secret to look at it, unable to restrain my longing. Sukemori's image appeared before my eyes, and once again they were dimmed with tears. It was more than I can describe.

The grounds, which had been so well tended, had now become "a plain of reeds," "a tangle of wormwood," with creepers and moss growing thickly everywhere.[32] They scarcely resembled the grounds of old. The young bush clover he had planted had grown rank and lay in wild profusion about the northern and southern gardens. Violet hempweed scented the air, and the single clump of pampas grass did indeed seem to be "an autumn field rich with the cries of insects."[33] I had my carriage drawn closer and alighted by the doors, where I gazed about me in solitude. The memories welled up in me, but to describe them would be more than I could bear. As usual, my heart was thrown into such turmoil that I could bring nothing clearly to mind:

Tsuyu kieshi	These last remains
Ato wa nohara to	Of one who vanished like the dew
Narihatete	Are now become wild moors;
Arishi ni mo nizu	No longer as they once were,
Arehatenikeri[34]	They have turned to utter ruin.

Ato o dani	Only the remnants of time past,
Katami ni min to	Yet I had hoped
Omoishi o	To find reminders here:
Sate shi mo itodo	But now that I have come,
Kanashisa zo sou	Grief and more grief is mine.

35. *Karenuru* is a pivot word meaning both "has withered" and "has gone, has departed." It forms word associations with *kozue*, "branches," and *tsuyukeshi*, "dew-covered."

36. The Taira had set fire to their residences before fleeing the capital.

In the eastern garden there were many willow and cherry trees planted together, all of the same height. Once, in the spring of a year long past, we two had gazed at them together, and now it seemed to me to have happened but a minute before. How it pained and grieved me to realize that only the branches of the trees remained as they had been:

Uete mishi	He who planted and gazed upon these trees
Hito wa karenuru	Is withered away and gone:
Ato ni nao	Amidst these ruins of the past
Nokoru kozue o	I look upon the branches that remain,
Miru mo tsuyukeshi[35]	And my tears well forth like dew.

Waga mi moshi	Should life but remain to me
Haru made araba	Until the spring,
Tazunemimu	Then I will come to gaze at you again.
Hana mo sono yo no	O flowers, do not forget
Koto na wasure so	How those days used to be!

On one occasion, as I was on my way somewhere I passed the ruins of Sukemori's mansion, which had long since vanished into smoke.[36] Only the foundation stones remained; the grasses were deep, here and there an autumn flower had come into bloom, the dew spilled from the leaves, and there came to me the sound of the mingled voices of the insects, filling me with sadness. I felt I could not pass by, and stopped my carriage for a while to gaze out. When, I pondered, would this sadness end:

Mata sara ni	And yet again I come
Uki furusato o	To gaze on this place of misery,
Kaerimite	Once dear to me.
Kokoro todomuru	How profitless, how stupid
Koto mo hakanashi	That I leave my heart to linger here!

Again and again the same thoughts came to mind, and not for a moment could they be dispelled. Yet my life went on

218

37. Kenreimon-in, Lady Daibu's former mistress, Tokuko, who had become a Retired Empress on the twenty-fifth day of the eleventh month of Yōwa 1 (Jan. 1, 1182). She had attempted to drown herself at the battle of Dannoura, but had been pulled from the water by Minamoto soldiers. She was brought back to the capital towards the end of the fourth month of Bunji 1 (1185). She took the tonsure on the first of the fifth month, and in the tenth month she moved to the Jakkōin, a convent at Ōhara, a few miles north of the capital.

38. *Miyako wa haru no nishiki*, an allusion to a poem by the priest Sosei, *Kokinshū* 56:

Miwataseba	As I look about,
Yanagi sakura o	Cherry blossoms and green willow fronds
Kokimazete	Are mingled into one:
Miyako zo haru no	The capital has now become
Nishiki narikeru	Brocade of springtime.

unending, and I heard of nothing but one misery piled on another, and all utterly beyond description:

Sadame naki	Well may they say
Yo to wa iedomo	This is a world of transience;
Kaku bakari	And yet there cannot be
Uki tameshi koso	Another instance
Mata nakarikere	Of such suffering as mine.

Though I had had no other news of the Retired Empress, I did hear that she was at Ōhara.[37] But without knowing the right people, there was no way for me to visit her. Yet in the end I set off regardless, trusting for my guidance in my deep devotion to Her Majesty.

As I gradually drew nearer, the mountain path looked so gloomy that my tears welled up to precede me along the way; my feelings were beyond description. But her hermitage and all about it, her whole way of life in this place, were more than I could bear to look upon. How could anyone, even one who had not known her in the old times, consider such an existence acceptable for her? But for someone like myself who had been in her service, was this reality, was it a dream? There was no way to describe it. The gales of late autumn blowing down the mountainside and raging through the tops of the nearby trees, the trickle of water from a bamboo pipe, the calling of the deer, and the crying of the insects, they sound everywhere the same; but here they filled me with a sadness I had never known. At court she had been served by more than sixty ladies-in-waiting, attired in layer upon layer of robes so beautiful they seemed to have been cut from "the brocade of springtime in the capital";[38] here she was attended by only three or four women, clothed in habits of inky black and so changed in appearance that I did not recognize them.

"Has it come to this?" was all that they or I could utter. Choked with our tears, we could say no more:

39. *Kakaru* is a pivot word meaning "such" when it modifies *miyama*, "mountain depths," and "hang" when it is a verb whose subject is *tsuki*, "moon." *Kage* is also a pivot word meaning "light (of the moon)," "form, appearance (of the Empress)," and "shadows." Murai Jun is the only commentator to propose the third meaning, but it is a common meaning, forms a word association with *miyama*, and comes naturally to mind on a reading of the poem. *Hyōkai*, p. 171. Other word associations are *kage, tsuki, kakaru,* and *aogimishi*, "I gazed up at."

40. There is the usual pivot on *sumu*, "to dwell" and "be clear," and a further Buddhist meaning of "to be tranquil, at peace," with overtones of entering religious orders.

Ima ya yume	Is this a dream?
Mukashi ya yume to	Or was that past a dream?
Mayowarete	I cannot tell.
Ikani omoedo	However I may think of it,
Utsutsu to zo naki	This is not reality.

Aogimishi	In awe I gazed
Mukashi no kumo no	Long, long ago
Ue no tsuki	At the moon above the clouds.
Kakaru miyama no	How desolate that its light should rest
Kage zo kanashiki[39]	In the shadows of these mountain depths.

As I thought back on the past, I wondered if this was indeed the same Empress whose beauty had of old been beyond compare with the splendor of the blossoms or the brilliance of the moon. Gazing at her wretched state, I asked myself why I was going back at all to a capital that held no inviting memories to draw me there. To have to leave her was disagreeable and cruel.

Yama fukaku	My heart, I leave you
Todomeokitsuru	Deep within these hills:
Waga kokoro	Become my guide,
Yagate sumubeki	Lead me at once to dwell with her
Shirube to o nare[40]	In purity and peace.

Everything made me feel that I wanted only to be done with this world:

Nagekiwabi	Unable to endure this grief,
Waga nakaramashi to	I even come to wish
Omou made no	That I might no longer live.
Mi zo warenagara	Do what I may, I can only feel
Kanashikarikeru	How sad is this fate of mine.

Was there absolutely no way, I wondered, that I could distract myself from my grief; and then, while I was visiting a place where I had never been before, I had the idea of going on

41. This follows Kubota's interpretation. "Hyōshaku," 24: 178. Other commentators favor an interpretation along the lines: "What memories brought me here?" "What memories was I searching for in coming here?" But Lady Daibu's intention in taking the trip was to escape from memories, so that interpretation does not seem appropriate. Furthermore, in the prose introduction to Poem 241 she uses a similar phrase: "a capital that held no inviting memories to draw me there." The Japanese in that case is *nani no omoide naki miyako*, compared with *nani mo omoide ni ka to* here.

42. *Kari* is a pivot word meaning "geese" and "impermanence."

43. The Ōsaka barrier. See Part Three, note 101.

44. *Iku kumoi* is a poetic expression for a great distance. *Kumoi* literally means "cloud being" or "cloud place" and was often used to refer to the sky, clouds, a distant place, or the court.

a distant journey. But that very thought immediately brought back memories of a different departure from the capital:

Kaerubeki	The road of my return
Michi wa kokoro ni	Is mine to take,
Makasete mo	Whenever I shall desire,
Tabidatsu hodo wa	And yet as I set forth
Nao aware nari	How heavy is my heart!

Miyako oba	Much as I loathe the capital,
Itoite mo mata	Parting from it
Nagori aru o	Still brings longing and regret.
Mashite to mono o	But how much keener was his pain,
Omoiidetsuru	I muse, as memories return!

The place I was heading for was close to Sakamoto on Mount Hiei. Snow fell, darkening the sky, and gave me the feeling that the capital was far off and remote. What pleasant memories could there be for me in the capital to make this place seem so desolate, I asked myself forlornly.[41]

Late that night there came the sounds of a line of geese flying over my lodgings. Their cries stirred me deeply, and for no reason I found the tears streaming down my face:

Uki koto wa	Thinking my miseries
Tokorogara ka to	Were of the place itself,
Nogaruredo	I fled,
Izuku mo kari no	Only to hear the geese proclaim
Yado to kikoyuru[42]	All places lodgings of impermanence.

I had crossed through only a single barrier,[43] which was no great distance to have come, yet the winds that swept through the treetops sounded far fiercer than in the capital:

Seki koete	Having crossed the barrier,
Iku kumoi made	I am not cut off
Hedatenedo	By wastes of cloud-filled sky,
Miyako ni wa ninu	Yet how different from the capital
Yamaoroshi kana[44]	Is the storm wind down the mountain side!

45. On the south side of the Great Hall of State (Shishinden) were two trees, a cherry tree by the southeastern corner and an orange tree by the southwestern. The southwestern corner was close to the Gekkamon gate, the station of the Bodyguard of the Right, and the orange tree was therefore known as The Orange Tree of the Bodyguard of the Right (*ukon no tachibana*). Late in 1178, perhaps not long before Lady Daibu left court service, Sukemori had been appointed Supernumerary Lieutenant of the Bodyguard of the Right (*ukon no gon no shōshō*), which was why he claimed an affinity with the tree. Sukemori probably broke his branch not from the orange tree by the Great Hall of State, but from another tree in the palace grounds, possibly one that was visible from Lady Daibu's rooms.

46. This poem alludes to the famous *Kokinshū* poem on orange blossom. See Part Three, note 18. Orange trees bloomed in the fifth month (*satsuki*, the month of rains), and there is no blossom on the tree that Lady Daibu is looking at. She wonders whether the tree recalls its summer scent, as she recalls her love.

With great devotion I performed the rites, and I prayed with all my heart that he whom I had loved might find repose in the world to come. For that and nothing else I prayed, but, as always, useless feelings rose up within me, and try as I might, how could I put them from me?

I rose and went to look outside, and caught sight of an orange tree thickly piled with snow. It reminded me of a time at the palace—what year would it have been, I wonder? It was a morning when the snow lay deep. Sukemori appeared in a casual court robe, rumpled after night duty; he broke off a spray from a snow-covered orange tree and brought it to me with the snow still clinging to it. Why, I asked him, had he taken a spray from that particular tree. He replied that the tree stood in a quarter he frequented a great deal, so he felt a close affinity with it.[45] The scene came back to me as clearly as if it were happening at that very moment, and my sorrow was more than I can express:

Tachinareshi	The orange tree
Mikaki no uchi no	That he knew so well
Tachibana mo	Within those sacred walls,
Yuki to kienishi	Does it too long for him
Hito ya kouramu	Who is vanished as the melting snow?

Such were the thoughts that immediately came to me. This tree that I now looked upon, the leaves grew thick upon it; but it bore no fruit, and its hue was one of loneliness:

Koto towamu	Something I would ask of you:
Satsuki narade mo	Though this be not the month of rains,
Tachibana ni	Yet still amidst your branches
Mukashi no sode no	Does that fragrance linger on
Ka wa nokoru ya to[46]	Of those sleeves of long ago?

226

47. *Naruko* is a pivot word meaning "bird rattle" and also functioning as *naru*, a verbal suffix meaning "seems to say." The bird rattle was a device of wooden boards and bamboo tubes suspended on ropes so that it could be rattled by someone pulling on connecting ropes from the edge of the field in order to scare away birds and other pests.

48. Between 1:30 A.M. and 2:00 A.M. (not 2:30–3:00 A.M., as older theories of Heian timekeeping maintained).

The blowing of the wind brought with it the sound of the bird rattle, and somehow this too was melancholy:

Arishi yo ni	It seems to say
Arazu naruko no	This world is not the world of old.
Oto kikeba	When I hear the rattle's sound,
Suginishi koto zo	Events that long have passed
Itodo kanashiki[47]	Bring yet more grief to me.

As I gazed away into the distance towards the capital, I realized how far beyond the cloud-banked horizon it lay:

Waga kokoro	Aimless and wretched,
Ukitaru mama ni	My heart drifts sunk in thought,
Nagamureba	And I gaze out;
Izuku o kumo no	All around the clouds stretch on,
Hate to shi mo nashi	Nowhere do they end.

It must have been around the beginning of the twelfth month. Darkness had set in, and sleet, neither quite snow nor quite rain, was falling intermittently. Banks of cloud pressed in silent tumult across the sky, which remained only partly overcast, while here and there groups of stars shone and were then snuffed out. I lay down and pulled the quilt up over my head. But later in the night—it must have been about the second quarter of the Ox[48]—I pushed the quilt off and looked up into the sky. It was unusually clear and had turned a lighter blue, against which large stars had appeared with unusual brilliance in one unbroken expanse. The sight was extraordinarily beautiful. It looked just as if pieces of gold and silver leaf had been scattered on paper of pale indigo. I felt as though I were seeing such a sky for the very first time that night. I had often before looked at starlit skies so bright that the moon might almost have been shining. But perhaps because of the time and place, that night made a particularly vivid impression on me, and I could only remain there sunk in thought:

49. Strictly speaking it was known as the Hie Shrine. It was at Hiyoshi, modern Ōtsu on the shore of Lake Biwa, Shiga Prefecture.

50. *Furu* (*furinishi*) "to grow old, move into the past," has a second meaning, "to fall," which forms a word association with *yuki*, "snow."

Tsuki o koso	The moon
Nagamenareshika	I have often gazed upon,
Hoshi no yo no	But the stirring beauty
Fukaki aware o	Of a night of stars
Koyoi shirinuru	I have understood this night.

As I made my way to the Hiyoshi Shrine,[49] snow darkened the sky and piled to a great depth on the front rail of my palanquin. Having spent the night in prayer, I returned to my lodging at dawn, and on the way back, when I lifted the blind, the driving snow blew inside my sleeves and into the front of my robes. I tried to brush it off my sleeves, but it had already frozen in little clusters here and there. It looked so lovely, and yet it only saddened me, for the one to whom I wanted to show it was not there:

Nanigoto o	What is there
Inori ka subeki	That I should pray for?
Waga sode no	Since there can be no way
Kōri wa token	To melt this ice that freezes
Kata mo araji o	On my tear-drenched sleeves.

At my cheerless traveler's lodgings, the snow lingered on unmelted, as though waiting for the companionship of a fresh fall. I gazed vacantly out at the sky, which was thinly overcast with clouds that threatened snow:

Sarade dani	Even without this,
Furinishi koto no	All that has befallen me
Kanashiki ni	Would still be sad.
Yuki kakikurasu	But now snow dims the sky,
Sora mo nagameji[50]	And I can no longer gaze at it.

And yet the whole night through I gazed out. At times clouds darkened the sky, at times they drew back, and never for a moment did they look the same:

51. *Uki*, "miserable, unhappy," has a second meaning, "floating," which forms word associations with *hare*, "clear," and *kumori*, "clouded over."

52. The text reads *musebinagara*, "choking, sobbing," but Hisamatsu and most other commentators consider it such an unusual expression that they prefer to interpret it as *musubinagara*, "forming, building up," a variant found in the GSRJ text. However, Kubota cites several examples to show that it is not such a strange expression after all in this context. It leads naturally to the "dismal sound" that Lady Daibu talks of immediately after. Hisamatsu, p. 486; "Hyōshaku," 25: 180.

Ōzora wa	The great vault of the sky,
Hare mo kumori mo	Now clear, now clouded over,
Sadamenaki o	Is in constant motion,
Mi no uki koto wa	While the drifting misery that is my life
Itsumo kawaraji[51]	Will never, never change.

The noise of the bird rattle outside made me feel still more lonely. The year was drawing to its end; the fields and all the trees about were withered and swept bare by the wind. The look of such a world, where not one trace of its past remained, had much to which my life might be compared:

Aki sugite	Autumn is past,
Naruko wa kaze ni	The noise of the bird rattle
Nokorikeri	Remains upon the wind.
Nani no nagori mo	No vestiges of old are there
Hito no yo zo naki	For me in the world of man.

Choked with ice, the tiny stream in the valley seemed to sob its way along.[52] Now and then I could hear the dismal sound of it; bringing many things to mind:

Tanigawa wa	The valley stream
Ko no ha tojimaze	Is choked with leaves,
Kōredomo	Frozen in the ice;
Shita ni wa taenu	And yet unceasing underneath
Mizu no oto kana	Is the sound of flowing water.

While it was still dark I started out for the capital. My road lay along the shore at Shiga, and in the inlets of the lake thin ice had formed. It seemed as though the waves had frozen as they rolled towards the shore and now could not draw back again. There was a thin covering of snow, and wherever I turned my eyes it was like a cloth of purest white:

Urayamashi	How I envy them!
Shiga no urawa no	The waves locked in the ice
Kōritoji	In the twists of Shiga Bay

53. The word associations are obvious in this poem. *Kaeru* (*kaeranu, kaerinamu*), "return," is the normal expression for the action of waves drawing back into the sea or lake. *Urayamashi*, "jealous," contains *ura*, "bay," linking it with other images of the shore.

54. The place-name Ōmi (written *aumi*) is a pivot word containing the verb *au*, "to meet," and can be expanded into *au umi*, "sea of meeting."

55. Not readily identifiable, but possibly a member of the Minamoto family.

| Kaeranu nami mo | Cannot now draw back, and yet |
| Mata kaerinamu[53] | They at least are certain to return. |

The surface of the lake was deep green, broken by black-looking patches of rough and frightening water. My view was limited by the horizon, no great distance away, but there, where the sky merged into the far waters of the lake, a tiny boat rowed in a straight line through the clouds till it vanished from my sight. From where I watched it was not an enticing spectacle, so wild were the wind and waves. Yet even so, I could not help musing, if I had heard that by some remote chance he who had sunk beneath the waves were dwelling in such a place, no matter how dismal it might be to live in, I would have come and stayed by his side:

Koishinobu	If only the Sea of Ōmi
Hito ni ōmi no	Were, like its name, a sea of meeting
Umi naraba	With the one for whom I yearn,
Araki nami ni mo	Then would I gladly mingle
Tachimajiramashi[54]	Even with these raging waves.

It was sometime after the middle of the first month: everything seemed somehow so springlike, mild and serene and gently veiled in mist. One of the late Retired Emperor Takakura's ladies-in-waiting, who was known as Chūnagon no Suke,[55] was now in service with the present court, and she suggested that we might meet. I felt very fondly towards her, for she was one who knew much of the old times. But while we were waiting for the day on which we were to meet, something occurred to interfere with our arrangements, and we were forced to cancel them.

On the night itself, as I kept thinking that this would have been the evening, the moonlight shone in through the eaves of the dilapidated house, and from time to time the scent of plum blossoms came wafting in. It was entrancing. I stayed up the whole night, gazing out, and in the morning I sent this:

56. *Ariake,* "dawn moon," is a pivot word containing *ari,* "to be," which is taken with *nagori,* "memories, regrets," to give *nagori ari,* "memories remain."

57. *Nehan-e,* a service to celebrate the anniversary of the Buddha Shakyamuni's entry into Nirvana.

Aware ika ni	With what longing, what regret,
Kesa wa nagori o	Would I gaze out this morning,
Nagamemashi	Sunk in reverie,
Kinō no kure no	If only last night's meeting
Makoto nariseba	Had truly taken place!

Her reply:

Omoe tada	But only think!
Sa zo aramashi no	Even thoughts of how it might have been
Nagori sae	Bring memories that remain
Kinō mo kyō mo	Yesterday, today, as I gaze out
Ariake no sora[56]	At the dawn moon lingering in the sky.

Once, while someone was talking about a quite ordinary matter, memories were stirred in me, and for no reason at all the tears began to flow so fast that I could not hold them back:

Uki koto no	At every moment
Itsumo sou mi wa	Sorrows cling to me,
Nani to shi mo	And even when
Omoiaede mo	I can find no cause for them,
Namida ochikeri	Still the teardrops fall.

On the fifteenth of the second month I went on a visit to a temple, having been invited to go there with someone for the Nirvana Service.[57] As I performed my devotions and continued to turn things over in my mind, I listened to the priests describing the moment of Shakyamuni's entry into Nirvana. It all merely brought home to me the unhappiness of life, and I felt powerless to hold back the tears that came welling up. I had often heard this sort of sermon, but just then it affected me with a special keenness; a sadness came over me, and my tears would not cease. Was it, I pondered, that my own life was not to last much longer. But that, it seemed to me, was no cause for grief:

58. For an explanation of "Reigning Empress" see Part one, note 15. Infukumon-in (1147–1216) was a daughter of Emperor Goshirakawa and the foster mother of Emperors Antoku and Gotoba.

59. *Nagame,* "to contemplate," can also mean "long rain" and is associated with *ame,* "rain."

60. See note 50, for *furu (furinishi).* Here it is associated with *ame,* "rain," rather than snow.

Yo no naka no	As a sign
Tsune naki koto no	That the world of men
Tameshi tote	Is one of impermanence,
Soragakurenishi	The Buddha is as a moon
Tsuki ni zo arikeru	That for a space is hidden in the sky.

There was a high-ranking lady-in-waiting who had been in service with Retired Empress Infukumon-in in the days when she had held the title of Reigning Empress.[58] We had known each other well and used to have the most friendly talks together. One day we chanced to meet, and we talked the whole day through. As she left me, rain was falling heavily, and my feelings of regret were especially intense. She had known the same sufferings as I, and I felt great affection for her. She brought back for me many tender memories, so I sent her this poem:

Ika ni sen	What can I do?
Nagamekanenuru	I cannot bear to contemplate
Nagori kana	These memories and regrets—
Saranu dani koso	Even were things not so,
Ame no yūgure[59]	This rain-filled dusk.

Her reply:

Nagamewaburu	In this dusk of rain,
Ame no yūbe ni	Which we cannot bear to contemplate
Aware mata	Alas, if only once again
Furinishi koto o	We two might speak together
Iiawasebaya[60]	Of these things long past!

As dawn broke on the twenty-third day of the fourth month, rain was falling lightly, and in the eastern sky a *hototogisu* flew by, singing the first song of the year. It sounded fresh and charming, and was profoundly moving:

61. The *hototogisu* was reputed to visit the land of the dead.

62. The translation follows Kubota's suggested emendation of the first line from *awazu* ("I do not meet") to *arazu* ("no longer as it was"), a reading found in other texts. "Hyōshaku," 26: 171.

63. The Buddha of Boundless Mercy who promises all beings salvation in the Pure Land of the Western Paradise if they only call on his name with faith. The repetition of the formula *namu Amidabutsu*, "Hail to the Buddha Amida," had become very popular in the late Heian period, and this is almost certainly the recitation Lady Daibu is referring to here.

Akegata ni	At break of day
Hatsune kikitsuru	I hear your first song of the year,
Hototogisu	O *hototogisu*.
Shide no yamaji no	I would ask you of that path
Koto o towabaya[61]	Through the mountains of the dead.

Arazu naru	Here at the end of my wretched life,
Uki yo no hate ni	No longer as it once was,
Hototogisu	O *hototogisu*,
Ikade naku ne no	How is it that your song
Kawarazaruramu[62]	Can remain unchanged?

The second day of the fifth month was the anniversary of my mother's death. Though I was feeling far from well, I performed ablutions, recited the name of Amida,[63] and summoned a priest to chant sutras. As I listened, I reflected that I would probably not be able to perform these rites the following year. This naturally upset me deeply, and my sleeves became soaked with tears:

Wakarenishi	When I think that this
Toshi tsuki hi wa	May be the last time I shall greet
Au koto mo	The year, the month, the day,
Kore bakari ya to	On which she parted from me,
Omou kanashisa	Oh, what grief and pain it brings!

Just after the twentieth of the third month came the anniversary of the day on which he with whom my time had been so brief had turned to foam upon the waters. As usual, alone and secretly within my own heart, I made the various preparations. But who would give such thought to these things after I was gone? It was so depressing, I could hardly bear to think that there would be no one to recall how devoted I had been, no one to perform these remembrances in my place. I could only sob bitterly. It was this fear that affected me, more than the thought that I myself might die:

Ika ni sen	What am I to do?
Waga nochi no yo wa	For my own fate in the world to come
Sate mo nao	I have not the least concern.
Mukashi no kyō o	But would there were someone who could pray
Tou hito mogana	For this day that belongs to long ago!

All around me the trees and the garden looked so cheerful with their rich green colors, and the small birds chirped as if they had not a single care. But all this quickly plunged me into a gloom of tears:

Harewataru	For one whose only thoughts
Sora no keshiki mo	Are those of wretchedness
Tori no ne mo	That will never end,
Urayamashiku zo	Even this clear, unclouded sky
Kokoro yukumeru	Is overcast with gloom.

Tsuki mo sezu	Over all its wide expanse
Uki koto o nomi	The sky is clear;
Omou mi wa	The birds are calling;
Haretaru sora mo	And how I envy them
Kakikurashitsutsu	For seeming so content!

1. Tanabata. According to a Chinese legend, the Heavenly Weaving Maid (the star Vega; J. Shokujosei) and the Heavenly Herd Boy (the star Altair; J. Hikoboshi) were lovers whose passion led them so to neglect their duties that the King of Heaven punished them by placing them on opposite sides of the Milky Way (Ama no Gawa, the River of Heaven) and allowing them to meet only once a year. On the seventh night of the seventh month, the Maid could cross the river on a bridge of magpies' wings.

The legend came to Japan at an early date and was soon adapted to fit Japanese custom. In the Japanese version, it is the Herd Boy who crosses the river to the Weaving Maid, and though he may use the traditional bridge of magpie wings, he may also cross by other means: by a bridge of red maple leaves or an ordinary bridge; by rowing a boat or being rowed by a boatman; or by fording the river on foot. The Maid begins to stand on the riverbank as soon as the autumn wind begins to blow, and on the seventh night she waits in great excitement. She prepares their bed on the riverbank by using her sleeves to wipe clean the rock that will serve as their pillow. When the lovers are reunited, they sleep (as did all Japanese courtly lovers) with their robes piled on top of each other as a covering; the robes are by tradition made of feathers or clouds. At dawn, the lovers must part, and the Herd Boy returns to his side of the river.

An alternative name for the Weaving Maid, or Weaver Star, was Maiden of the Loom (Tanabatatsume), whence comes the name of the festival. The shortened form *tanabata* was also used for either of the two stars or even for both at once, and it is sometimes difficult to tell which is being referred to. In Lady Daibu's case, failing evidence to the contrary, it is best to assume *tanabata* means the Maid, because she would naturally have put herself in the woman's place. The festival's official name was *kikōden*, but the name Tanabata Festival (*tanabatamatsuri*) was generally preferred.

People participated in the happy night by watching the sky directly and by watching the reflection of the sky in a bowl of water or a pool. To help the Maid, ladies would offer to lend her their robes, but they were always afraid that she would reject as unlucky a robe that was rough, or for mourning, or in any other way unsuitable for this auspicious occasion. Each person wrote his wishes on seven mulberry leaves, using ink mixed with dew gathered from the cuplike leaves of the *satoimo* (*Colocasia antiquorum*, a type of sweet potato). The mulberry leaves were then hung as offerings on bamboo poles. Five-colored thread was also twisted and hung on poles or on the leaves of dwarf bamboo as an offering, while one prayed for the stars to bless one's artistic talents. The thread was associated with the occasion because of the Maid's normal occupation of weaving. Lovers could adopt one of two attitudes: either they deliberately did not meet that night for fear of sharing the fate of the two stars or they made a point of meeting in order to participate in the happiness of the reunited couple. Most of these beliefs and observances are to be found in the poems in this section.

2. The idea of wrapping one's joy in one's sleeves is to be found at least

Part Five

Year by year I have composed poems for the Festival of the Seventh Night,[1] and I include here a few of the ones I can remember:

Tanabata no	Today the Weaving Maid
Kyō ya ureshisa	Will keep her treasured joy
Tsutsumuran	Wrapped safely in her sleeves,
Asu no sode koso	But tomorrow, I already know,
Kanete shirarure[2]	Those same sleeves will be soaked with tears.
Kane no oto mo	You temple bells whose sound announces dawn,
Kakoe no tori mo	You cocks that crow to tell of morning,
Kokoro araba	If you know what feeling is,
Koyoi bakari wa	At least for this one night
Mono wasurenare	You will forget what you should do.
Chigirikeru	I know not why
Yue wa shiranedo	The stars have made this pledge,
Tanabata no	And yet I am impatient
Toshi ni hitoyo zo	For the meeting of the two,
Nao modokashiki	Which comes but once a year.

as early as the *Kokinshū* (which contains poetry mostly from 850 to 900) and probably comes from the practice of enfolding precious things in one's sleeves in order to carry or protect them. Sleeves were a common image in love poems, since they refer to the robes with which the lovers covered themselves as bedclothes, and they were also used to catch the tears shed at parting or any other time of unhappiness caused by love.

3. One name for grasshoppers was *hataorimushi*, literally "loom weaving insects," presumably because of the sound they make. They were often referred to in poems on the Tanabata Festival. There are word associations between *hataori*, "weaving," *aya*, "pattern," and *nuki*, "cross thread, weft." *Aya* is a pivot word meaning "pattern (on cloth)" and "tone, texture (of voice)."

4. Such a sad occasion required tears of blood, hence the reference to colors.

Koe no aya wa	With a noise of looms,
Oto bakari shite	Grasshoppers cry and weave
Hataori no	Patterns that are only sound;
Tsuyu no nuki o ya	Is it because they lend the Weaving Maid
Hoshi ni kasuramu[3]	The dew of which they form their strands?
Samazama ni	I imagine all
Omoiyaritsutsu	That they feel and do this night.
Yoso nagara	And though I am no part of them,
Nagamekanenuru	I find it too distressing
Hoshiai no sora	To gaze at the two stars meeting in the sky.
Ama no gawa	My thoughts are fixed
Kogihanareyuku	On the color of those tears
Fune no naka no	That flow for love unsatisfied
Akanu namida no	In the boat that rows in parting
Iro o shi zo omou[4]	Across the River of Heaven.
Kikabaya na	How I would like to hear
Futatsu no hoshi no	The words of love
Monogatari	Exchanged by those two stars.
Tarai no mizu ni	If only words could be reflected
Utsuramashikaba	In the bowl of water as their image is.
Yoyo futo mo	Year after year for certain,
Taen mono kawa	It will never break,
Tanabata ni	The lovers' vow of these two stars,
Asa hiku ito no	A vow as long as hempen threads,
Nagaki chigiri wa	Which I draw out to offer them this night.
Oshinabete	The dew falls equally
Kusamura goto ni	In every place
Oku tsuyu no	And on all the clumps of plants,
Imo no ha shi mo no	But why does it chance this very night
Kyō ni auramu	To lie so thick upon the tuber leaves?

5. *Kokorozukai*, "fretfulness," is a pivot word, since the last part contains the word *tsukai*, "messenger" (*zu* is a voiced variant of *tsu*), and this meaning forms a word association with *yukikaeru*, "pace back and forth."

Hitokazu ni
Kyō wa kasamashi
Karagoromo
Namida ni kuchinu
Tamoto nariseba

Today, like everybody else,
I would lend the Weaving Maid
My Chinese robe,
But for the moldering of its sleeves
From the dampness of my tears.

Hikoboshi no
Yukiai no sora o
Nagamete mo
Matsu koto mo naki
Ware zo kanashiki

Though I stare in reverie
At the sky where the Herd Boy
Goes to meet his love,
I, who have no man for whom to wait,
Am filled with grief.

Toshi o matanu
Sode dani nureshi
Shinonome ni
Omoi koso yare
Ama no hagoromo

In the dawn, which brings forth tears
To soak the sleeves even of those
Who do not have to wait a year to meet,
I imagine well the dampness
Of the Weaver's heavenly robe.

Aware to ya
Omoi mo suru to
Tanabata ni
Mi no nageki o mo
Ureetsuru kana

In the hope that she
Will think of me with pity
I make lament
To the Weaving Maid
And tell her of my grief.

Tanabata no
Iwa no makura wa
Koyoi koso
Namida kakaranu
Taema narurame

For the stony pillow
Of the Weaving Maid
Tonight at least
Will surely make an interlude
When it will not be splashed with tears.

Ikutabi ka
Yukikaeruramu
Tanabata no
Kureisogu ma no
Kokorozukai wa[5]

How many times
Does she pace back and forth
In fretfulness,
The Weaving Maid who tries
To hurry on the coming of the night?

248

6. There is a word association between *kasanu*, "mount, pile up," and *koromo*, "robe." The thought is more compressed and suggestively expressed in the Japanese, which uses an old image for the Weaving Maid's robe, *kumo no koromo*, "robe of clouds," as a metaphor for the rain clouds. This metaphor automatically leads to an identity of dew and rain, and the word "rain" is not necessary in the Japanese, where it is so clearly implied.

Hikoboshi no	This is the day
Aimiru kyō wa	The Herd Boy meets his love;
Naniyue ni	Yet why do we scoop the water for our bowls
Tori no wataranu	Before the birds have even built
Mizu musuburamu	Their bridge for him to cross the river?
Aware to ya	Surely the Weaving Maid
Tanabatatsume mo	Will feel the pity of it,
Omouran	This fate that denies to me
Ōse mo matanu	Even the long wait
Mi no chigiri oba	For a meeting with my love.
Tanabata ni	Today, perhaps the insects
Kyō ya kasuran	Will lend the Weaving Maid those robes
Nobe goto ni	That in every field
Midareoru naru	The loud confusion of their cries
Mushi no koromo mo	Proclaims them to be weaving.
Itouramu	I know not what aversion
Kokoro mo shirazu	May be in her heart,
Tanabata ni	But I shall behave as others do
Namida no sode o	And lend the Weaving Maid my robe,
Hitonami ni kasu	Soaked though its sleeves may be with tears.
Nanigoto o	What words will he first say,
Mazu kataruramu	The Herd Boy to his love,
Hikoboshi no	As he lays his head with hers
Ama no kawara ni	Upon the stony pillow
Iwamakura shite	On the Heavenly River's bank?
Tanabata no	Their love unsatisfied,
Akanu wakare no	The two stars part—
Namida ni ya	Can it be the dew of tears
Kumo no koromo no	Covering the robe of the Weaving Maid,
Tsuyu kasanuran[6]	This rain that fills the clouds?

7. *Kuru* (*kureba*), "to grow dark," can also mean "to reel, spin thread" and thus forms word associations with *ito*, "thread," *tayu* (*taen*) "break," and *nagaki*, "long."

Nanigoto mo	In all this world
Kawarihatenuru	Where nothing now
Yo no naka ni	Remains unchanged,
Chigiri tagawanu	Their pledge goes on unbroken,
Hoshiai no sora	And the stars meet in the sky.

Kyō kureba	As twilight falls tonight
Kusaba ni kakuru	I drape upon the leaves
Ito yori mo	These offerings of thread.
Nagaki chigiri wa	Longer even than that thread,
Taen mono ka wa⁷	Could their promise ever end?

Kokoro to zo	It was of their own accord
Mare ni chigirishi	They made the pledge
Naka nareba	That they would seldom meet,
Urami mo seji na	So surely they cannot resent
Awanu taema o	The intervals when they must be apart.

Aware to mo	To make the Weaving Maid
Katsu wa miyo tote	See how I, myself,
Tanabata ni	Am also sunk in grief,
Namida sanagara	I take off my robe to lend to her,
Nugite kashitsuru	Drenched though it is with tears.

Ama no gawa	When the lovers meet tonight
Kyō no ōse wa	Across the River of Heaven,
Yoso naredo	It is no concern of mine,
Kureyuku sora o	And yet I wait with eagerness
Nao mo matsu kana	For dusk to steal across the sky.

Urayamashi	How I envy them!
Koi ni taetaru	For their hearts are strong
Hoshi nare ya	To endure the pangs of love,
Toshi ni hitoyo to	If they can pledge themselves
Chigiru kokoro wa	For only one night in the year.

8. The expression *ama no to*, literally "the door of heaven," is a common image for the dawn and leads to a double meaning of *aku* (*akeyuku*), "to dawn" and "to open."

9. *Koke*, "moss," is closely associated with *iwa*, "rock."

10. Based on an anonymous poem, *Shūishū* 722:

Itsu shi ka to	As I wait and wait
Kure o matsu ma no	Impatient for the evening,
Ōzora wa	Wondering when it will come,
Kumoru sae koso	The vast sky dims with cloud,
Ureshikarikere	And even that is cause for joy.

11. Based on an anonymous poem, *Kokinshū* 488:

Waga koi wa	It seems my love
Munashiki sora ni	Has covered over
Michinurashi	All the empty sky,
Omoiyaredomo	For though I try to ease my thoughts,
Yuku kata mo nashi	There is nowhere they can go.

Ai ni aite	They meet at long last;
Mada mutsugoto mo	Yet before they can exhaust
Tsukiji yo ni	Their tender words of love
Utate akeyuku	The dawn breaks cruelly through the night,
Ama no to zo uki[8]	And now how hateful is the rising of the sun.
Uchiharau	Soaked they must be
Sode ya tsuyukeki	With a dew of tears,
Iwamakura	The sleeves that now wipe clean
Koke no chiri nomi	The rocky pillow
Fukaku tsumorite[9]	Where dust alone lies thick upon the moss.
Kumoru sae	Even as the sky
Ureshikaruran	Grows dark with cloud
Hikoboshi no	He must feel joy:
Kokoro no uchi o	I can imagine what the Herd Boy
Omoi koso yare[10]	Feels within his breast.
Yoi no ma ni	Early in the evening
Irinishi tsuki no	The moon sets; its brief light
Kage made mo	Must make more bitter still
Akanu kokoro ya	All the frustration
Fukaki tanabata	That the Weaving Maid feels in her heart.
Tanabata no	Such is the outcome of my life
Chigiri nagekishi	That I, who used to grieve
Mi no hate wa	At the fate of the Weaving Maid,
Ōse o yoso ni	Now hear of the lovers' rendezvous
Kikiwataritsutsu	As something of no interest to myself.
Nagamureba	In distraction I gaze up,
Kokoro mo tsukite	And my heart is void,
Hoshiai no	But the sky where the two stars meet
Sora ni michinuru	Has now grown full
Waga omoi kana[11]	Of my own thoughts.

254

12. There is a double meaning in *tachiwakare*, "to depart, separate," since *tachi* can also mean "cut out (cloth)" and is thus associated with *hagoromo*, "robe."

13. The Taira flight from the capital, the last time Lady Daibu saw Sukemori, took place in the seventh month, the month of the Tanabata Festival, and also the first month of autumn.

Tsuyukesa wa	Deeper than the dew
Aki no nobe ni mo	That lies on the autumn fields
Masarurashi	Must be the dew of tears
Tachiwakareyuku	That, at the lovers' parting,
Ama no hagoromo[12]	Falls on her heavenly robe.

Hikoboshi no	In his heart the Herd Boy
Omou kokoro wa	Must be wondering how,
Yo fukakute	While still in the depths of night,
Ika ni akenuru	The gate of heaven could have opened
Ama no to naramu	To admit the dawn.

Tanabata no	Would that the autumn wind
Aimiru yoi no	That blows this evening
Akikaze ni	When the Weaving Maid meets with her love
Mono omou sode no	Might dry this dew of tears,
Tsuyu harawanan	Which anguished thoughts make fall upon my sleeves.

Aki goto ni	Surely the stars will see
Wakareshi koro to	What is in my heart
Omoiizuru	As I recall each autumn
Kokoro no uchi o	That this was the very season
Hoshi wa miruran[13]	When I parted from my love.

Tanabata ni	Though I lament,
Kokoro wa kashite	Though I feel sympathy
Nageku to mo	For the sadness of the Weaving Maid,
Kakaru omoi o	Not in the least can I describe to her
E shi mo kataranu	The torment of my own unhappy heart.

Yo no naka wa	This world has come to be
Mishi ni mo arazu	No longer as I once knew it,
Narinuru ni	And yet the sky
Omogawarisenu	Where the two stars meet tonight
Hoshiai no sora	Looks as of old, unchanged.

14. *Utakata* is a pivot word in which the first half, *uta*, means "poem,"
while the whole word means "foam."

Kasanete mo	Though her heavenly robe
Nao ya tsuyukeki	Is piled in sleep upon her lover's,
Hodo mo naku	Shortly their sleeves must part—
Sode wakarubeki	How damp they must be
Ama no hagoromo	With the dew of tears!
Omou koto	Though I write my thoughts
Kakedo tsukisenu	Each year on these mulberry leaves,
Kaji no ha ni	Never can I exhaust my grief.
Kyō ni ainuru	Would that I might know why
Yue o shirabaya	I live on to do the same today!
Yoshi kasaji	So be it! I shall not lend my robe,
Kakaru uki mi no	For such is my wretchedness
Koromode wa	That my sleeves are drenched,
Tanabatatsume ni	And no doubt the Weaving Maid
Imare mo zo suru	Will turn from them in disgust.
Kata bakari	Only in form I write
Kakite tamukuru	And offer up these poems
Utakata o	From one who is shorter-lived than foam.
Futatsu no hoshi no	With what thoughts will the two stars
Ikaga miruramu[14]	Look upon my words?
Nani to naku	Deep in the night
Yowa no aware ni	A sadness indefinable
Sode nurete	Brings dampness to my sleeves—
Nagame zo kanuru	And no longer can I contemplate
Hoshiai no sora	The sky where the two stars meet.
E zo shiranu	I cannot understand!
Shinobu yue naki	The Herd Boy had no cause
Hikoboshi no	To bear the pains of separated love.
Mare ni chigirite	Yet he promised such rare meetings
Nageku kokoro o	And now he fills his heart with grief.

258

15. "Crossing" (*watari*) refers, of course, to Sukemori's death. The word is associated with *kawa*, "river."

16. The first line, *hiku ito no*, "like thread that I draw out," is a rhetorical introduction to *tada hitosuji*, "single-minded and intense," through a pivot on *hitosuji*, which can also mean "a single strand (of thread)." *Suji*, "strand," and *ito*, "thread," are associated.

17. This interpretation follows Kubota ("Hyōshaku," 26: 177), whereas other commentators interpret the poem as follows:

> How long shall I go on
> Writing the seven poems
> Of the Festival?
> If you know, tell me,
> Herd Boy of the heavens!

The problem lies in the word *shirabaya*, the ending of which may be construed as the desiderative suffix *baya*, giving the meaning "Would that I knew," or as the conditional ending *ba* followed by an exclamatory particle *ya*, giving the meaning "If you know." The first interpretation seems grammatically more natural and gives the poem more of the "cry from the heart" that is characteristic of Lady Daibu.

Nagekite mo	Though she laments, she can still rely
Ōse o tanomu	On a meeting with her love
Ama no gawa	Across the River of Heaven.
Kono watari koso	The crossing that parts me from my love
Kanashikarikere[15]	Is truly cause for grief.

Kakitsukeba	When I write things down,
Nao mo tsutsumashi	Reserve holds back my words.
Omoi nageku	But, Weaving Maid,
Kokoro no uchi o	I wish that you could know
Hoshi yo shiranan	My heart and all its anguished thoughts.

Hiku ito no	Like the single strands of thread
Tada hitosuji ni	That I draw out as my offerings,
Koikoite	Their love is single-minded and intense.
Koyoi ōse mo	Oh, how I envy them
Urayamaretsutsu[16]	The tryst that is theirs this night!

Tagui naki	The Weaving Maid, perhaps,
Nageki ni shizumu	Will shun these words
Hito zo tote	That I write for her,
Kono koto no ha o	Looking on me as one
Hoshi ya itowan	Sunk in misery beyond compare.

Yoshi ya mata	Well then, Weaving Maid,
Nagusamekawase	Let us each one from the other
Tanabata yo	Take our consolation
Kakaru omoi ni	For hearts that wander
Mayou kokoro o	In the midst of such unhappy thoughts.

I thought each year would be my last, yet the number of years has gone on piling up:

Itsu made ka	Would that I knew
Nanatsu no uta o	How long I shall go on
Kakitsuken	Writing the seven poems
Shirabaya tsuge yo	Of the Festival.
Ama no hikoboshi[17]	Oh, tell me, Herd Boy of the heavens!

Part Six

I had been convinced ever since I was young that my life had little point to it, and now I hated it for dragging on when I had no desire to live. I need hardly add that I had no thought at all of mixing with society. However, some well-connected people made arrangements for me that I could not refuse, and unexpectedly after so many years, I found myself once again at court. This was a fate entirely unforeseen, and one to which in the depths of my heart I could never reconcile myself.

When I looked towards the Wisteria Hall, I could only recollect unhappily how I had lived there of old. The furnishings and the whole appearance of the court were the same as ever; the only change was the increasing sadness in my heart. How miserable I was! As I gazed at the unobscured moon, memories never failed to well up in me, and then my eyes would be dimmed with tears.

Those whom I had known in the old days as courtiers of no great eminence were now in the highest ranks, and I could not help imagining constantly how things might have been if Sukemori had only lived. I now felt even more heartbroken and

1. Emperor Gotoba (1180–1239; r. 1184–98), fourth son of Emperor Taka-kura.

2. On the Gosechi Celebrations, see Part Three, note 9. The banquet, known as *gosechi no enzui*, was held in the palace on the second day of the celebrations (the day of the tiger) and was for all courtiers who were permitted into the Imperial Audience Chamber (collectively known as *tenjōbito*), up to and including the First Secretaries of the Emperor's Private Office, which effectively meant courtiers of the fourth and fifth ranks. The word *enzui* means something like a carousal or revelry, and was used for a number of such banquets following court festivals. The banquets seem to have been rather like modern Japanese parties, consisting mainly of heavy drinking and singing.

3. "Shirausuyō," a song traditionally performed at the *gosechi no enzui*.

4. There were two famous clumps of bamboo in the garden in front of (i.e. on the east side of) the Emperor's Apartments (Seiryōden), one at the northern end and one at the southern.

miserable than before I had come to court. Was there anything that could compare with this?

The Emperor[1] bore a very strong resemblance to the late Retired Emperor Takakura. The sight of him set me longing unbearably in the solitary depths of my own insignificant heart for all that was past. Catching sight of the moon, I wrote:

Ima wa tada	Still now by force alone
Shiite wasururu	I banish from my mind
Inishie o	Those times of old—
Omoiide yo to	But it bids me to remember them,
Sumeru tsukikage	The tranquil brightness of the moon.

At the time of the Gosechi Celebrations, the banquet for the junior courtiers was being held in the Empress's Apartments.[2] The moon still hung in the frosty dawn, as I heard voices singing the song "Thin White Paper."[3] How could I help reminiscing of the way I once used to listen to that song year after year?

Shimo sayuru	When I hear the voices
Shirausuyō no	Singing "Thin White Paper,"
Koe kikeba	Clear in the crisp frost,
Arishi kumoi zo	The court I once knew, distant as the clouds,
Mazu oboekeru	Comes before all else to mind.

As I let my mind drift on, absorbed in my various cares, I glanced outside and saw a spotted dog scampering round the base of one of the bamboo clumps.[4] It looked just like a dog that had lived in the Emperor's Apartments in the old days. Whenever I had gone there on an errand, I had called it to me and draped my sleeves over it. It had always recognized me and used to frisk about wagging its tail. Now, at the sight of this new dog, a vague sorrow came over me:

264

5. This is the festival known as *tango no sechie*. See Part Three, note 37. A palanquin loaded with irises was placed on either side of the steps leading up to the Great Hall of State.

6. *Ukine* is a double pivot word: *uki* means "grief" and "mud"; and *ne* means "root" and "cries, sobs." Hence the word means both "mud-covered roots" and "sobs of grief." Iris roots were hung on the sleeves, and from this there is a suggestion of tears falling on the sleeves.

7. Goshirakawa reigned from only 1155 to 1158 but exercised power as a Retired Emperor (*in*) until his death in 1192. Sukemori was a First Secretary for the six months preceding his flight from the capital in August 1183.

Inu wa nao	This dog is, after all,
Sugata mo mishi ni	The very image
Kayoikeri	Of the one I knew;
Hito no keshiki zo	But people's faces bear no likeness
Arishi ni mo ninu	To what once they were.

There must have been people around who had lived through or at least knew something of those times, but I had no way of arranging to talk to them. I could only continue to brood in my own heart, unable to relieve my sorrow:

Waga omou	Oh, for some companion
Kokoro ni nitaru	Whose thoughts would match
Tomo mogana	Those that are in my heart!
So yo ya to dani mo	Then we might share our stories,
Katariawasen	Were it but to say, "Yes, thus it was."

On the fifth day of the fifth month the ceremonial palanquins piled with irises had been placed as usual near the steps of the Hall of State, and with the decorations on the eaves of the building, it all looked just as it had of old:[5]

Ayame fuku	Decked with irises, the eaves
Nokiba mo mishi ni	Have the same look as they had of old.
Kawaranu o	But sad are my sleeves,
Ukine no kakaru	Adorned with mud-covered roots
Sode zo kanashiki[6]	And heavy with cries of grief.

I once heard an official giving judgment on a lawsuit that someone had brought before the court. Referring to a pronouncement from the time of Retired Emperor Goshirakawa, he said that it had been written down by Sukemori when he had been a First Secretary to the Emperor[7]—he whom I now looked on as part of a dream from which I had not yet awakened! How were my feelings to remain calm, as I heard that name?

8. Fujiwara no Takafusa. See Part One, note 20.

9. This poem has the same pivot word as Poem 326. See note 6. *Ne,* "sobs," is associated with *namida,* "tears."

10. In addition to the pivot word *ukine,* there is a pivot word in *ayame,* which means iris (or sweet flag; see Part Three, note 37), and contains the word *aya,* "pattern, discernment."

11. Fujiwara no Sanemune. See Part One, note 5. His death occurred on the eighth of the twelfth month of Kenryaku 2 (Jan. 1, 1213) and is the latest datable event in the *Memoirs* with the exception of the epilogue. Sanemune's son Kintsune was born in 1171 and died in 1244.

Mizu no awa to	The name of him
Kienishi hito no	Who vanished as the foam
Na bakari o	Upon the waters—
Sasuga ni tomete	Merely to hear it lingering on
Kiku mo kanashiki	Is misery itself.

Omokage mo	His image, his name,
Sono na mo saraba	If only they were gone!
Kie mo sede	But every time
Kikimirugoto ni	I see and hear them, still unfaded,
Kokoro madowasu	What turmoil is in my heart!

Ukarikeru	A bitter dream
Yume no chigiri no	Is the fate that binds me to him
Mi o sarade	And will not let me be:
Samuru yo mo naki	No moment is there when I wake from it;
Nageki nomi suru	No course is there for me but grief.

When Counsellor Takafusa[8] was confined to his house because of some misfortune, I sent him this poem of condolence on the fifth day of the fifth month, for he was a person to whom I could quite easily speak of the past:

Tsuki mo senu	As well as iris roots,
Ukine wa sode ni	I also hang upon my sleeves
Kakenagara	My endless sobs of grief,
Yoso no namida o	But I think with feeling too
Omoiyaru kana[9]	Of your tears unseen.

His reply:

Kakenagara	As you adorn yourself
Ukine ni tsukete	With iris roots, amid your sobs of grief,
Omoiyare	Think what is in my heart,
Ayame mo shirazu	For I know nothing of irises,
Kurasu kokoro o[10]	In such distraction do I spend my days.

When the Ōmiya Grand Minister passed away, his son Counsellor Kintsune[11] secluded himself in mourning and did not pre-

12. On the Feast of Abounding Light, see Part Three, note 115. *Kokoro no yami*, "darkness of the heart," is a common expression for the deep attachment between parents and children, which impeded their chances of Buddhist salvation.

13. Taira no Chikamune (1144–99), brother-in-law of Kiyomori and hence well known to Lady Daibu, but not involved in the Taira downfall. Like his father, Chikanaga, mentioned in the next sentence, rose to high position; his dates are unknown.

sent himself at the palace even for the Gosechi Celebrations.
On behalf of someone who was sending him a message, I wrote
this poem on thin white paper decorated with a pattern of
combs:

Mayouran	We feel for you
Kokoro no yami o	In the darkness of your heart,
Omou kana	As it wanders lost—
Toyo no akari no	Even amidst the brightness
Sayaka naru koro[12]	Of the Feast of Abounding Light.

His reply:

Kakikumoru	Even this darkness
Yami mo yoso ni zo	That wraps me in its shroud
Narinubeki	Is sure to be lifted from me,
Toyo no akari ni	For glimmers now reach through
Honomekasarete	From the Feast of Abounding Light.

The death of Counsellor Chikamune[13] affected me deeply,
for he was someone I had known closely in my early days. So
towards the end of the ninth month I sent the following poems
to his son Chikanaga. The sky, filled with the rain of late autumn, brought forth many melancholy thoughts that were almost too much to endure, and I could well imagine how he
felt, in his dark robes of mourning:

Kuraki ame no	At the sound of dark rain
Mado utsu oto ni	Beating at the window,
Nezame shite	I wake from sleep,
Hito no omoi o	And I think of you
Omoi koso yare	And what is in your heart.

Tsuyukesa no	I think of you,
Nageku sugata ni	Also of the flowers
Mayouramu	Drenched in dew,
Hana no ue made	Which you misapprehend, no doubt,
Omoi koso yare	For the shapes of weeping men.

14. *Shigeki* is a pivot word meaning "numerous" and "dense (growth of plants)." *Nageki*, "laments," is also a pivot word, since its last syllable *ki*, means "trees"; it is thus modified by each of the meanings of *shigeki* in turn. There are word associations between *tsuyu*, "dew," *kusaba*, "grasses," *uragarete*, "withered away," *shigeki*, and *ki*.

15. *Karetsutsu* is a pivot word meaning both "departed" and "withered." In the second sense it forms word associations with *ueokishi*, "planted," *hana*, "flowers," and *chiru*, "scatter."

Tsuyu kieshi　　　　　Withered away now
Niwa no kusaba wa　　Are the grasses of that garden
Uragarete　　　　　　Where the dew has vanished,
Shigeki nageki o　　　But my thoughts dwell
Omoi koso yare[14]　　On the dense growth of regrets.

Wabishira ni　　　　　Under the night rain
Mashira dani naku　　When even the monkeys
Yoru no ame ni　　　Raise their cries of desolation,
Hito no kokoro o　　　I think of the feelings
Omoi koso yare　　　In your heart.

Kimi ga koto　　　　At the end, the very end
Nagekinageki no　　　Of my grieving grief,
Hatehate wa　　　　I gaze in reverie;
Uchinagametsutsu　　And I think of you
Omoi koso yare　　　And what is in your heart.

Mata mo kon　　　　It will come again,
Aki no kure oba　　　So I shall not grieve
Oshimaji na　　　　For autumn's passing;
Kaeranu michi no　　We have partings on that road
Wakare dani koso　　Along which no one shall return.

His replies:

Itabisashi　　　　　In the wood-planked gallery
Shigure bakari wa　　The only sounds
Otozurete　　　　　Are those of the autumn rain.
Hitome mare naru　　How desolate this house,
Yado zo kanashiki　　Where visitors come rarely.

Ueokishi　　　　　Gone is the master
Nushi wa karetsutsu　Who planted them,
Iroiro no　　　　　And as I watch,
Hana sae chiru o　　The many bright flowers scatter too,
Miru zo kanashiki[15]　To leave me desolate.

16. Between this poem and the next, the GSRJ text includes an additional poem:

> Aki no niwa   In the autumn garden
> Harawanu yado ni   Where the broom has now been stilled,
> Ato taete   All trace of man is gone.
> Koke nomi fukaku   Only the moss grows deep,
> Naru zo kanashiki   Bringing me desolation.

17. This poem is not a reply to any of the ones Lady Daibu sent, and at the time of Chikamune's death, Chikanaga was not of the correct rank to wear a robe of gardenia yellow, which suggests the poem may be spurious.

18. One of the two nights of the year considered especially good for viewing the moon. The other, as noted earlier, was the fifteenth of the eighth month.

19. Daibandokoro, a room at the rear of the Emperor's Apartments used for the preparation of food and as a duty room for ladies-in-waiting.

Harema naki	No break is there
Uree no kumo ni	In these clouds of grief;
Itsu to naku	And the ceaseless falling
Namida no ame no	Of the rain of tears
Furu zo kanashiki[16]	Fills me with desolation.
Yomosugara	The whole night I pass
Nagekiakaseba	In vigil with my grief,
Akatsuki ni	Then through the dawn I hear
Mashi no hitokoe	The monkey's solitary cry—
Kiku zo kanashiki	How desolate it is!
Kuchinashi no	Changing my robe
Hanairogoromo	Of bright gardenia yellow,
Nugikaete	I put on the mourning sleeves
Fuji no tamoto ni	Of wisteria's somber hue—
Naru zo kanashiki[17]	How desolate it is!
Omouramu	Griefs of your own
Yowa no nageki mo	Must surely fill your heart
Aru mono o	In the depths of night,
Tou koto no ha o	Yet you send words of consolation.
Miru zo kanashiki	As I gaze at them, how desolate I am!
Kurenutomo	Would we had means to turn
Mata mo aubeki	These partings from one another
Aki ni dani	Into a mere autumn season,
Hito no wakare o	Which, though it pass away,
Nasu yoshi mogana	Will visit us again.

The thirteenth night of the ninth month was fine and clear, just as tradition demanded.[18] Chikanaga had no time to spare from his duties and did not look as though he was going to relax that evening. But suddenly he turned to one side and scribbled on a small scrap of paper; then, pushing his way through the young people gathered in the Table Room,[19] he came up behind me, drew out a poem from the front of his robe, and gave it to me:

20. *Nagatsuki*, "the month of long (nights)," is the name of the ninth month and functions as a pivot word: its first part, *naga*, "long," is read with the word *yo*, "night." *Miyo* is a pivot word meaning "see, look at" (imperative) and "three nights" or "third night," in which sense it is read with *tōka amari*, "past ten," of the preceding line, to give "three nights past ten," the normal expression for "thirteenth night."

21. There is the same pivot on *nagatsuki* as in the preceding poem. *Yoshi* is also a pivot word: it means "well may it be (bright)" and "even if," and thus completes the first half of the poem and begins the second half. There are two conceits in this poem: if the moon sees Lady Daibu being so miserable, it will hide itself in cloud; the dimming of Lady Daibu's eyes by tears is compared, as so often before, to the dimming of the sky by clouds.

22. Minamoto no Michimune (1167–97). His full title is Captain Imperial Advisor (*saishō chūjō*).

23. Reeds were well known for making a noise when stirred by the slightest wind, and were often used in such similes as this one.

24. A place just to the south of the capital, where Michimune had a villa.

Na ni shi ou	True to its name
Yo o nagatsuki no	Is this thirteenth night,
Tōka amari	Long in the month of long nights.
Kimi miyo tote ya	And is it just to bid you gaze at it
Tsuki mo sayakeki[20]	That the moon shines with such limpid radiance?

My reply:

Na ni takaki	Bright it may be,
Yo o nagatsuki no	The moon on this night of high renown,
Tsuki wa yoshi	Long in the month of long nights;
Uki mi ni mieba	Yet were it looked on by this wretched self,
Kumori mo zo suru[21]	It would be dimmed in cloud.

Imperial Advisor Michimune[22] was always coming to the palace and calling for ladies-in-waiting, but they would be some little way off and unable to go to him immediately. "What should I do, when I want to talk to ladies-in-waiting?" he complained. So I told him that as long as he coughed in front of my curtain, I would be sure to hear him. "That doesn't sound likely!" he said, to which I replied that I was always on duty at this one spot and never left it day or night.

Sometime after that, I was told that one morning he had presented himself at that spot so early the dew had not even dried. So I then sent off a messenger with the following poem and instructions to follow Michimune wherever he might have gone:

Ogi no ha ni	I am not one to whisper
Aranu mi nareba	Hastily, like leaves of reeds,
Oto mo sede	So without a sound I watched.
Miru o mo minu to	Yet it would seem
Omou narubeshi[23]	You thought I saw you not!

Having quickly discovered that Michimune had gone to Koga,[24] the messenger delivered the letter and started back.

25. One of the imperial detached palaces, situated between Koga and the capital.

Michimune sent a servant after him, but I had told the messenger that he was on no account to accept a reply. He had been pursued as far as the south gate of the Toba Palace,[25] but there had escaped into a thicket, getting himself caught up in briars as he did so; and he had finally hidden among some baggage carts. When he reported this to me, I told him how well he had done.

Afterwards, Michimune contended that he had seen no such letter. He also maintained that though he had come, there had been no one behind my curtain, so he had just gone away again. I objected to this. I had been sitting there motionless and watching him, I said, but he had left too hastily. And so the time of the Gosechi Celebrations came around, but there were still ladies who did nothing but tease him about the incident.

On the night of the Feast of Abounding Light he came to the palace as the moon shone down through the clear and frosty dawn. He looked magnificent. But not long after that he was dead. It was so pathetic, so depressing. Later on, people always said that the moon, which had lingered in the sky that morning, and even the shapes of the clouds were something to remember him by:

Omoiizuru	Memories return with it,
Kokoro mo ge ni zo	And our hearts in truth
Tsukihatsuru	Are full to breaking;
Nagori todomuru	It holds remembrances of him,
Ariake no tsuki	The moon that lingers in the dawn.

These reflections also made me write:

Kagiri arite	Even when life ends
Tsukuru inochi wa	At its ordained and natural time,
Ikaga sen	What can we do?
Mukashi no yume zo	That ancient dream of mine, then,
Nao tagui naki	Is indeed unique!

26. This birthday party is well documented. It took place on the twenty-third of the eleventh month of Kennin 3 (Dec. 27, 1203) at Retired Emperor Gotoba's palace in the second ward of the capital. Fujiwara no Toshinari (1114–1204, also known as Fujiwara no Shunzei) was the greatest poet of his generation and the chief arbiter of poetic taste until his death. His full title here is *gojō no sanmi nyūdō*, Third Rank Lay Priest of the Fifth Ward.

27. A well-known poet of her day. Her dates are unknown, but she is thought to have died in 1204 or soon after. Her father, Minamoto no Moromitsu (dates unknown), was also a well-known poet.

28. *Kesa* is a pivot word meaning "this morning" and "stole."

29. The translation is more explanatory than the original Japanese, which merely says: "*zo* of *kesa zo* [this morning] should have been *ya*, and *n* of *tsukaen* [I shall serve] should have been *yo*." The alterations change the poetic speaker from Toshinari to Retired Emperor Gotoba and make the poem an imperial command to Toshinari to live yet longer. The altered poem is as follows:

Nagaraete	For your long life
Kesa ya ureshiki	You must be pleased this day!
Oi no nami	Serve your Lord
Yachiyo o kakete	Through a thousand ages,
Kimi ni tsukaeyo	As your years mount like the waves!

30. Fujiwara no Norimitsu (1154–1213), a successful courtier and something of a scholar.

Tsuyu to kie	At least with those
Keburi to mo naru	Who vanish as the dew
Hito wa nao	Or turn to smoke of pyres,
Hakanaki ato o	We may gaze in our distraction
Nagame mo suramu	At reminders of their death.

Omoiizuru	Whenever I hear of one
Koto nomi zo tada	Who dies an ordinary death,
Tameshi naki	It seems to me
Nabete hakanaki	Mine are the only memories
Koto o kiku ni mo	So utterly beyond compare.

It must have been just after the twentieth of the eleventh month in the third year of Kennin [1203] that the Retired Emperor, having heard that Lay Priest Toshinari was going to be ninety years old, arranged a celebration.[26] The formal Buddhist stole that would be presented to Toshinari was to bear a poem, and Lady Kunaikyō,[27] the daughter of Lay Priest Moromitsu, was asked to compose it. At the request of the Retired Emperor himself, I embroidered the poem on the stole in purple thread. This was how it ran:

Nagaraete	For my long life
Kesa zo ureshiki	How pleased I am this day!
Oi no nami	Though my years mount like the waves,
Yachiyo o kakete	I shall serve My Lord
Kimi ni tsukaen[28]	For a thousand ages.

Secretly, I felt that if it was meant to be a poem from the person who was receiving the gift, it ought to have been a little better. It was supposed to be embroidered just as it was, however, so that was the way I did it.

But late on the evening of the celebration, a message came from the Retired Emperor to say that the poem would have to be changed, since it should have read as a poem from him to Lay Priest Toshinari.[29] I was to go to the palace in the second ward, using Counsellor Norimitsu's[30] carriage. When I

arrived, I reembroidered the necessary syllables. I thought that while I was there I would like to see the celebration, so I stayed the whole night through to watch. Memories of old came back to me, and I thought what an extraordinary honor this was for the art of poetry.

The next day I wrote to Lay Priest Toshinari to tell him of my feelings:

Kimi zo nao	Still more, My Lord,
Kyō yori nochi mo	From this day forward
Kazoubeki	The course of your life to come
Kokonokaeri no	Shall number yet again
Tō no yukusue	Nine times ten years.

In his reply he said: "Because of His Majesty's most gracious summons, I came crawling to the palace, feeling how repulsive I must appear to everyone. But when I receive a message of congratulation such as yours, I realize that there are those who know about my younger days and really understand things. Then there are those who are ignorant. The two are truly not the same!"

Kameyama no	Nine times one thousand years
Kokonokaeri no	On the Mount of Immortality
Chitose o mo	I would relinquish,
Kimi ga miyo ni zo	Could I but add them to the reign
Soeyuzurubeki	Of His Gracious Majesty.

1. In the GSRJ and other texts the second line reads *omoi no hoka no,* "beyond imagining." The first two lines of the translation would then read "Heartrending grief / beyond imagining." One argument in favor of this reading is that Lady Daibu often uses the phrase *omoi no hoka* in connection with her circumstances, and its use here would create a last echo in the work.

Conclusion

Though life has brought me nothing but painful recollections one after another, the years have piled upon me, and in the course of this vain existence I have written down little by little those things that have chanced to come to mind. Once in a while people would ask me whether I had any such writings, but what I had written was so much my own personal thoughts that I felt embarrassed, and I would copy out just a little to show to them. I wrote these things, intending that my eyes alone should look on them; and now, as I gaze at them years later, I feel:

Kudakikeru	Grief enough
Omoi no hodo no	To break one's heart!
Kanashiki ni	Yet as I gather up my thoughts
Kakiatsumete zo	To write them down,
Sara ni shiraruru[1]	I feel the pain anew.

1. *Minbukyō* is the title used.

2. Fujiwara no Sadaie (1162–1241, also known as Fujiwara no Teika) was a son of Toshinari and like his father before him, the greatest poet and the poetic arbiter of his generation. The collection of poems referred to is the *Shinchokusenshū*, the ninth imperial anthology, which was commanded in 1232 and completed in 1235.

3. In its second meaning of "leaves" the *ha* of *koto no ha*, "words," is associated with *chiru* (*chiraba*), "scatter."

Epilogue

In my old age I was approached by Lord Sadaie, the Minister of Civil Affairs,[1] who told me he was making a collection of poems and asked if I had anything suitable already written down.[2] I was most grateful for this kindness of his in thinking of me as a poet along with all the others; but I was even more moved by his consideration in asking under what name I would like to be known. I could not forget that past, which was now so far away from us, so of course I replied, "Just as I was known in those days."

Koto no ha no	*If my words, like leaves,*
Moshi yo ni chiraba	*Should scatter through the world,*
Shinobashiki	*Would that I might leave behind*
Mukashi no na koso	*The name that was mine*
Tomemahoshikere[3]	*In the unforgettable days of old.*

He replied:

Onajiku wa	*If it is all the same,*
Kokoro tomekeru	*Let us bequeath*
Inishie no	*To worlds that are yet to come*
Sono na o sara ni	*That name from days of old,*
Yo ni nokosanan	*To which your heart still clings.*

At that I felt so happy.

Appendixes

Appendix A
The Date of Compilation

There are many theories, all unfortunately inconclusive, about the date and the process of compilation of the *Memoirs*, which I will briefly summarize here. No scholar today believes that Lady Daibu compiled her *Memoirs* suddenly and in one step when Fujiwara no Sadaie asked her for contributions to the *Shinchokusenshū* in 1232.[1] The exchange has the unmistakable air of an epilogue added quite some time after the completion of the work proper; the wording of the conclusion implies that Lady Daibu already had ordered material to hand, from which she would make excerpts as necessary; the *Memoirs* differ considerably from the type of collection that would have been produced purely in response to such a request for poems; and there is a large gap in time between this exchange of poems and the latest datable poem in the *Memoirs* proper.[2] There can therefore be little doubt that the *Memoirs* proper were complete before this exchange with Sadaie. Moreover,

1. One troubling point in the dating of this exchange is Lady Daibu's reference to Sadaie as the Minister of Civil Affairs (*minbukyō*), a title he ceased to hold in 1227. But there are other instances in the *Memoirs* where she uses titles for people after they had officially relinquished them. There is certainly very strong circumstantial evidence that Sadaie was here asking for poems for the *Shinchokusenshū*, and no doubt at all that the command to compile the anthology was given in the sixth month of 1232. See *Zenshaku*, pp. 70–72; and Itō Yoshio et al., p. 562. The occasion and the dating of this exchange with Sadaie are therefore almost beyond question. be recalled in this connection. See Kusakabe, pp. 26–27.

2. Kusakabe's view that the epilogue was added by another hand may

since it is clear that the exchange must have taken place in late 1232 or early 1233, we at least have a conclusive date by which the *Memoirs* were completed.

The simplest view of compilation is that Lady Daibu composed her *Memoirs* immediately after the death of Retired Empress Kenreimon-in, which occurred in January 1214. This would explain why there is no poem that can be dated later than the end of 1213 (Poems 332 and 333). The death of the Retired Empress would have marked the final passing of the old days and would have been an understandable motive for working on the *Memoirs*.[3]

Most scholars suggest a more complex process of compilation, proposing that various parts of the *Memoirs* were written at various times. The most obvious theory is that the first volume was composed at a fairly early date, around 1183, and the second sometime after 1213.[4] A further break in compilation is also postulated at the end of Part Two, the section of poems on topics.[5] Another theory views the work as being completed through the end of Part Five (the Tanabata section) in one stage, around 1187 or 1188, with Part Six being added after 1213.[6]

The most complex theories suggest that the *Memoirs* were first written in an order quite different from the one we see today, beginning with the poems on Sukemori's death, then moving to other sections, whose raw material may already have been collected into some sort of rough order.[7] One of the scholars who is of this view proposes a further break in the middle of Part Six, between Poems 329 and 330.[8]

All of these theories are inconclusive, and all have the same

3. Tomikura 1942, p. 102; Shimada 1950, pp. 14–15.
4. Shinoda, pp. 82–89; Ikari 1964, pp. 1–11.
5. Ikari 1964, pp. 1–11.
6. *Zenshaku*, pp. 67–72; Hon-iden 1964, pp. 20–35.
7. Ōbayashi 1973, pp. 20–28; Hisatoku 1961a, p. 4.
8. Ōbayashi 1973, pp. 20–28.

weakness, namely, that they tend to interpret structural breaks as breaks in the process of writing. It is impossible in merely looking at the work as we have it today to decide whether a structural element is due to a conscious shaping by the author or to the manner of compilation, or both. To show that parts are structurally distinct is not to show that they were compiled at different times. Yet their subject matter and themes are different enough to account for different structure and treatment, even if they were composed at the same time.

One is on safer ground in dating individual poems and incidents, though the best that can be done is to discover the earliest that a particular poem or prose introduction, and hence the final version of a particular part, could have been written. All such dating in the *Memoirs* is done by reference to the use of titles or official posts for persons mentioned in the text. It can often be accurately determined when a title first came into use for a particular person and when it was relinquished. Unfortunately, the use of a title long after it had officially been relinquished cannot be ruled out, especially in a work such as Lady Daibu's, in which she may be casting her mind back over a considerable number of years; so the fact that a title was not officially used after a certain year is not proof that an entry in the *Memoirs* was not written after that date. On the other hand, official posts and titles are reliable in showing the earliest possible date that the extant version of a certain entry can have been written. The most significant discovery in this respect is that the title Ōinomikado Priestess, which is used for Princess Shikishi in the prose introduction to Poems 72 and 73, could not possibly have been in use before 1192 and, to judge from contemporary sources, was not actually used until 1196.[9] This means that Part Three was not completed in its present form until at least 1196, though a draft form may well have existed earlier.

An accurate dating of Parts Four and Five is impossible. Op-

9. *Ibid.*

posing theories have been advanced on the number of years covered by, and hence the probable date of, the section of Tanabata poems; and Part Four is generally considered to have been composed at the same time as this section.[10] But these theories, along with Murai Jun's tentative suggestion (on the basis of a single, rather unreliable source) that the collection was complete up to Part Six by 1206,[11] must be viewed with considerable doubt. In fact, the only thing we can say with certainty about the second volume is that Part Six was not compiled in its entirety until after 1213.

Not one of the theories put forward can be completely accepted or rejected. I myself am inclined to believe that Lady Daibu gathered her material over a period of time and had several drafts of different parts of her *Memoirs* before she arrived at the final form; and that she did begin with the material centering on Sukemori's death, then gradually brought in her other material to fill in the background and complete her story, eventually producing the sequence as we have it today, replete with introduction and conclusion.

Whatever view is taken of the process of compilation, all scholars tentatively agree that the *Memoirs* were completed in their present form, with the exception of the epilogue, between 1213 and 1219. A date before 1220 makes sense for at least two reasons. For one thing, the wording of the epilogue suggests a considerable interval between the completion of the work and the exchange with Sadaie. For another, it is generally felt that there cannot have been too long a gap between the compilation of the work and the latest event mentioned in it. Some would further argue that Lady Daibu would surely have mentioned the political upheavals of 1220 and 1221, years marked by the Jōkyū War and the banishment of Retired Emperor

10. Hon-iden 1964, pp. 20–35; Gotō 1971, pp. 7–18; Ōbayashi 1972, pp. 11–13.

11. Murai 1963, pp. 233–35.

Gotoba, had she compiled her collection after those events. This argument is a shaky one, however, since she persistently ignores events outside the narrow theme of her own personal losses. Consequently, even the final date of the work is in some doubt. But though a completion as late as 1233 is conceivable, the first reason given above seems to me to make a persuasive case for 1220 or a few years earlier.

Appendix B
Textual History

The textual history of Lady Daibu's *Memoirs* is relatively free of complications. Ikari Masashi, author of the only detailed and comprehensive textual study,[1] found no major variants among the almost 50 different manuscripts and old printed texts he studied. This account is based on Ikari's work, which is almost uniformly accepted at authoritative.[2]

Ikari distinguishes six basic types of text, which he groups into two families as follows:

Family A	Type 1: Kyūshū Daigaku Text; Kunaichō Text; Mukyūkai Text
	Type 2: Yoshimizu Jinja Text
	Type 3: Shōkōkan Text
Family B	Type 4: Kan-ei Printed Text
	Type 5: Tenri Text
	Type 6: Gunsho Ruijū Text

The texts listed for each type are the only important examples; other texts in the same category, if any, are either derivative

---

1. *Kenreimon-in Ukyō no Daibu shū: kōhon oyobi sōsakuin.* This book uses a dual pagination system; the numbers cited here are for the book as a whole.

2. Indeed, such is the recognition of Ikari's work that scholars tend to refrain from textual discussion and to accept his judgment on the most reliable text. Murai, for instance, follows Ikari in his choice of basic text, though he includes two poems found only in other texts and makes changes based on other texts where they seem to him desirable.

or of demonstrably less importance.[3] The Shōkōkan Text is the only extant example of Type 3, and there is only one other Type 2 text besides the Yoshimizu Jinja Text, a copy from the mid-Edo period (eighteenth century).

Ikari distinguishes these types primarily on the basis of the various colophons, and the differences and similarities in the texts.[4] Type 1 has a simple and straightforward colophon. Type 2 has no colophon, since the text consists only of Volume One of Lady Daibu's *Memoirs*. Type 3 has essentially the same colophon as Type 1, though with many additions showing further copyings and collations. Type 4 has a colophon that is quite different from the colophon of Type 1 and includes a genealogical table of the Sesonji family. Type 5 has no colophon, only a genealogical table like the one in Type 4. Type 6 has the same genealogical table followed by a distinctive short colophon.

Comparison of the texts themselves clarifies the distinctions between these types. Type 3 has sufficient textual differences from Type 1 to be called a type of its own. Type 2 merits its own separate classification because it lacks the second volume and because of textual differences from Type 1. However, it is classified as a Family A text because it possesses Poems 29–32, whose presence or absence is one of the distinguishing features of the textual families. Type 4 texts, with features of Type 1 and Poems 29–32, belong to Family A. But they also have features in common with Types 5 and 6, and thus in some ways fit into Family B. In addition, they have one distinctive feature of their own: they include two quotations from the *Azuma kagami* (c. 1266), a historical tale recounting the rise to power of Yoritomo. Types 5 and 6 share features quite different from other texts, so they form Family B. But, as noted, Type 6 texts have a colophon and Type 5 texts do not.[5]

3. For details on the minor texts, see under the various subheadings in Ikari 1969, pp. 3–92.

4. A chart showing the major points of similarity and difference is to be found in *ibid.*, pp. 8–10.

5. *Ibid.*, pp. 7–11 has details of the textual differences and similarities.

Of the six types outlined, Type 1 is shown by Ikari to be the line nearest to the original of Lady Daibu; and of the three important texts in this type, he considers the Kyūshū Daigaku Text to be the best and most reliable. The paper, brushwork, and format of the manuscript indicate that it is an early Muromachi (fourteenth century) copy, making it one of the two oldest extant texts (the Yoshimizu Jinja Text is also from the early Muromachi period). The colophon of the Kyūshū Daigaku Text reads as follows:

Transmission of the text:

THE COLLECTION OF KENREIMON-IN UKYO NO DAIBU

This book is said to have been copied out by Shichijōin Dainagon, who was especially intimate with the author and was shown the author's own copy.
This copy was made on the second day of the second month of the second year of Shōgen [1260] from the text of Shōmeimon-in Kosaishō.

Therefore, if the colophon is to be believed, the Kyūshū Daigaku Text is in direct line from Lady Daibu's own copy. It is not clear whether Shōmeimon-in Kosaishō made a copy of Shichijōin Dainagon's text or received the actual text by inheritance or gift; the former is more likely, and the line of descent probably runs from Lady Daibu's own copy to Shichijōin Dainagon's to Shōmeimon-in Kosaishō's to the Shōgen copy and finally to the Kyūshū Daigaku Text. There were probably several recopyings between the Shōgen Text and the Kyūshū Daigaku Text in view of the interval of time between the Shōgen copying and the copying out of the Kyūshū Daigaku Text. But it is not inconceivable that the copyist of the Kyūshū Daigaku Text worked from the original Shōgen Text. With present sources this question cannot be decided; it is safer to assume several intervening copies.

One of the main criteria for establishing an authoritative text is the number of recopyings it has undergone. In this respect, the Kyūshū Daigaku Text is superior to the Kunaichō Text, which possesses the same colophon but with additions showing that it is at least the third copy after the Shōgen Text. Moreover, it is a late Edo manuscript and is therefore likely to be the product of numerous recopyings.

The Mukyūkai Text has the same colophon as the Kyūshū Daigaku Text except for the entries mentioning Shōmeimon-in Kosaishō or the Shōgen copying. This abbreviated colophon suggests the Mukyūkai Text is only once removed from the Shichijōin Dainagon Text. However, it dates from the late Edo period, and although age is not necessarily a criterion for authenticity, the earlier the manuscript, the less the opportunity for recopying; thus the Kyūshū Daigaku Text is probably nearer the original. Furthermore, the fact that the Mukyūkai Text has a very high incidence of *kanji*, or Chinese characters, rather than *kana*, or native Japanese syllabic signs, suggests considerable influence from late recopyings, during a time when *kana* tended to be replaced by *kanji*.

Apart from all this, one of the main reasons for preferring the Kyūshū Daigaku Text to others is the text itself. The writing is by the same hand throughout, except for the colophon, which appears to have been written by a different person, though at about the same time as the text proper. The standard of calligraphy is extremely high and there are few emendations (all made by the copyist himself, as far as can be judged). Ikari feels that this shows great care on the part of the copyist. His table of the mistakes in the various texts—omissions, superfluous characters, and errors of fact—indicates that the Kyūshū Daigaku Text has far fewer mistakes than any other, save for the Mukyūkai Text, which comes a close second.[6] The text of the Kunaichō Text is greatly inferior to the other two Type 1's, but is cited as representative and important because it appears to have had considerable influence on other types of text.[7]

Of the remaining texts, the most interesting, and perhaps the most important, is the Yoshimizu Jinja Text. In Ikari's

6. *Ibid.*, pp. 16, 17.
7. *Ibid.*, pp. 12–19, 30–32, has more detail about these manuscripts.

view, the number of corrections in the text, which appear to
have been made by the copyist himself, suggest that great care
was taken to obtain a correct copy. Moreover, since there are
very few alternative readings given, Ikari believes that the
copyist may have used only one text to copy from. He notes
approximately 160 points of difference between this text and
others that appear to be unique variations, suggesting that it
has a different ancestor from the texts that are descended
through the Shōgen copying. However, many of the differences
are such that it is difficult or impossible to decide which version is correct, and the text should be ranked with the Kyūshū
Daigaku Text in this respect, particularly in view of its age.
But though it is important for this reason and for the influence
it has apparently had on later texts of other types, it has the
serious disadvantage of lacking the second volume.

Ikari is inclined to believe that this text never had the other
volume, and that the text from which it was copied did not
have it, either. His arguments, however, are far from conclusive, and the best we can say is that this text existed in its
present form, without the second volume, by the late Edo period. Whether it originally had the other volume and lost it
at some time between the early Muromachi and late Edo periods, or whether the ancestors of this text were all without
the second volume or lost it at some stage of transmission is
impossible to decide.[8]

A more interesting question is the relationship of the Yoshimizu Jinja Text to the Kyūshū Daigaku Text. Ikari is of the
view that the Yoshimizu Jinja Text derives from an early unpolished version of the first volume. But its ancestor could have
been an early unpolished version of the collection, regardless
of whether it contained both volumes or only the first. The
variations between the volumes cited by Ikari, together with
his arguments, are quite convincing. But the evidence is not
conclusive.[9] Hon-iden, for one, disagrees with Ikari. He main-

8. *Ibid.*, pp. 36–41, has the details of Ikari's arguments.
9. *Ibid.*, pp. 38, 39, gives details of variations, and Ikari 1964, pp. 1–11,
gives details of his arguments.

tains that the Yoshimizu Jinja Text could be merely an ex-
cerpted version that Lady Daibu made from her finished copy,
in the manner she describes in her conclusion.[10] This problem
is unlikely to be solved, but in any event the Kyūshū Daigaku
version is unquestionably clearer or preferable in many cases,
which is what prompts Ikari to consider it the more polished
version.

The Shōkōkan Text is extremely unreliable, since it is rid-
dled with mistakes. But as a collation of many texts and a
heavily commented text, it is valuable in the study of the
work's history of textual criticism. Its ancestry seems to be
basically a mixture of Types 1, 2, and 5, and it dates from the
late Edo period.

The Kan-ei Printed Text, dating from Kan-ei 21 (1644), is
the first printed text of the *Memoirs* and gave rise to many
other printed texts and even manuscripts, all of them alike.
The special features of this type of text have been described
above. It is not a particularly good text, being a mixture of
other types, notably Types 1, 2, and 5. Ikari convincingly shows
that the Tenri Text (Type 5) influenced the Kan-ei Text, not
the reverse.[11]

The Tenri Text itself is of unclear ancestry. It bears little
similarity to Types 1 and 2, though it has much in common
with Types 4 and 6. What agreements it does have with the
Type 1 texts are with the Kunaichō Text, not the Kyūshū Daigaku Text. It contains a great many mistakes and is unreliable.

The Gunsho Ruijū Text, representing the Type 6 texts, is
significant because it was the one on which many scholars relied when Lady Daibu's *Memoirs* began to be studied in ear-
nest at the beginning of the twentieth century. Ikari considers
this regrettable, since the text is not particularly good. The
colophon indicates that it is a collation of various manuscripts
and printed versions, and Ikari's studies suggest that it was
based on Type 5 texts and collated with texts of Types 1 (Ku-

10. Hon-iden 1964, p. 35.
11. Ikari 1969, pp. 50–53.

naichō Text), 2, and 4.[12] Since some manuscripts were made from the Gunsho Ruijū printed text, it did, in a sense, start a line of its own.

It is clear from Ikari's study that the Kyūshū Daigaku Text is the most authoritative of the many known today. This is the text used in most modern studies and editions, including the *Nihon koten bungaku taikei* edition, on which I have relied for this translation. The usefulness of the other texts should not be overlooked, however. Even the best text has its deficiencies, and editors often amend the Kyūshū Daigaku Text where a different reading seems to improve the meaning or to be more acceptable from a literary point of view.

The comparatively large number of extant texts, particularly from the Edo period, testifies to a steady interest in Lady Daibu's *Memoirs*. Yet the colophon of the Kyūshū Daigaku Text strengthens the view that Lady Daibu did not allow her text to circulate widely. It emphasizes that Shichijōin Dainagon was a particular friend of Lady Daibu's. Hon-iden's researches into the identity of Shichijōin Dainagon indicate that she was probably the lady-in-waiting mentioned in the prose introduction to Poems 12 and 13 under the name of Dainagon no Tsubone.[13] It is quite likely that Lady Daibu showed her collection only to such close friends from her younger days, and that it was almost unknown outside a small circle of intimates. That Fujiwara no Sadaie had to ask her for poems suggests that they did not circulate freely, although it was not uncommon for even major poets to be asked to submit poems when imperial collections were being compiled. Since no "Sadaie version" has been discovered, she may have given him only a short excerpt from her work, retaining the whole for herself and her closest friends. Certainty is impossible on this point, for such a "Sadaie version" could well be the ancestor of one of the lines of texts, and the Kyōgoku-Reizei poets who compiled the *Gyokuyōshū* and the *Fūgashū* undoubtedly had

12. *Ibid.*, pp. 87–89.
13. *Zenshaku*, pp. 76–78.

access to a complete text of the *Memoirs*. This may even have been a "Sadaie version" that descended to their faction of Sadaie's descendants rather than to the rival Nijō line.[14] Whether the *Memoirs* passed into posterity via the Shichijōin Dainagon copy alone, or via that and a "Sadaie version," or via several copies made from Lady Daibu's own, there is no doubt that the work enjoyed a quiet popularity and was often recopied up until the Meiji period and the beginnings of modern scholarship and interest in the work.

14. Suzuki Minoru, p. 9.

Bibliography

Place of publication is Tokyo unless otherwise noted.

Abe Akio et al., eds. 1970–74. *Genji monogatari*. 6 vols. Shō-gakkan.

Brower, Robert H., and Earl Miner. 1961. *Japanese Court Poetry*. Stanford, Calif.: Stanford University Press.

Cranston, Edwin A., trans. 1969. *The Izumi Shikibu Diary*. Cambridge, Mass.: Harvard University Press.

Freedman, Ralph. 1963. *The Lyrical Novel*. Princeton, N.J.: Princeton University Press.

Frye, Northrop. 1957. *Anatomy of Criticism*. Princeton, N.J.: Princeton University Press.

———. 1963. *The Well-Tempered Critic*. Bloomington: Indiana University Press.

Fukuda Yuriko. 1967. "Kenreimon-in Ukyō no Daibu shū no sekai," *Nihon Bungei Kenkyū* (Kansai Gakuin Daigaku), December.

———. 1968. "Kenreimon-in Ukyō no Daibu shū kenkyū," in Hisamatsu Sen-ichi et al., eds., *Nihon bungei no sekai*. Ōfūsha.

Gakutōsha, ed. and pub. 1979. *Kokubungaku: Kaishaku to Kanshō*, August. This issue, devoted to the study and comparison of *The Poetic Memoirs of Lady Daibu* and *The Confessions of Lady Nijō (Towazugatari)*, appeared after this book was in press. It contains illuminating articles on Lady Daibu and her work.

Gotō Shigeo. 1970. "Kenreimon-in Ukyō no Daibu shū ni kansuru ichikōsatsu," *Nagoya Daigaku Bungakubu Kenkyū Ronshū (Bungaku)*, no. 17, March.

——. 1971. "Kenreimon-in Ukyō no Daibu shū tanabata no uta ni kansuru ichikōsatsu," *Nagoya Daigaku Bungakubu Kenkyū Ronshū (Bungaku)*, no. 18, March.

——. 1972. "Kenreimon-in Ukyō no Daibu shū daieikagun ni kansuru ichikōsatsu," *Nagoya Daigaku Bungakubu Kenkyū Ronshū (Bungaku)*, no. 19, March.

GSRJ, see *Shinkō gunsho ruijū*, listed.

Hagitani Boku. 1957–69. *Heianchō utaawase taisei*. 10 vols. Privately published.

Hall, John W. 1970. *Japan from Prehistory to Modern Times*. New York: Dell.

Hall, John W., and Jeffrey P. Mass, eds. 1974. *Medieval Japan: Essays in Institutional History*. New Haven, Conn.: Yale University Press.

Hattori Kimiko. 1962. "*Kenreimon-in Ukyō no Daibu shū* no honshitsu to *Gyokuyō-Fūgashū*," *Aichi Kenritsu Joshi Daigaku Kiyō*, no. 12.

Hisamatsu Sen-ichi, ed. 1964. *Kenreimon-in Ukyō no Daibu shū*, in *Heian Kamakura shikashū*. Iwanami Shoten. (*Nihon koten bungaku taikei*, vol. 80.)

Hisamatsu Sen-ichi and Kubota Jun, eds. 1978. *Kenreimon-in Ukyō no Daibu shū*. Iwanami Shoten.

Hisatoku Takafumi. 1961a. "Kenreimon-in Ukyō no Daibu shū no kōsō ni tsuite," *Nagoya Shiritsu Joshi Tankidaigaku Kiyō*, no. 10.

——. 1961b. "*Kenreimon-in Ukyō no Daibu shū* hochū," *Kinjō Kokubun*, March.

——. 1968. *Kenreimon-in Ukyō no Daibu shū*. Ōfūsha.

Hon-iden Shigeyoshi. 1950. *Hyōchū Kenreimon-in Ukyō no Daibu shū zenshaku*. Musashino Shoin. Also rev. ed. 1974. Unless otherwise indicated, all citations are for the 1950 edition, which contains useful material deleted from the 1974 edition.

——. 1964. "Kenreimon-in Ukyō no Daibu shū tsuikō: shū toshite sono seiritsu to denrai ni tsuite," *Kansai Gakuin Daigaku Kinen Ronbun Shū*, September.

——. 1977. *Kodai waka ronkō*. Kasama Shoin.

Hyōkai, see Murai Jun 1971, listed below.

"Hyōshaku," see Kubota Jun 1968–71, listed below.

Iida Shōichi. 1951. "Kenreimon-in Ukyō no Daibu shū no sei-kaku," *Kansai Daigaku Bungaku Ronshū*, March.

Ikari Masashi. 1963. "Kenreimon-in Ukyō no Daibu shū kōsō-ron no tame no oboegaki 1," *Gobun*, June.

———. 1964. "Kenreimon-in Ukyō no Daibu shū kōsōron no tame no oboegaki 2," *Gobun*, March.

———. 1965. "Kenreimon-in Ukyō no Daibu to sono kashū," *Kokubungaku*, October.

———. 1969. *Kenreimon-in Ukyō no Daibu shū: kōhon oyobi sōsakuin*. Kasama Shoin. This work uses a dual pagination system; numbers cited are for the book as a whole.

———. 1975. "Kenreimon-in Ukyō no Daibu shū shichū," in Suzuki Chitarō Hakase no koki o iwau kai, ed., *Kokubun-gaku ronkō*. Ōfūsha.

———. 1977. "Kenreimon-in Ukyō no Daibu shū oboegaki: kin-dai no chūshakusho to kenkyū bunken," *Gobun*, May. This article contains an excellent bibliography on Lady Daibu and her work from 1961 to 1977.

Ikeda Kikan. 1977. *Heian jidai no bungaku to seikatsu*. Shi-bundō.

Itō Yoshio et al., eds. 1962. *Waka bungaku daijiten*. Meiji Shoin.

Itoga Kimie. 1961. "Kenreimon-in Ukyō no Daibu shū no nikki bungeiteki seikaku," *Bungei Kenkyū*, March.

———. 1969. "Kenreimon-in Ukyō no Daibu," in Hisamatsu Sen-ichi, ed., *Nihon joryū bungaku shi: kodai chūsei hen*. Dōbun Shoin.

———. 1979. *Kenreimon-in Ukyō no Daibu shū*. Shinchōsha. (*Shinchō nihon koten shūsei*.)

Karaki Junzō. 1964. *Mujō*. Chikuma Shobō.

Kojima Michiko. 1967. "Kenreimon-in Ukyō no Daibu shū no kōsō ni kansuru ichishiron," *Nagoya Daigaku Kokugo Kokubungaku*, November.

Kokka taikan, see Matsushita Daisaburō and Watanabe Fumio, eds., listed below.

Konishi Jin-ichi, Robert H. Brower, and Earl Miner. 1958. "Association and Progression: Principles of Integration in Anthologies and Sequences of Japanese Court Poetry, A.D. 900–1350," *Harvard Journal of Asiatic Studies*, vol. 21.

Kubota Jun. 1967. "Kenreimon-in Ukyō no Daibu," *Kokubungaku*, January.

———. 1968–71. "Kenreimon-in Ukyō no Daibu shū hyōshaku," 28 parts, *Kokubungaku*, Oct.–Dec. 1968, Feb.–Nov. 1969, Jan. 1970–March 1971.

Kunaichō Shoryōbu, ed. 1959–67. *Katsura no Miyabon sōsho*, vols. 1–13. Yōtokusha.

Kuroita Katsumi, ed. 1959–64. *Shintei zōho kokushi taikei*. 60 vols. Yoshikawa Kōbunkan.

Kusakabe Ryōen. 1978. *Ukyō no Daibu kashū*. Kasama Shoin.

Kuwabara Hiroshi. 1965. "Shikashū no kenkyū hōhō: gendankai to mondaiten 1, Heian zenki," *Kokubungaku*, October.

McCullough, Helen C., trans. 1968. *Tales of Ise*. Stanford, Calif.: Stanford University Press.

Mass, Jeffery P. 1974. *Warrior Government in Early Medieval Japan*. New Haven, Conn.: Yale University Press.

Matsuda Takeo. 1968. *Heianchō no waka*. Yūseidō.

Matsushita Daisaburō, ed. 1958. *Zoku kokka taikan*. Kadokawa Shoten.

Matsushita Daisaburō and Watanabe Fumio, eds. 1951. *Kokka taikan*. Kadokawa Shoten.

Miner, Earl. 1969. *Japanese Poetic Diaries*. Berkeley: University of California Press.

Morris, Ivan. 1964. *The World of the Shining Prince*. New York: Oxford University Press.

Murai Jun. 1963. *Tsurezuregusa jōenbon*. Koten Bunko.

———. 1971. *Kenreimon-in Ukyō no Daibu shū hyōkai*. Yūseidō.

Nakamura Shin-ichirō. 1972. *Kenreimon-in Ukyō no Daibu*. Chikuma Shobō.

Namie Michi. 1954. "Kenreimon-in Ukyō no Daibu no uta to tōji no kafū," *Kokubun* (Ochanomizu Joshi Daigaku), June.

Ōbayashi Jun. 1972. "Kenreimon-in Ukyō no Daibu shū seiritsu ni kansuru ichisuiron," *Kokubungaku Kō*, December.

———. 1973. "Kenreimon-in Ukyō no Daibu shū seiritsu ni kansuru ichisuiron 2," *Kokubungaku Kō*, June.

Ōhara Tomie. 1975. *Kenreimon-in Ukyō no Daibu*. Kōdansha.

Okamura Sumiko. 1971. "Kenreimon-in Ukyō no Daibu shū no kōsō," *Fuji Joshi Daigaku Kokubungaku Zasshi*, February.

Ōno Susumu et al., eds. 1974. *Iwanami Kogo Jiten*. Iwanami Shoten.

Saiga Mie. 1972. "Kenreimon-in Ukyō no Daibu shū no hairetsu ni tsuite," *Nōtorudamu Seishin Joshi Daigaku Kokubunga-kuka Kiyō*, March.

———. 1973. "Kenreimon-in Ukyō no Daibu shū," in Akabane Kiyoshi et al., eds. *Waka no honshitsu to tenkai*. Ōfūsha.

———. 1974. "Kenreimon-in Ukyō no Daibu shū ni okeru 'aware'," *Nōtorudamu Seishin Joshi Daigaku Kiyō (Koku-bungakuka)*, no. 7.

———. 1975. "Kenreimon-in Ukyō no Daibu shū no kafū ni kansuru ichikōsatsu," in Suzuki Chitarō Hakase no koki o iwau kai, ed., *Kokubungaku ronkō*. Ōfūsha.

———. 1977. "Kenreimon-in Ukyō no Daibu no kafū ni tsuite," *Nōtorudamu Seishin Joshi Daigaku Kiyō: Kokugo Koku-bungaku Hen*, n.s. vol. 1, no. 1 (o.s. no. 10).

Sansom, George. 1958. *A History of Japan to 1334*. Stanford, Calif.: Stanford University Press.

Sasaki Nobutsuna. 1908. *Kagaku ronsō*. Hakubunkan.

———. 1948. *Chūko sanjo kajin shū*. Asahi Shinbun Sha. (*Nihon koten zensho*.)

Scholes, Robert, and Robert Kellogg. 1966. *The Nature of Narrative*. New York: Oxford University Press.

Seki Misao. 1950. "Kenreimon-in Ukyō no Daibu shū," *Koku-bungaku: Kaishaku to Kanshō*, November.

Sekino Kasumiko. 1958. "Kenreimon-in Ukyō no Daibu shū kenkyū," *Nihon Bungaku* (Tōkyō Joshidai), February.

Shimada Taizō. 1934. "Kenreimon-in Ukyō no Daibu ni tsuite," *Kokugo Kokubun*, May.

——. 1950. *Shinchū Kenreimon-in Ukyō no Daibu shū.* Kawara Shoten.

Shinkō gunsho ruijū. 1928–37. 24 vols. Naigai Shoseki Kabushikigaisha.

Shinmura Izuru. 1931. "Seiya sanbi no josei kajin," in *Gendai nihon bungaku zenshū,* vol. 58: *Shinmura Izuru shū.* Kaizōsha. Originally published in *Nanban sarasa.* Kaizōsha, 1924.

Shinoda Amane. 1963. "Kenreimon-in Ukyō no Daibu shū kō: jōge ryōkan no aida ni okeru kakuhitsu no sōtei o megutte," *Gengo to Bungei,* September.

Suzuki Hideko. 1959. "Shinchokusenwakashū to Kenreimon-in Ukyō no Daibu," *Atomi Gakuen Kokugoka Kiyō,* no. 8.

Suzuki Minoru. 1962. *Kenreimon-in Ukyō no Daibu ni kokoro o yoseta hitobito.* Kyoto: Hatsune Shobō. This work contains a very full bibliography from the early 1900's until 1961.

Suzuki Shigeko. 1955. "Kenreimon-in Ukyō no Daibu shū to sono hito," *Nihon Bungaku Ronkyū,* December.

Tamai Kōsuke. 1965. *Nikki bungaku no kenkyū.* Hanawa Shobō.

——, ed. 1927–31. *Kōchū kokka taikei.* Kokumin Tosho Kabushikigaisha.

——. 1929. "Ukyō no Daibu kashū," *Chūko shokashū,* in *Kōchū kokka taikei,* vol. 13. Kokumin Tosho Kabushikigaisha.

Tōda Goryō. "Kenreimon-in Ukyō no Daibu shikō," *Kokugo Kokubun Kenkyū,* October.

——. 1962. "Kenreimon-in Ukyō no Daibu shikō 2: kashū hensan jiki o megutte," *Kokugo Kokubun Kenkyū,* June.

——. 1966. "Kenreimon-in Ukyō no Daibu to tanabata no uta," *Kokugo Kokubun Kenkyū,* September.

Tomikura Tokujirō. 1942. *Ukyō no Daibu—Kojijū.* Sanseidō. The half of this work dealing with Lady Daibu has been reissued as *Ōchō no hika.* Athene Shobō, 1970.

——. 1957. "Kenreimon-in Ukyō no Daibu shū hyōshaku," 5 parts, *Kokubungaku,* August–December.

Tsuji Kunio. 1972. *Kenreimon-in Ukyō no Daibu shū,* in Hisamatsu Sen-ichi et al., eds., *Izumi Shikibu, Saigyō, Teika.* Kawade Shobō Shinsha. (*Nihon no koten*, vol. 11.)

Wagner, James G. 1976. "The *Kenreimon'in Ukyō no Daibu Shū*," *Monumenta Nipponica*, vol. 31, no. 1.

Wakashi Kenkyūkai, ed. 1973–76. *Shikashū taisei.* 7 vols. Meiji Shoin.

Watanabe Shizuko. 1964. "*Kenreimon-in Ukyō no Daibu shū* no tokushitsu," *Tōyō Daigaku Daigakuin Kiyō*, March.

———. 1967. "Shinkokinshū to Kenreimon-in Ukyō no Daibu no uta," *Bungaku Ronsō* (Tōyō Daigaku), no. 37, November.

Yamada Shōzen. 1958. "Kenreimon-in Ukyō no Daibu shū zakkō: sono kaisō no seikaku o chūshin ni," *Kokubungaku Tōsō* (Taishō Daigaku), March.

Yamaguchi Michiko. 1960. "Kenreimon-in Ukyō no Daibu shū ni okeru shi to sanbun," *Jinbun Ronkyū*, vol. 11, No. 1.

Zenshaku, see Hon-iden Shigeyoshi 1950, listed above.

Zoku kokka taikan, see Matsushita Daisaburō, listed above.

General Index

Index of First Lines

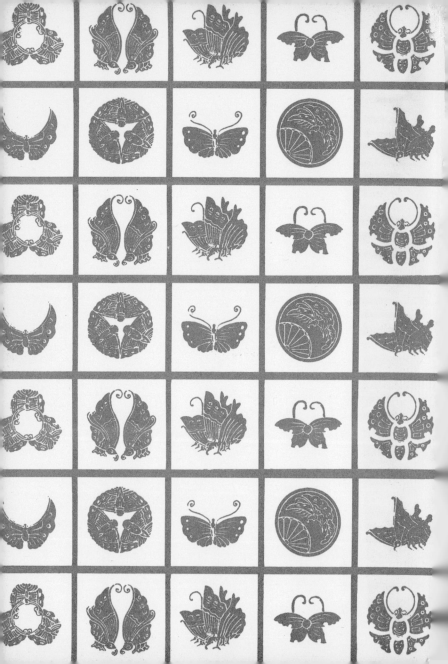